My Heart Is Bound Up with Them

MY HEART IS BOUND UP WITH THEM

How Carlos Montezuma Became the Voice of a Generation

DAVID MARTÍNEZ

THE UNIVERSITY OF
ARIZONA PRESS
TUCSON

The University of Arizona Press
www.uapress.arizona.edu

We respectfully acknowledge the University of Arizona is on the land and territories of Indigenous peoples. Today, Arizona is home to twenty-two federally recognized tribes, with Tucson being home to the O'odham and the Yaqui. Committed to diversity and inclusion, the University strives to build sustainable relationships with sovereign Native Nations and Indigenous communities through education offerings, partnerships, and community service.

ISBN-13: 978-0-8165-4817-0 (hardcover)
ISBN-13: 978-0-8165-4816-3 (paperback)
ISBN-13: 978-0-8165-4818-7 (ebook)

Cover design by Leigh McDonald
Cover photograph of Montezuma courtesy of Carlos Montezuma Photograph Collection, Greater Arizona Collection, Arizona State University; photograph of Verde River by Finetooth
Typeset by Sara Thaxton in 10/14 Warnock Pro with Archetype and Hardwick WF

Publication of this book is made possible in part by support from the Institute for Humanities Research, Arizona State University, and by the proceeds of a permanent endowment created with the assistance of a Challenge Grant from the National Endowment for the Humanities, a federal agency.

Library of Congress Cataloging-in-Publication Data
Names: Martinez, David, 1963– author.
Title: My heart is bound up with them : how Carlos Montezuma became the voice of a generation / David Martínez.
Description: Tucson : University of Arizona Press, [2023] | Includes bibliographical references and index.
Identifiers: LCCN 2022016282 (print) | LCCN 2022016283 (ebook) | ISBN 9780816548170 (hardcover) | ISBN 9780816548163 (paperback) | ISBN 9780816548187 (ebook)
Subjects: LCSH: Montezuma, Carlos, 1866–1923. | Yavapai Indians—Biography. | Indian activists—Biography. | Fort McDowell Yavapai Nation, Arizona—Biography. | LCGFT: Biographies.
Classification: LCC E99.Y5 M66 2023 (print) | LCC E99.Y5 (ebook) | DDC 323.1197/5724092 [B]—dc23/eng/20220616
LC record available at https://lccn.loc.gov/2022016282
LC ebook record available at https://lccn.loc.gov/2022016283

Printed in the United States of America
♾ This paper meets the requirements of ANSI/NISO Z39.48-1992 (Permanence of Paper).

Dedicated to the memory of Peter Iverson (1944–2021),
a much-valued friend and colleague as well as an exemplary historian,
whose work on Carlos Montezuma was an influence on my own.

Thank you.

Contents

Acknowledgments

In many ways, I have been thinking about this book since I began researching and writing *Dakota Philosopher* during my fellowship year (2003–2004) at the Newberry Library. That year-long immersion in Progressive Era Indigenous history taught me much about an incredible generation of men and women who defined, at least for me, what it means to be an Indigenous writer and activist. At the time, Charles A. Eastman, Ohiyesa, was foremost on my mind. Yet Carlos Montezuma always stood close to my heart because he was Eastman's friend and because his work took me back to Arizona, which my Akimel O'odham family and community called home. Thus, on December 17, 2003, I presented on Montezuma's work and legacy for the first time at a brown-bag organized by Dan Cobb, who was the assistant director of what was then called the D'Arcy McNickle Center for American Indian History. I later presented at the American Society for Ethnohistory on two successive occasions. First, during the November 12–15, 2008, meeting in Eugene, Oregon, I presented "The Myth of Two Worlds: Carlos Montezuma, Arizona, and the Fight Against Bureauism." Then at the September 30–October 3, 2009, meeting in New Orleans, Louisiana, my talk became "The Myth of Living in Two Worlds: Carlos Montezuma and the Salt River Pima." What resulted from these two presentations were the discursive threads that eventually grew into the book in hand.

During the fall of 2011, Chad Allen, author of *Blood Narrative: Indigenous Identity in American Indian and Maori Literary and Activist Texts*, was at Ohio State University at Newark, where he invited me to present on Eastman and Montezuma in separate panels at the Society of American Indians Centennial Symposium. My Montezuma presentation subsequently appeared as "Carlos Montezuma's Fight against 'Bureauism': An Unexpected Pima Hero," in a joint issue of the *American Indian Quarterly* and *Studies in American Indian Literatures* published in the summer of 2013. That publication led Joyce Martin to invite me to be a part of her Montezuma Collection digitization project. During the fall of 2014, Joyce was the curator of the Labriola National American Indian Data Center, located in Hayden Library at Arizona State University, Tempe Campus. More specifically, Joyce asked me to be her humanities scholar for her application to ASU's Institute for Humanities Research. When our project was awarded a seed grant, we collaborated with our colleague Jodi Reeves Flores, lead digital curator at ASU's Center for Digital Antiquity, in addition to hiring some capable student workers, Mark Langenfield and Nagarjuna Myla. Mark, who held an MLS degree, assisted Joyce with processing digitized items into ASU's Digital Repository; Nagarjuna assisted Jody with developing an online exhibit. At the end of our funding year, Joyce and I organized a public event, held at the Labriola on April 23, 2015. The event was titled "Carlos Montezuma's *Wassaja* Newsletter," and I was joined by Peter Iverson, author of *Carlos Montezuma and the Changing World of American Indians*; Raphael Bear, former president of the Fort McDowell Yavapai Nation; Jacque McCalvin, librarian, Fort McDowell Yavapai Nation Library; and Jacqueline Hettel, assistant director, Nexus Lab (ASU). In addition to a capacity audience at the Labriola, we were pleased to include Karen Ray (Yavapai), director, Fort McDowell Yavapai Nation Cultural Center and Museum, as a guest presenter. Arriving with members of the Yavapai community was Carolina Castillo Butler (Mexican American), who played a leadership role in the historic battle against Orme Dam. Indeed, it was Carolina who gave me a signed copy of *Oral History of the Yavapai*. Then, in its May 2015 issue, *The Yavapai News* reported on this event in an article titled "ASU Hosts Panel on Dr Carlos Montezuma's WASSAJA Newsletter." The article noted that "a number of FMYN [Fort McDowell Yavapai Nation] staff and residents were in attendance," including "Donald Beckman, Erika McCalvin, Dr Bill Myhr, Shaunai Miller, Angel Moreno and Lataisha Dini." Just before the Labriola event, I presented "Carlos Montezuma: Arizona History, Wassaja and the Struggle for Justice" at the Western Social Sciences Association annual conference, April 8–10, 2015, in Portland, Oregon.

In the ensuing years, I was honored to share my ongoing Montezuma research at "Indians in the Midwest: Representations in the Arts and Archives," a one-day conference held at the Newberry Library and hosted by the D'Arcy McNickle Center for American Indian History, in Chicago, Illinois, on October 1, 2016. With this event in mind, I want to say a special word of gratitude to Patricia Marroquin Norby (Purépecha), then director of the McNickle Center, who invited me. Patricia was a student of mine at the University of Minnesota, Twin Cities campus, where she took a course I taught on American Indian Studies on Indigenous Aesthetics. Since then, I have had the honor of watching her grow as a thinker and leader in her own right. Recently she was appointed associate curator of Native American Art at the Metropolitan Museum of Art in New York City. As for "Indians in the Midwest," on the program with me were Kate Beane (Mdewakanton Dakota), David Beck, Rosalyn Lapier (Blackfeet Tribe of Montana and Métis), Amy Lonetree (Ho-Chunk Nation), Phillip Round, Susan Sleeper Smith, and Kelly Wisecup. My paper was titled "From Fiery Apache to Yavapai Cousin: Carlos Montezuma's Role in Arizona Indian History." A month later, I was at the American Society for Ethnohistory annual conference in Nashville, Tennessee, November 9–12, 2016, where I presented "Carlos Montezuma and the Impact of Arizona Statehood: His Journey from Assimilated Indian to Yavapai Kinsman." At this panel, I had the privilege of sharing the lectern with Patience Collier (University of Oregon) and Sarah Carmen Moritz (McGill University). Dan M. Cobb, now at UNC–Chapel Hill and author of *Native Activism in Cold War America: The Struggle for Sovereignty*, served as moderator. Also, I want to acknowledge Maurice Crandall, the author of *These People Have Always Been a Republic: Indigenous Electorates in the U.S.-Mexico Borderlands, 1598–1912*, who was in my audience, and whom I had the pleasure of meeting at the end of the presentations. Two years later, at the Southwest Popular/American Culture Association annual conference in Albuquerque, New Mexico, February 7–10, 2018, I presented "Carlos Montezuma's Role in Arizona Indian History." Joyce Martin was my copresenter. Also presenting were Shannon McRae, State University of New York at Fredonia, and Toanui Tawa, Southern Utah University. Margaret Vaughan, Metropolitan State University, served as moderator.

During the summer of 2018, I began the epic task of transcribing all of the handwritten letters contained in the Carlos Montezuma Collection. However, at this time Hayden Library, which held the Collection, was undergoing a two-year shutdown for a major renovation project. Consequently, the Labriola was temporarily relocated to the Fletcher Library on ASU's West Campus. Fortunately, because of the excellent intra-library service between ASU's four campuses, Joyce Martin was able to arrange for the Collection to be sent to the Design and the Arts Library on the Tempe Campus, where Archivist Specialist Harold Housley made certain that I could access the archived correspondence, complete with a space in which to do my work. This book would not exist without these transcriptions, which would not have happened without the superb assistance of Joyce and Harold.

As for the development of this manuscript into a book, I immediately turned to Kristen Buckles, whose superlative talents as my editor enabled me to rise above my limitations as a writer and researcher and excelled at finding the numerous points at which I needed to revise my work and get my narrative on Montezuma to say what I needed it to say. In addition to the compassion and insight that Kristen brought to the discussion on my work, she did a commendable job of finding me superb individuals to write the peer reviews. Indeed, I want to express a special word of gratitude to my anonymous readers. Their supportive comments gave me courage and inspiration to complete this project. More importantly, their constructive criticisms were the medicine that I needed in order to see, through their eyes, the true nature of what I had done and what I had to do if I wanted this rough draft to mature into a fully refined piece of scholarship. I worked very hard at honoring the many helpful recommendations for revision that I received. Having said that, any flaws that remain in this work are solely mine to own. At the same time, a heartfelt word of thanks to Jennifer Manley Rogers, who did an incredible job copyediting my manuscript. Copyeditors like her are not appreciated enough for what they do to enhance an author's work.

In the end, it is plain to see that the book in hand is the result of nearly two decades of work, in which numerous developments occurred in a variety of places and events, where all of the people enumerated above played roles, great and small, in helping me build my research, refine my ideas, and shape this intellectual biography of an Indigenous mind whose opinions, activism, and compassion for others are still informing and influencing the Indigenous community today. To everyone, thank you! However, I cannot end these acknowledgments without paying homage to my muse and my angel. Sharon Suzuki-Martinez, my wife of nearly thirty years, is not only a superb poet and artist who constantly amazes me but also an irreplaceable partner in my life's work as a scholar. She has been there during all of the ups and downs I have experienced during this long process of weaving all of my messy strands of thought into a (hopefully) coherent narrative. In addition to listening to me talk endlessly about my latest insights into Montezuma's life and work, she provided gentle but poignant observations of what I was doing. For that, I will be forever grateful.

My Heart Is Bound Up with Them

Introduction

A Trunkful of Papers Arrives at ASU

> Much has been written about this full blood Yavapai because he had an unbelievable life and left an inspiring legacy. Wassaja was not born into a world of peace. In 1866 there was an extermination policy on Indians. His mother gave birth to Wassaja on the ground somewhere in Kewevkepaya (Southeastern Yavapai)[1] country, probably within view of Four Peaks or the Superstition Mountains. For his aboriginal parents, he was the new generation and the continuation of their native race.[2]

Such was how anthropologist Sigrid Khera described the legacy of one of the more extraordinary lives of the Progressive Era struggle for Indian rights. Nearly a century after his death in 1923, the name of Carlos Montezuma still stands prominently in modern American Indian history. For the Fort McDowell Yavapai community, in particular, Montezuma is remembered as a revered ancestor, whose memory is preserved in the names of the Wassaja Memorial Health Center, Wassaja Family Services, and the Fort McDowell Yavapai Nation Wassaja Scholarship at Arizona State University. For those outside of the Yavapai community, such as the author of the book in hand, Montezuma is remembered through his corpus of writings, most importantly the political essays that appeared in his self-published newsletter *Wassaja*. Speaking of which, the scholarship on Montezuma's work and legacy is possible largely because of the archives (held at the Wisconsin Historical Society, the Newberry Library, Arizona State University, and the University of Arizona) that nearly perished after his death, when Montezuma's name fell into relative obscurity. Indeed, at the time of the Red Power movement (1964–1973), which rose to overshadow the Progressive Era, Montezuma was all but forgotten. During this period, Montezuma appeared in books by Edward H. Spicer (1962) and Hazel W. Hertzberg (1971). However, neither volume did much to reaffirm Montezuma's place in Indian rights history. It was a different story, of course, in Fort McDowell, Camp Verde, and Prescott, where Montezuma's descendants invoked his name in their battle against the Orme Dam during the 1970s, which pitted them against the Central Arizona Project.

During the early years of the struggle against Orme Dam, specifically in spring 1974, the *Arizona Statesman* ran a story titled "Seeds of Wounded Knee? Carlos Montezuma Collection, a Timely Acquisition, Boosts Stature of ASU's Hayden Library." Wounded Knee in this context referred to the 1973 confrontation between the American Indian Movement and federal forces at the historic site of the 1890 massacre of unarmed Ghost Dance prisoners. As for the Carlos Montezuma Collection, its contents, which were literally contained in a trunk that was nearly lost to posterity, documented the Yavapai activist-intellectual's battle on behalf of Fort McDowell against the Indian Bureau during the 1910s, when it sought to forcibly remove the "Mohave-Apache" to the Salt River Pima-Maricopa Reservation for the purpose of opening the land to local developers.[3] Six decades after Montezuma's battle, the "Fort McDowell Mohave Apache Tribe" was opposing the proposed construction of the Orme Dam—a part of the Central Arizona Project—that threatened to flood Yavapai land.[4] Montezuma's name would be invoked by those fighting to protect Fort McDowell. Could the Montezuma Collection aid in the struggle for justice?

Complementing the Montezuma Collection's arrival at Hayden Library was the work that Khera began during the early 1970s, which became *Oral History of the Yavapai*. The volume, published in 2012—twenty-eight years after Khera's untimely death—bears the names of the Yavapai elders who asked for help with creating an oral history: Mike Harrison and John Williams, as authors, and Carolina Castillo Butler, as editor. Montezuma is referenced multiple times.[5] The first is in regard to his gravestone at Fort McDowell, which was illustrated with a photograph that is now in the Labriola National American Indian Data Center, a part of Hayden Library's special collections, and for which Khera is credited as the photographer. The photo caption informs the reader: "Fort McDowell Cemetery. Mass burial of Yavapai victims of the Skeleton Cave massacre is marked by a circle of rocks next to the fenced grave of Wassaja, the famed Yavapai Carlos Montezuma. On May 25, 1985, the Yavapai conducted a ceremony and dedicated a formal marker for the mass grave."[6] Second, Montezuma is referred to in the context of Yavapai history, when his cousins George and Charles Dickens wrote to their cousin in Chicago for help against the Indian Bureau, in letters dated March 20 and 29, 1910, respectively.[7] The Dickens brothers would be two of Montezuma's most loyal correspondents, along with Mike Burns, another Yavapai community member, whose accounts of life and politics at Fort McDowell will drive much of the historical narrative that follows in the present discourse.

The additional references to Montezuma in *Oral History* consisted of personal anecdotes that Harrison and Williams shared as they recounted episodes of Yavapai history.[8] Naturally, because of the existential threat that the Indian Bureau posed to the "Mohave Apache" during the early decades of the twentieth century, the struggle to remain on their homeland along the Verde River was recalled with great urgency. At the same time, it is fair to say that Harrison and Williams were aware that the effort to force the Yavapai off of their reservation during Montezuma's day had been largely forgotten by their own time. The Yavapai, on the other hand, as Harrison and Williams confirm, had not forgotten. Indeed, insofar as an archive can be said to retain memories, the Carlos Montezuma Collection had not forgotten Montezuma's legacy either. So, what was in there? Getting back to the Hayden Library story, historian and journalist Edward H. Peplow Jr. observed:

> It [the Carlos Montezuma Collection] contains some 2000 letters, pamphlets, photographs, notes and newspaper clippings that belonged to Dr. Carlos Montezuma, the Arizona Mohave Apache Indian who became nationally famous as a wealthy and fashionable Chicago physician who spent his fortune and ultimately his life fighting the white man's treatment of the Indian.[9]

Nearly 120 of the approximately 2,000 items enumerated are correspondence sent to Montezuma from 1901 to 1921.[10] Fittingly, an additional final letter was written by Montezuma and addressed to Mike Burns, and it sheds light on the other missives, in particular the concern for the Indian Bureau's mistreatment of the Yavapai. The historical discourse that these letters generated will form the basis of the following seven chapters—in addition to

numerous primary and secondary sources, including a dozen archive sources—in which the voices of Montezuma's family and friends, acquaintances,
and readers add to one's understanding of the 1910–1922 Yavapai land- and
water-rights crisis. These voices will also complicate Montezuma's historic
image in unexpected ways, which will compel a fresh reading of his editorials, essays, and speeches.

An additional complication to the discourse on Montezuma and Indian
rights is what I call the "Reservation English" in which correspondents such
as the Dickens brothers and Mike Burns expressed themselves, yet which
is no less meaningful and insightful than the discourse of their "educated"
peers, such as Montezuma. More to the point, it was commonplace for turn-
of-the-twentieth-century denizens of the reservation system to speak and
write in "Broken English," which was a result of limited English-language
education, typically acquired at boarding schools, reinforced by the social
dynamics of an Indigenous enclave, a given tribe's reservation, in which the
non-Western Indigenous language was still spoken by community members
on a daily basis, precluding the need for English-language fluency. Thus,
a kind of pidgin English emerged, which was perfectly comprehensible to
community members, but difficult for outsiders to understand, until their
ear grew accustomed to the regional dialect.[11] In the case of Montezuma,
while he lost his fluency in Yavapai, he exposed himself to the English spoken
at Fort McDowell, which meant that he developed his sensitivity for how his
family and community communicated their thoughts, feelings, and opinions, orally and in writing, thus informing his understanding of his Yavapai
community's values.

With respect to Peplow, his article curiously omitted any reference to
Montezuma's role as a cofounder of the Society of American Indians or his
self-published newsletter, *Wassaja*. Except for Spicer and Hertzberg, noted
above, Montezuma as a historic figure was barely visible at this point (1974).
Nonetheless, Peplow did highlight some remarkable events in Montezuma's
work on behalf of the Fort McDowell Mohave Apache against the Salt River
Valley Water Users Association and the Indian Bureau.[12] More to the point,
during the 1910s, as "the [Mohave] Apaches on Arizona's Ft. McDowell Reservation were about to be deprived of their water rights and removed to the
Salt River Reservation to live with their traditional enemies, the Pimas, they
appointed him [Montezuma] their representative."[13] In collaboration with Indian rights advocate, Illinois attorney, and compiler of *The Rape of McDow-*

ell Reservation, Arizona, by the Indian Bureau (1921),[14] Joseph W. Latimer,[15] Montezuma waged an arduous but ultimately successful campaign against the Indian Bureau, thus enabling the Yavapai to remain on what was left of their ancestral lands.[16] In turn, archivist Charles C. Colley warned, in the same *Arizona Statesman* article with regard to contemporary Yavapai affairs: "Once again history is repeating itself. Plans for the Central Arizona Project call for the building of Orme Dam, and the waters it impounds will flood the reservation." Consequently, "as this problem develops the Montezuma Collection easily could prove a valuable and timely source of background information germane to its solution."[17] The force of circumstances—the latest crisis along the Verde River and the fortuitous recovery of an important archive—was revitalizing Montezuma's legacy for a new generation.

Although Montezuma has long been remembered in his home community, his contributions to the struggle for Indian rights—like those of many of his Progressive Era friends and associates—had largely been lost to history. Peter Iverson remarked in his 1982 biography:

> While largely forgotten for many years by most Americans, Montezuma during his lifetime ranked as one of the most important Indians in the country. After his death in 1923, he remained a vital figure within the memories of his people, the Yavapais or Mohave-Apaches of the Fort McDowell reservation in southern Arizona; his opinions continued to influence some of the Pimas [Akimel O'odham] and Papagos [Tohono O'odham] of the same region. But by the time Spicer's book was published [in 1962], he had receded from the prominence he had enjoyed in the eyes of Arizonans and people interested in Indian affairs.[18]

As of the 1970s, when the fight against the Orme Dam erupted, Montezuma and the Progressive Era generation he represented were relics of the past, remembered more by a handful of historians than by the young people energizing the Red Power movement.[19]

In his revised and expanded 1971 edition of Jennings C. Wise's *The Red Man in the New World Drama*, Vine Deloria Jr. (Standing Rock Sioux) said in passing: "The Indian Bureau had been the exclusive domain of non-Indians for nearly a century. With the exception of a handful of well-educated Indians such as Carlos Montezuma, an [Mohave] Apache, and Charles Eastman, a Sioux, both doctors, few Indians had been employed in government service."[20] Deloria's portrayal of Montezuma and Eastman was typical of how Progressive Era American Indian intellectuals were regarded, namely as accepting of assimilation rather than leading a resistance. Montezuma and Eastman were Indian Bureau employees, and nothing more. Years later, in *Tribal Secrets: Recovering American Indian Intellectual Traditions* (1995), Robert A. Warrior (Osage) reinforced this stereotype when he characterized his intellectual predecessors: "[Richard] Pratt [founder of the Carlisle Indian School], whose program of educational reform began with Indian prisoners held captive in Fort Marion in the 1870s had as his slogan 'Kill the Indian and save the man!' [Charles] Eastman was for a time the 'outing officer' at Carlisle, and Dr. Carlos Montezuma (Wassaja) was staff physician. The work of both important figures bears the mark of Pratt's influence."[21] As will be demonstrated, the historical evidence tells a different, more nuanced story.

As for the Red Power generation and its progeny, if one knew anything of Montezuma during, say, the 1970s and 1980s, he was likely little more than an old black-and-white photograph in a book or museum, if even that. I personally grew up without ever hearing Montezuma's name among my Akimel O'odham relatives, even though he played a significant role in protecting the Gila River Indian Community, in addition to Salt River, from being forcibly relocated to Oklahoma.[22] Needless to say, working on this book enabled me to learn more about O'odham history and politics, which is prominently featured in the last chapter of the present volume.

For many, the name Carlos Montezuma appeared for the first time in 1971 when Hazel W. Hertzberg published *The Search for an American Indian Identity: Modern Pan-Indian Movements*, which was about the emergence of the Society of American Indians (SAI). Although Montezuma's name did appear briefly in Edward H. Spicer's 1962 *Cycles of Conquest*, a comprehensive history of Hispanic and American colonization of the Sonoran Desert region spanning the years 1533–1960, the epic scope of Spicer's historical narrative precluded Montezuma's legacy from being more than the proverbial footnote to larger events. In Hertzberg's discourse, on the other hand, Montezuma was highlighted as an influential force shaping the SAI, as well as the organization's most vocal critic, as exemplified in his 1915 address "Let My People Go," which he delivered at the SAI annual conference in Lawrence, Kansas.[23] In fact, Hertzberg characterized Montezuma as more of a troublemaker than an intellectual leader, especially when she contrasted him with Arthur C. Parker, the Seneca historian and archaeologist whom she greatly admired. Throughout her thirteen chapters, Hertzberg made at least three dozen references to Montezuma, the majority of which were about his vehement disdain for the reservation system. In chapter 2, for example, while summarizing Montezuma's life and work as one of the "Red Progressives," Hertzberg gave her appraisal of his legacy:

> Montezuma was by temperament and conviction a factionalist. He helped to found the Society of American Indians and then spent most of the rest of his life attacking it. Even as a Pan-Indian, he was combative, without any gift for compromise. He was perhaps at his best as editor of Wassaja, his personal newspaper to which he gave his [Mohave] Apache name meaning "beckoning" or "signaling."[24]

As was typical of the way Montezuma's advocacy work on behalf of his Fort McDowell community was overlooked by historians, Hertzberg only made an oblique reference to the Yavapai's fight against the Indian Bureau while recounting the imminent demise of the SAI, which was evident at its 1920 conference in Saint Louis, Missouri, an event that she called a "sad affair": "Much of the remaining conference time was taken up by the complaints of a delegation from several Arizona reservations led by Carlos Montezuma, who had been spending a good deal of time advising Arizona tribes. . . . Clearly, the SAI had lost all sense of direction and was in rapid disintegration."[25]

As for Montezuma's alleged role in the SAI's decline, what Hertzberg dismissed as a proclivity for factionalism, Montezuma asserted was a necessary critique of the national Indian rights organization. Indeed, the climax of the SAI movement, in Montezuma's estimation, was its 1919 annual conference in Minneapolis, Minnesota, where two things happened: One, Eastman presided over the conference as SAI president. Two, the SAI no longer waffled on its attitude toward the Indian Bureau—it unequivocally called for its abolition. Unfortunately, these two things emerged after nearly a decade of Parker's influence. More to the point, Montezuma attributed the SAI's decline after 1919 to the SAI being seen for too long as an ally to the Indian Bureau, which he accused of being the source of all the problems in the reservation system. Nonetheless, Hertzberg argued that the SAI diminished as a political force because it drifted from the pan-Indian and gradualist approach to Indian Bureau reform that Parker promoted and moved toward the abolitionist agenda that Montezuma advocated and Eastman, as president, endorsed.

What was quite clear in the above quotations from *The Search for an American Indian Identity* was Hertzberg's ignorance of the significance of Montezuma's "advising" of these "Arizona reservations," which included Fort McDowell. Unsurprisingly, Hertzberg was equally insensitive to the meaningfulness of Montezuma's reconnection with his Yavapai tribe and family, even though she referred to this in her remarks about Montezuma's legacy. This reconnection began in earnest at the turn of the century, then became increasingly important throughout the remainder of his life. Because of his worsening health, Montezuma had to forego the opportunity to organize the SAI's Chicago conference, leaving instead with his wife Marie for Arizona, specifically the "McDowell Reservation . . . where he died on January 31, 1923, in a primitive hut on the reservation." Seeing this as at best ironic, at worst hypocritical, Hertzberg judged Montezuma's career thusly: "After so many years of asserting that he would not 'go back,' he did indeed 'go back' to die among Indians. Montezuma was still deeply committed to Pan-Indianism, but he chose to die an [Mohave] Apache. In the end he tried to honor his devotion both to the Indian race and to the [Mohave] Apache."[26]

Montezuma's life and activist career would not be the subject of a historical biography until 1982 when Peter Iverson (author of *The Navajo Nation* [1981]) published *Carlos Montezuma and the Changing World of American Indians.*[27] According to Iverson, he was encouraged to work on his book during the 1976 meeting of the American Society for Ethnohistory in Albuquerque, New Mexico:

> While there, I talked with Professor Alfonso Ortiz of the University of New Mexico's Department of Anthropology. Ortiz, a Tewa, had recently urged more regard be given by scholars to the lives of such Native Americans as Charles Eastman and Carlos Montezuma. Ortiz encouraged me to write the biography and I began to work.[28]

Unfortunately, as important as Iverson's work was to American Indian intellectual history, it did not spawn another major work on Montezuma's legacy until twenty-one years later when Leon Speroff published his monumental *Carlos Montezuma, M.D.: A Yavapai American Hero: The Life and Times of an American Indian, 1866–1923.*[29] Speroff was a medical doctor, distinguished in the field of reproductive endocrinology, menopause, hormone replacement therapy, and contraception,[30] who took on the task of writing about Montezuma because of a chance encounter in 1975 on a flight from Minneapolis to New York.

> As we flew through the night, Leon Summit [medical editor of Pfizer Phar-maceutical's monthly periodical] told me Carlos Montezuma stories. In the 1960s, he was in Chicago researching an article on the great Chicago fire, and he kept encountering Carlos Montezuma in old newspapers. Intrigued, he set out to learn more and eventually with the help of the Chicago Historical Society obtained and saved from being lost a significant collection of Mon-tezuma material. His intention was to write a biography.[31]

It is unclear whether or not Summit's Montezuma archival collection is in any way related to the collection that Hayden Library acquired, not to men-tion the one at the Newberry Library, the Wisconsin Historical Society, or the University of Arizona. Speroff did not clarify this, even though he did acknowledge Wisconsin's collection, along with the papers and ephemera assembled by John William Larner Jr., after he decided to write his own book upon learning that Summit never published his biography. Summit passed away in 1998.[32]

In between Iverson's and Speroff's work, Robert A. Warrior's *Tribal Se-crets* appeared in 1995, containing several brief but significant references to Montezuma's political legacy.[33] In addition, there was a 1952 novel by Oren Arnold, *Savage Son*, which was based on Montezuma's much-told life story.[34] Arnold's wife, Adele, then published her own fictionalized version of Mon-tezuma's story in her 1974 novel *Red Son Rising*.[35] A decade later, in 1984, William S. Burroughs made an implicit reference to Montezuma's legend-ary abduction by "Pima Indian" raiders in *The Place of Dead Roads*.[36] Then, in 2007, Kevin Bruyneel briefly but poignantly placed Montezuma within a spectrum of Progressive Era American Indian intellectuals in *The Third Space of Sovereignty: The Postcolonial Politics of US-Indigenous Relations*, in which Montezuma stood between Parker and Eastman, on one side, and Zitkala-Sa (Gertrude Bonnin) on the other. Altogether, they represented dif-ferent notions of citizenship and Indian-affairs reform at a time when most Indigenous people in the United States did not possess citizenship status, in spite of the Fourteenth Amendment or the provisions in the 1887 General Allotment Act.[37] A year later, in 2008, Gina Capaldi published a children's book also inspired by Montezuma's story titled *A Boy Named Beckoning:*

The True Story of Dr. Carlos Montezuma, Native American Hero.[38] All of the foregoing works were in addition to several scholarly and general-audience articles that appeared in peer-reviewed journals and other venues over the years.[39] Yet in spite of the number of works on Montezuma's life and career that have accumulated, there is still much work to be done. Toward that end, four works have recently appeared, including my article "Carlos Montezuma's Fight Against 'Bureauism': An Unexpected Pima Hero" (2013),[40] Julianne Newmark's "A Prescription for Freedom: Carlos Montezuma, *Wassaja*, and the Society of American Indians" (2013),[41] Maurice Crandall's (Yavapai-Apache Nation of Camp Verde) "Wassaja Comes Home: A Yavapai Perspective on Carlos Montezuma's Search for Identity" (2014),[42] and Kiara Vigil's *Indigenous Intellectuals: Sovereignty, Citizenship, and the American Imagination, 1880–1930* (2015), which contains a chapter titled "Tracing Carlos Montezuma's Politics: Progressive Reform and Epistolary Culture Networks." Collectively, these four works complicate Montezuma's legacy in terms of his relation to the Pima, or Akimel O'odham; the Society of American Indians; the Yavapai community; and other Progressives. It is noteworthy that while the present volume was undergoing peer review during the summer of 2021 two additional works were added to the growing body of Montezuma scholarship. Cristina Stanciu published "'Americanism for Indians': Carlos Montezuma's 'Immigrant Problem,' *Wassaja*, and the Limits of Native Activism"[43] and Thomas C. Maroukis published *We Are Not a Vanishing People: The Society of American Indians, 1911–1923.*[44]

When examining the ASU Library's Montezuma Collection, in Box 1 one finds an assortment of items summarizing the Yavapai doctor's political beliefs: short notes about the endemic conditions in the reservation system, a handmade *Wassaja* masthead, more notes equating reservation and prison, and a comment about how the reservation system will be around as long as there is an Indian Bureau. Then, in another handwritten note, Montezuma proclaimed: "Wassaja is like a bomb, when it blows up the Indian Bureau, it will be no more."[45] As for what motivated his hostility toward the Indian Bureau, in Box 3 one finds letters from Montezuma's cousin, Charles Dickens, in addition to a January 30, 1911, letter to Secretary of the Interior R. A. Ballinger, in which was highlighted the demand "do not remove Camp McDowell Indians!"[46] Furthermore, there is a copy of HR 6294, titled "A Bill Pertaining to Camp McDowell, 62nd Cong., 1st Sess.," dated April 20, 1911, and a copy of the 1911 program of the Society of American Indians' inaugural meeting.[47] A little further on, in Box 4, one finds a letter from Fort McDowell community member Mike Burns asking for Montezuma's help with fighting the Indian Bureau's plans for building a dam on the Verde River.[48] For anyone familiar with Montezuma's life story, these items resonate with the heroic image that has developed over time of Montezuma as an Indian rights fighter. Such was the nature of social justice and Indian affairs during this era. As for the impression these items may make on subsequent generations, including the one reading this text, if one knew nothing about Montezuma before seeing the Montezuma Collection, one's first impression might be mixed, even conflicted. In one regard, Montezuma was a person proclaiming his desire to "blow up the Indian Bureau," not to mention abolishing the reservation system it ran. In another regard, Montezuma was honestly concerned for his relatives, such as Charles Dickens and Mike Burns, at "Camp McDowell." Folder after folder, in fact, contains numerous letters from Montezuma's family back home, imploring their cousin to help with their predicament with the Indian Bureau and doing so as community leaders upon whom the Yavapai were depending. More exactly, George Dickens was a Yavapai chief, who took over this role upon Yuma Frank's death in 1914; Charles Dickens, who coordinated Montezuma's annual hunting trips, was a community member well-known for his money-making schemes; and Mike Burns, who was despised for having led soldiers to his people's hideout at Skeleton Cave, later redeemed himself as a valued translator and tribal historian.

Although Iverson and Speroff, not to mention other scholars, have cited the correspondence extensively from the four existing Montezuma archival collections, the one-man diatribe against the Indian Bureau and the Society of American Indians in the pages of *Wassaja*, along with an assortment of speeches, most notoriously "Let My People Go," has overshadowed the more personal record expressed by Montezuma's Yavapai family and friends, which is the main focus of the discourse here. Consequently, it has been commonplace to portray Montezuma in terms of two distinct, not to mention linear, stages of his political career. First, he has been defined by his denouncement of the Indian Bureau, which he carried out repeatedly in the pages of *Wassaja*, complete with a call to abolish the Bureau and terminate the reservation system, thereby ending the segregation of Indians and allowing them to live, work, and go to school anywhere they pleased. Second, he has been further defined by his work for the Yavapai community, influenced by his reunion with his extended family, an effort in which, contrary to the first stage, Montezuma's objective was preserving—not abolishing—the reservation articulated in Theodore Roosevelt's 1903 executive order. Since Montezuma ended his life serving the Yavapai valiantly, it is tempting to think of these two sides in chronological terms, in which the latter repudiates the former. However, such a thesis is confounded by the fact that Montezuma began returning to Arizona many years before delivering his seminal speech at the 1915 SAI meeting in Lawrence, Kansas. Indeed, Montezuma undertook an unexpected effort in pursuit of tribal membership, most notably at San Carlos, where he believed he was from due to his family being forcibly detained there during the 1880s.[49] For someone who advocated U.S. citizenship for all Indians so passionately, complete with an assimilationist political agenda, Montezuma's sincere interest in tribal membership was one of these contradictions that only make sense within the context of his life story.

Because Montezuma was abducted at a young age, then spirited away by Carlo Gentile to New York before moving to Chicago, one might expect that Montezuma had utterly lost his Yavapai identity that had, up until his legendary abduction, been nurtured by his biological family and community in their homeland near Four Peaks during the mid-nineteenth century. How much of his Yavapai origins Montezuma remembered after graduating from medical college in the late 1880s can only be conjectured. Despite recovering his name, Wassaja, Montezuma never demonstrated knowledge of his language, nor did he display any cultural knowledge.[50] In fact, during a confrontation between Montezuma and Pima Agency Superintendent Byron A. Sharp, Montezuma needed to ask Chief George Dickens, a fluent Yavapai speaker, to testify about his relationship with the Camp McDowell Indians. Nellie H. David (a.k.a. Davis), another Yavapai community member, was obliged to translate. Montezuma wrote about this in the October 1920 issue of *Wassaja*, in which he recalled saying to Sharp: "'You say I create bad influence with these Indians. I do not believe you. You are a hireling, but I believe George Dickens, who is the chief of the Indians under your charge. I will ask Mrs Nellie Davis to interpret to George Dickens what you have said about my influence.' In Apache tongue, Mrs Davis conveyed my question."[51] In *Oral History of the Yavapai*, Harrison and Williams recalled an anecdote about three boys, taken from their Yavapai homeland after the Skeleton Cave Massacre and raised by Whites, whose knowledge of their language was broken. One of the boys was Montezuma: "Carl [Carlos] he cannot say anything in Yavapai. All he remembers is his name, Wassaja."[52]

Like many intellectual leaders of his generation, Montezuma likely re-garded his heritage as something that was now a thing of the past. Conse-quently, the series of correspondences from Charles Dickens, George Dick-ens, and Mike Burns, which made up the vast majority of the letters in the archives sent to Montezuma, shed light on how Yavapai community leaders portrayed their reservation, the urgent issues confronting it, and their expe-riences under early twentieth-century federal Indian policy. Indeed, one can argue that the letters between Montezuma and his Yavapai relatives were his main source of understanding of the perils and predicament of the reserva-tion system that the Indian Bureau ran on behalf of its so-called wards. More specifically, one can claim that what Montezuma learned about life under the Indian Bureau from his family was the spark that lit the fire in Montezuma's soul, instigating his passionate drive to abolish the reservation system and its oppression of Indian people everywhere.

As for the letters contained in the Montezuma Collection at ASU, they can be arranged in at least two ways: First and most obviously, in chrono-logical order, from May 1, 1901, to February 12, 1921. Second, in terms of the letter writers: Charles Dickens, George Dickens, and Mike Burns were the primary correspondents with Montezuma; far fewer letters were written by an assortment of relatives and other non-Yavapai senders, both Indian and non-Indian. Collectively, the correspondence can further be analyzed ac-cording to particular themes or topics that appear recurrently, such as the Indian Bureau's plan to relocate the Yavapai to the Salt River Pima-Maricopa Reservation. Consequently, there was much concern for maintaining land and water rights at Fort McDowell while dealing with the pressure to accept allotments at Salt River as a barbed-wire fence was installed around Fort McDowell farms and homes. Complementing the ongoing legal and political battle that the Yavapai were having with the Indian Bureau was the steady stream of news that Montezuma received about daily life at Fort McDowell, such as marriages, births, and deaths, not to mention regular plans made for an annual hunting trip, which Montezuma's cousins clearly looked forward to year after year. Except for a fraction of the letters, Montezuma was always addressed as "Dear Cousin."

The thesis guiding the present discourse is that Montezuma / Wassaja can be seen more clearly as an integral part of Yavapai history when viewed through the lens of the correspondence he received from his family and friends at Fort McDowell. More specifically, the accumulation of personal narratives expressed in the letters written by George Dickens, Charles Dickens, and Mike Burns, which are augmented by the range of other letters (the majority of which were from Arizona), generates a historical discourse that, when privileged as the grounding narrative on the Yavapai experience, ultimately casts Montezuma in the light of the people, places, and events contained in these letters. In a way, what follows takes a proposition articulated in Crandall's brief essay on Montezuma, in which he emphasized Wassaja's familial relations and how he was always remembered as a member of the Yavapai community. For anyone familiar with Indigenous society, kinship ties are abundantly important to understanding not only personal identity but also political principles and values. More exactly, taking Montezuma's kinship ties to Fort McDowell seriously is imperative to understanding his Indian rights agenda, especially his call to abolish the Indian Bureau.

It is common for scholars to emphasize Montezuma's role in the Pan-Indian movement for citizenship rights, as exemplified by Hertzberg as well as Bruyneel, who placed Montezuma's anti–Indian Bureau agenda on a spectrum of Progressive Era trends in Indian affairs. Toward that end, Bruyneel cited Homi Bhabha's notion of a "nation's narrative" as a way of explaining Montezuma's critique of American history. Bruyneel saw Montezuma as underscoring the perception of Indigenous peoples in the United States as the "first Americans" in order to cause white Americans to rethink their assumptions about who and what was "American."[53] Taking into account that Bruyneel's comments about Montezuma's politics are brief, Montezuma's connection with his Yavapai family and community was not mentioned at all. The same is true of Vigil's discourse on the "epistolary culture" generated out of Montezuma's correspondence. Of primary interest here was Montezuma's voluminous exchange of letters with a variety of Progressive Era leaders, both within and outside of the SAI. Vigil took a literary studies approach to Montezuma's work and legacy, regarding the cited correspondence as an ancillary discourse to the public statements expressed through *Wassaja* and his speeches. As an example of Indigenous modernity, the correspondence was a kind of group email thread that served the purpose of keeping the drive to abolish the Indian Bureau and obtain citizenship rights moving forward. However, Vigil did not cite any letters from any of Montezuma's Yavapai family and community, such as the Dickens brothers or Mike Burns. Instead, working through the correspondence held at the Wisconsin Historical

Society, Vigil maintained her focus on Montezuma's correspondence with non-Yavapai.

> When letters became pamphlets that became newsletters that became jour-
> nals and magazines, Montezuma's ideas (and those of other Indian writ-
> ers) traveled along an important continuum. For instance, the letters Native
> people sent to Montezuma when he was editor of *Wassaja* produced an
> important form of internal and national dialogue across Indian Country.
> Montezuma's personal letters and ideas expressed in *Wassaja* demonstrate
> an emerging pan-Indian public sphere that diverged from American repre-
> sentative democracy, even as individuals like Montezuma aimed to incorpo-
> rate themselves into that system in order to reform it.[54]

What Vigil called "epistolary culture" in her work will also be prevalent in the work that follows. However, the emphasis will be inward toward Mont-ezuma's Yavapai family and community in Central Arizona, along the Verde River, which was where his heart belonged. As Crandall asserted: "By switch-ing the narrative to tell the story from his relatives' point of view, we see what it meant to be Yavapai and what they hoped for and expected from their kinsman. This reorients Wassaja's story back to Arizona, even while Wassaja himself was still living in the Windy City."[55] In this book, unlike other treat-ments of his work as an Indian rights advocate, Montezuma's relation to the outside, non-Yavapai, world will largely be limited to the Akimel O'odham at the Salt and Gila River Reservations. For it was the work he did on be-half of the O'odham, my people, in which Montezuma most successfully and convincingly demonstrated his pan-Indian political beliefs. Yavapai and O'odham may be historic rivals, but they/we were united in the battle against Indian Bureau injustice.

With the foregoing in mind, the reader will embark on a path that the men and women who wrote to Montezuma—and whose letters were thankfully preserved in the Carlos Montezuma Collection—created as they called on him for help, advice, and comradery. Indeed, the argument guiding this book is that one cannot fully understand Montezuma's political agenda, as when ex-pressed passionately in "Let My People Go" (1915), unless one sees it within the context of his Yavapai kinship relations, which formed the basis of his kinship-like relationship with the O'odham and ultimately with all American Indians.

As of 1901, which is when chapter 1 begins, Carlos Montezuma was already a recognized Indian rights advocate, a commitment that began while he was a medical student in the late 1880s, which is reflected in the letters he received. In fact, this chapter opens with a plea from an Apache man living in Arizona who wanted help returning his two sons from the Carlisle Indian Industrial School in Pennsylvania. More prominent, however, are the letters from his Yavapai family, in particular his cousins, the brothers George and Charles Dickens, and Mike Burns, the latter of whom may be regarded as the black sheep of the family. Together, through personal correspondence that spanned roughly two decades, they wrote a compelling history of the Fort McDowell Mohave Apache Reservation, as seen from their own unique points of view, as expressed in the idiomatic English of their community. On the whole, two factors become apparent from the outset in the letters. One, Montezuma was a valued and respected member of the Yavapai community. Two, the Indian Bureau, in reaction to Arizona's growing population and drive for statehood, was plotting to accommodate the non-Indigenous political and business interests in Arizona's land and scarce water resources at the expense of Indigenous peoples, in particular the Yavapai and the O'odham.

Chapter 2 sees Montezuma take on the "American Kaiser," which was one of the ways Montezuma expressed his disdain for Cato Sells, the commissioner of Indian Affairs under President Woodrow Wilson. Sells, more bluntly, was the villain in Montezuma's story. Because of his bureaucratic insensitivity to Yavapai rights and humanitarian needs, Sells promoted relocating them to Salt River as an opportunity for prosperity. He refused to acknowledge the calamity he was creating. The Yavapai crisis was also the reason why Montezuma became an unrelenting critic of the SAI, which he denounced as utterly useless as an Indian rights organization. In Montezuma's opinion, the SAI was too cozy with Indian Bureau employees, even electing them to high office within the organization's ranks, hence the need for *Wassaja: Freedom's Signal for the Indian.*

Chapters 3 and 4 document the concurrent battles that Montezuma waged to defend Yavapai land and water rights and to abolish the Indian Bureau. The Yavapai crisis was ignored not only by the SAI but also by politicians and the media of the day. Arizonans may have heard about Arizona Senator Carl Hayden's promotion of what became the Salt River Project and

Arizona's growing economy but likely heard little to nothing about the impact this was having on the Yavapai. For that, one needed to be a part of the Indian rights movement. But even then, one needed to read *Wassaja* for all of the problems that the Indian Bureau created for Indians in the reservation system. Indeed, for many, it was only when they read Montezuma's essays on "Camp McDowell" that they finally learned what had been happening. Montezuma's reputation as a radical voice for Indian rights grew during the years overlapping with WWI. One can say moreover that Montezuma emerged as a notorious figure in the eyes of the Indian Bureau. Under Sells, the Bureau was adamant about land allotment, controlling water rights, and disrupting Indian lives in the name of progress. Montezuma did not hesitate to fight back. Speaking of which, it was during this epoch that attorney Joseph W. Latimer appeared as Montezuma's most important ally and collaborator. Despite his importance in this story, Latimer remained a little-known figure but nonetheless made his mark when he made Sells look foolish at the 1911 congressional hearing. This was the only time a Yavapai delegation presented its case before Congress; subsequent efforts to go to Washington, D.C., never materialized, mostly because of a lack of funds.

Chapters 5 and 6 document Montezuma, Latimer, and the Yavapai's effort to reverse the plan to relocate the Yavapai to Salt River. In spite of obtaining a reversal from Interior Secretary Walter L. Fisher, who had served under President William H. Taft, once the Wilson administration took over, there was a new secretary of the interior, Franklin Lane, and a new commissioner of Indian Affairs, Cato Sells, who reactivated the earlier plan for Yavapai relocation. Even after another change in presidential administration, the Yavapai were still threatened with removal. Letters from home illustrated what life was like under this ongoing threat to Yavapai well-being. In addition, the O'odham and Piipaash (Maricopa) appeared as a growing concern for Montezuma.

Chapter 7, in turn, recounts how Montezuma was an unexpected hero for the O'odham. Highlighted is the advocacy work he did for the Salt and Gila River Reservations. Montezuma saw Yavapai and O'odham rights as tied together. As one went, so did the other, at least when it came to their antagonistic relation with the Indian Bureau. As a result of defending O'odham rights, Montezuma was fondly remembered in the writings of George Webb and Anna Moore Shaw.

With that I hope that I have provided my reader sufficient motivation for continuing on to the first chapter of this epic story, and that she/he/they may learn as much as I did from researching and writing this uniquely Indigenous story.

The Reservation System as a Humanitarian Crisis

Montezuma Emerges as an Indian Rights Hero

Correspondence sent to Montezuma, as preserved in ASU's Carlos Montezuma Collection, began dramatically on May 1, 1901, when Manuel Ruiz beseeched the learned doctor for help in getting Ruiz's children returned from the Carlisle Indian Industrial School in Carlisle, Pennsylvania. At this point in Montezuma's career, he was in Chicago, running a private medical practice. After serving as an Indian Bureau physician at Fort Stevenson, the Western Shoshone Agency, and the Colville Agency, Montezuma had worked at the school under Carlisle founder Richard Pratt but had left in 1896.[1] If Ruiz knew this, he did not state it in his short missive, perhaps hoping that the only address he had for Montezuma, which was at Carlisle, would suffice. As Ruiz explained in exasperated tones:

> I will take the pleasure of writing you a few lines to let you know that I have been sick for several months at the same time one of my sons is sick to at Carlisle Pa so I have had a very bad luck since last year my wife died to last year [1900] in the month of may the 6 of may and since then I have been with very bad luck so I wish you could send me my two sons home because one is sick and I am sick my self and cant not get well and I think I wount get over this sickness the poor boys lost there mother and dident see her so I guess I migt die to and [they] wount see me to so I hope you would pleas send the boys because I havent got nobody els to see me I got two children more but they are to small one is 10 years and the other is 1 they cant do any

thing for me so pleas do the best you can to send me my two boys because
it seems that I am getting wors and worse every day so I hope you will have
pations to send down the boys that is all for to night a letter to you Dr Montezuma[. . .]the boys are out in the country now but no matter do the best
you can to send them[.][2]

It was unclear from the archival record if Montezuma did anything to help
Ruiz with his plight. Did Montezuma ever see this letter? According to the
Carlisle Indian School Digital Resource Center, there were two Apache students with the surname Ruiz. First, Juan Ruiz, age 12, whose hometown
was Globe, Arizona, with "Manuel Ruiz" noted in the address line of his
student record (the letter quoted above was sent from Globe). In fact, both
parents were noted as "living," and Juan was designated a "half blood"; it
is unclear if "half blood" referred to the mother being white, Mexican, or
another impossible-to-determine identity. What is clear is that Juan arrived
at Carlisle on November 17, 1897, and was discharged on June 30, 1903,
having completed his five years at the school.[3] A nearly identical student
information card was listed for Manuel Ruiz, age 15, complete with the same
entry and discharge dates.[4] Nothing on either boy's student record indicated
their mother's demise or any special dispensation for a family emergency.
In all likelihood, the father's effort at getting his sons returned home was
to no avail.[5]

Subsequent letters sent to Montezuma prior to 1911 are sparse. In fact,
there are only three such letters in the Montezuma Collection, dated 1901,
1903, and 1908—two from Charles Dickens and one from Mike Burns, both
of whom (along with George Dickens, Charles's brother) would go on to become Montezuma's most frequent correspondents. From the outset, Charles
Dickens and Burns addressed Montezuma as "Dear Cousin," affirming a familial relationship with Montezuma that preceded the correspondence.[6] In
the case of Charles, that familiarity included asking for favors without hesita-
tion, something that recurred throughout his missives. For example, Charles
asked on November 2, 1901, for Montezuma's help in arranging the return
of his sister Grace Thumbo,[7] who had been at Carlisle since 1899, along with
wanting "$3.25" for an accordion from the Montgomery Ward's catalog, say-
ing "I know how to play accordions, alright, Cousin."[8] Then, on December 7,
1908, Dickens asked for "$250.00" to start a store, explaining "I am going to
put a store here on the reservation their is no store here now. the store is here

close last 3 months ago. The Agent want some boby put store here who got money." At the same time, Montezuma did not hesitate to ask his cousin for help, in one instance requesting "three baskets," which, Charles assured him, "my close relative," were on their way.[9] In between, on August 6, 1903, Mike Burns wrote inviting Montezuma to travel around Arizona with him, identifying himself in the end as Montezuma's "long lost cousin."[10] Taken together, these four letters affirmed Montezuma as a valued resource, a person with influence, and as a relative, three attributes that characterized Montezuma's correspondence until the end of his life.

> There is no evidence in these letters that they viewed him as "assimilated," or scorned him for his education and profession. There is not a hint that this thought entered their minds. This is not to say that it never happened, but to the relatives with whom he formed these powerful, personal connections, he was simply the boy Wassaja, a Yavapai who had been kidnapped but was never truly gone.[11]

It is worth observing, before proceeding, that in between the lines that he received from back home, Montezuma sought to ameliorate the wounds created by his 1871 abduction. "During the autumn of 1901, Montezuma returned to the places of his boyhood." Thirty years had passed since he was handed over to Carlo Gentile for thirty silver dollars, in a transaction that took place in Florence, Arizona. Montezuma was an accomplished physician and a longtime resident of Chicago. Yet, the experience of setting foot to homeland was transformative.

> Montezuma felt the loss of his father, mother, and sisters all the more, having retraced their steps. He regained firsthand contact with Yavapai relations, including Mike Burns and Charles Dickens. Burns had quite a bit of knowledge about recent Yavapai history. He had corresponded with Montezuma before the 1901 trip. Dickens and his brother George, both would be important people in Fort McDowell reservation affairs. They were first cousins to Montezuma.[12]

Between 1911 and 1916, prior to the United States entering World War I, Montezuma saw a steady flow of letters from home. Coincidentally, 1911–1916 marked the height of the influence of the Society of American Indians

(SAI) on Progressive Era Indian affairs, at the end of which, in 1916, Montezuma launched his one-man newsletter *Wassaja* after scolding the SAI for
its ineptitude in his 1915 "Let My People Go" speech.

Paralleling the above events was growing anxiety back at Fort McDowell
over the Indian Bureau's plans for relocating the Yavapai to the Salt River
Pima Reservation. As for the correspondence, during the SAI's inaugural
year 1911, Montezuma received three letters, one each from Charles Dickens, Yuma Frank, and Charles C. Cook. Each made clear that the assault on
Yavapai land and water rights was well underway, including the intention
for forced removal to the Salt River. Pima Agency Superintendent Charles E.
Coe, according to Dickens and Frank, was known for illegally seizing Montezuma's letters from community members. Dickens wrote, for example: "Mr.
Coe say to me I got you[r] letter and he say he saw a letter from Chicago.
he want to see the letter and Mr. Coe he take my letter in my pant pocket."[13]
Moreover, according to Frank, Coe did no good for the Indians, instead
talking only about "forcing Indians to move to Salt River." This is the first
time that the Indian Bureau's plans for the Yavapai are mentioned in this
correspondence.[14]

Montezuma was clearly perceived as a threat to the Indian Bureau's interests at Fort McDowell. Nevertheless, the Reverend Charles Cook, the Presbyterian missionary serving the Gila River Reservation, wrote to Montezuma
as an ally in the field, encouraging him to persevere in his work for Indian
rights. Reflecting on the travails that the Akimel O'odham faced after the
illegal annexation of the Gila River during the 1870s, Cook wrote on June 10,
1911: "I am not acquainted with the Apache Mohaves. Only I feel certain that
if they have any good lands and water for irrigation the whites & Mormons
will do their best to get it away from them." Cook counseled Montezuma
about his Indian rights work, which pitted him against formidable opposition: "The Indian Office at Wash[ington] spends much money here to help
the Grafters but little really to help the Indians. Many of our Indians are
christians (Presbyterians), they could make a comfortable living if the government would restore the Gila river water, taken from them, by building the
San Carlos reservoir. You may rest assured that if your people have water,
some pasture and good lands, the whites will try & get it."[15]

In a sense, Cook represented the kind of compartmentalization that many
missionaries practiced, in which they saw themselves, as representatives of
their churches, as disconnected from the evil done by secular forces, whether

corporate or government, that appropriated and exploited Indian land and people. To put it more bluntly, Cook could not see how he was a tool of colonization. At best, he thought of himself as a more humane face to "Indian civilization." Montezuma, however, later scolded church leaders for their complicity in harm done to Indians.

The battle over water rights that plagued Indian affairs throughout the American West reached crisis level in southern Arizona, where Indigenous nations suffered the grinding effects of population growth, economic development, and a shrinking land base, all of which was exacerbated by an inhumane reservation system that treated Indians more like stock animals than human beings.[16] Consequently, the racist deprivation of Indian water in Arizona was a recurring problem for not only the Akimel O'odham but also the Yavapai. Both nations were the victims of river reclamation projects that deliberately and dangerously overlooked the needs of Indigenous peoples. Indeed, there is an abundance of evidence that the Indian Bureau intentionally used water as a way of controlling the Indian population for the purpose of forwarding its agenda. In the case of the Yavapai, a mere three years after their reservation was established in 1903, the Indian Bureau intervened to disrupt the Yavapai's supposedly irrevocable right to the land and water:

> In 1906 the Indian Irrigation Service of the Bureau of Indian Affairs [then known as the Office of Indian Affairs] recommended that no more funds be spent on the irrigation system of McDowell. Instead, it was proposed to relocate the McDowell farmers onto the neighboring Salt River Pima-Maricopa Reservation; this land was under the Bureau of Reclamation's Salt River Project canal. According to the Indian Irrigation Service, such a move would have been less expensive for the government than developing a permanent irrigation dam at McDowell. This recommendation assumed that the McDowell water rights could be legally transferred to the Salt River Reservation and that the McDowell farmers would agree to removal.[17]

The assumption that Yavapai water rights could be transferred to the Salt River Reservation was likely based on the assumption per *Lone Wolf v. Hitchcock* (1903) that Congress has plenary power over Indian Affairs. The Winters Doctrine of Indian water rights would not be articulated until 1908.

With respect to the San Carlos Reservoir, David H. DeJong, in *Stealing the Gila* (2009), explains the role of William H. Code, whose name appeared multiple times in the correspondence sent to Montezuma and who served as chief irrigation engineer for the Pima Agency during the time period in question. Indeed, it was Code's recommendations regarding water management that were the source of much distress across central Arizona:

> Code served as the "engineer member" of the Salt River Valley Water Users Association (SRVWUA), which met weekly to consider means of securing water for the Salt River valley. Code was adamant that groundwater was the only means of restoring water to the Pima, and it was at his behest the Indian Service no longer recommended construction of a dam at San Carlos, which Code saw as "wasteful and unsuitable." . . . [Instead,] Code proposed wells in place of water stored in the San Carlos Reservoir . . . [which became part of] a scheme that was deleterious to the Pima. . . . It was at this time, Presbyterian missionary Charles Cook opined, that the Reclamation Service went into the hands of big speculators.[18]

On Columbus Day, October 12, 1911, as the Yavapai-O'odham crisis grew, the Society of American Indians held its inaugural meeting, which Montezuma played a role in organizing. Yet Montezuma did not appear on the conference agenda. As Hertzberg recounts, Montezuma was vehemently against including Indian Bureau employees: "The anti-Indian Bureau forces in the new organization were well represented by Dr. Carlos Montezuma—'Wassaja' or 'Monty'—known as 'the fiery Apache.'" Hertzberg adds: "Like Eastman he [Montezuma] was uprooted from tribal life, went to white schools, and married a white woman," which suggests an attempt to explain why Montezuma was opposed to the Indian Bureau presence in the SAI. With his life story in mind, Hertzberg analyzes Montezuma's character profile:

> [Richard] Pratt's ideology—"to civilize the Indian, put him in civilization and keep him there"—suited him exactly and he took it over as his own. He admired Pratt deeply, perhaps because he and Pratt were somewhat alike— intolerant men of simple, unchanging, but strongly held views.
>
> Montezuma, like Pratt, hated the Indian Bureau and reservation life. He believed in public education and instant assimilation. He was a self-made man, an individualist, a fiery speaker, and a writer with a polemical pen. But unlike Pratt he was, after all, a "full-blooded" Indian, and in him the conflict between being an Indian and living in the white world ran very deep.

As an example of Montezuma's inner turmoil, Hertzberg points to a paradox in his attitude toward reservation life, namely that he developed a loathing for the reservation system during his experience as a government physician, yet "when . . . mortally ill, he returned to the reservation to die."[19]

What Hertzberg's analysis does not take into consideration is that Montezuma was suffering from trauma. Although Hertzberg identifies all of the crises in Montezuma's life, in particular his abduction, being separated from his siblings, the death of his parents, being held captive by the Akimel O'odham, his purchase by Carlo Gentile, and his forced removal to New York, then Chicago, where he grew up in a world that had little regard for Indigenous people, Hertzberg enumerates these hardships without reaching the crucial insight that Wassaja, the boy, paid a psychological toll that informed his sense of self and his relationship with the American Indian community. Hertzberg instead focuses on his intransigence as an anti–Indian Bureau thinker and activist. "Montezuma was one of the few men with whom another founder of the SAI, the Reverend Sherman Coolidge, ever quarreled publicly."[20] By contrast, Crandall argues in his Yavapai-centric discourse on Montezuma that

> [Wassaja's abduction] shaped everything that came after: his search for family, the evolution of his identity as an Indian and as a Yavapai, and his return to Arizona later in life. . . . The period of most intense trauma for Wassaja was during his most important formative years. When viewed through this lens, the events of his early childhood assume their proper significance.[21]

The year 1912 was a momentous one in Arizona, as it became the last of the forty-eight contiguous states to be admitted into the Union, an event marked on February 14. George W. P. Hunt became the new state's first governor,[22] while Carl Hayden, progressive Democrat from Tempe, was elected its first congressman.[23] Hayden's name appears repeatedly in Arizona Indigenous history during this period, not only because of the role he played in Indian affairs as a congressman, but also due to his advocacy for what became the Salt River Project.[24] At the same time, there was no acknowledgement of Arizona statehood in the letters sent from Arizona to Montezuma. One way of interpreting this omission is in terms of how distressed the Yavapai were at the growing domination that Arizonans had over the lands and lives of the Yavapai. Statehood was not something worth celebrating. Nevertheless, the Yavapai were quite aware of the population and economic growth occurring around them, from Prescott to Phoenix, which was driving the effort to remove them from their Yavapai homeland. Within this context, Charles Dickens dominated Montezuma's attention throughout 1912, as eight of the nine letters were from him, the exception being Grace Pelcher. It should also be noted that Montezuma was awaiting word from Secretary of the Interior Walter L. Fisher in response to the appeal that he and others representing Fort McDowell had made before the House Committee on Expenditures during the summer of 1911. Insofar as the Yavapai at Fort McDowell were struggling to protect their water rights, in addition to remaining on their executive-order reservation, the impact of both the Winters Doctrine and the Kent Decree could influence Interior's decision on the fate of the Yavapai. The Winters Doctrine (articulated in *Winters v. United States* [1908]) stipulated that "Indian land reserved by treaty included the reservation of water necessary for the [present and future] irrigation of the land,"[25] and the Kent Decree (articulated in *Hurley v. Abbott* [1910]) "established the water priorities for the Salt River Valley," including Fort McDowell, which was granted from the Verde River "sufficient water to irrigate 3,000 acres of land."[26] Presently, the Indian Bureau was refusing to honor the Yavapai's request for an irrigation dam, saying that "at least 5,000 acres were necessary to justify a dam."[27]

As for the letters from Charles Dickens, a person named "Goodrich" and plans for building a dam at Fort McDowell recurred throughout his messages, as did references to a "Mrs Grey" and Harry Temple.[28] Otherwise, Dickens only reported that the Yavapai were always working, as they anxiously awaited news from Washington, D.C., about the Indian Bureau's plans for them. In the meantime, some of the Fort McDowell Yavapai had moved to the Salt River Reservation.

> George Dickens Mother she is now died. Can You make out and put in a new paper about her and let the peoples know there[?][29]

> Mr. Goodrich was here last month with his wife and looking [for] the place to build a dam. He found the place alright. You know the place to. Up to right on reservation line.[30]

> Did you hear any news from Washington Congress yet?[31]

I just received aletter [*sic*] from Mrs. Grey . . . I told her everythings is alright here[.] Nothing going on. and I told her we working every days our land puting Grain in. We all well.[32]

I am sorry you did not send me the $65.00 That I want you loan me to pay for my wagon. . . . My work is down there at Arizona Canal Reclamation Service[33] we all through working down there. if I still working right along this month I will pay all on my wagon. . . . You know we all help each other when we was Washington in Committee Cousin & Cousin[.] Please do it what I ask you[.] I cannot wait for my bills[.][34]

General [Richard H] Pratt is here to-day from Phoenix and he return back this after noon with Supt. Goodman. we were very glad to see Gen. Pratt and he say I can write you and let you know that he is here. and he say he want you to buy are O Basket and he say you can buy good one here.[35]

[Latimer] send us a letters that he received from Secretary Fish[36] & First Secretary Samuel Adams[37] that allotments at McDowell.[38]

Also we glad to hear that You coming out here again and see us in Sept 10/12. I hope you come soon . . . About Mr. Harry Temple[39] as we want him to be Agt here at Camp McDowell reservation still we want him yet. He is good man as we know him very well indeed when he was Teacher at San Carlos when I was aboy [*sic*].[40]

Before continuing with the above correspondence, it is worth noting that Charles Dickens's reference to a "Committee" in Washington was in regard to the opportunity that Yavapai community leaders, including Montezuma, had to plead their case before congressional members. Iverson documents this seminal 1911 event before the Committee on Expenditures in the Interior Department of the House of Representatives. The results of this hearing, specifically Secretary of the Interior Fisher's 1912 reversal of the Indian Bureau's plan to relocate the Yavapai, formed the basis of Fort McDowell's effort to stay on their 1903 reservation:

Montezuma and the other Yavapais appeared in Washington before the committee in June. [Charles] Coe and [William] Code testified in July. While the testimony of these various individuals revealed little new information or perspectives that had not surfaced in private communication, the hearings afforded Montezuma and his allies a wonderful opportunity for national publicity and attention. Montezuma had recently retained an attorney, Joseph W. Latimer, to assist him. It marked the beginning of a lifelong association between the two. Latimer figured significantly in the ensuing, continuing debate over McDowell. From this point on, the Indian Service had to deal with persistent questioning from both men. At the hearings, the committee members even allowed Latimer to interrogate witnesses. The attorney had a pleasant time exposing the limited knowledge of some individuals, such as former commissioner Francis E. Leupp.[41]

The publicity and attention to which Iverson makes reference included a front-page story in the *Arizona Republican*. On August 24, 1912, Montezuma was featured in a story headlined "Indians Hold Reservation of M'Dowell," in which the fight to remain on the reservation was reported as a decisive victory for Montezuma and the Yavapai:

> After two years of the hardest fighting the Mohave and Apache Indians of Camp McDowell reservation in Arizona have won their battle against being ousted from their present quarters and transferred by the Indian bureau to a barren waste in the Salt River district. Chief Yuma Frank of the Mohave Apaches will receive the decision made by Secretary Walter L. Fisher of the department of the interior tomorrow provided he calls at the postoffice in Phoenix, Arizona.[42]

One of the reasons, if not the main reason, this story garnered as much attention as it did is the fact that the land in question was regarded as "some of the richest irrigated irrigable land in the southwest."[43] In light of which, it is not surprising that the business interests that wanted the Yavapai removed and the land entered into the public domain got a more sympathetic ear from Fisher's successor, Franklin Lane, complete with a different federal Indian policy, during the administration of Woodrow Wilson, which also saw Cato Sells appointed as Indian commissioner. The latter development, recounted below, is what instigated Montezuma's historic battle against the Indian Bureau.

As for the remainder of Montezuma's 1912 correspondence, Grace Pelcher identified herself as one of Montezuma's cousins. The purpose of her letter was to update Montezuma on the new farm that she and "Max," presumably her husband, acquired "here," in which she apparently meant Camp McDowell. Among their recent visitors were a "Mr & Mrs Goodrich," whom "George," likely George Dickens, took into Mesa. Montezuma must have been hoping to learn about the plans for building a dam at the Verde River, but the Goodriches' visit was foiled by the weather: "I did not have any chance to speak to them. For the day they came it was raining and so very cold that they thought it was best to go to the Agent where they could have a comfortable beds to sleep. I have not heard what he (Mr. Goodrich) thought of building a dame up a bove." The rest of her letter replied to Montezuma's inquiries about "Miss Julia Brown," replies in which it is unclear who this person was to Montezuma.[44]

The year 1913 was a more robust year for correspondence. Montezuma received eighteen letters altogether, half of which were from Charles Dickens while the rest came from Mike Burns (5), George Dickens (2), and Chief Yuma Frank (2). Noteworthy is the copious amount of Yavapai history that Montezuma learned from Burns during this time. Perhaps because of renewed concerns over the Indian Bureau's plans for the Yavapai, in addition to Burns's admiration for his renowned cousin, Burns felt compelled to assert himself as a tribal historian. In a letter dated January 7, Burns wrote about a "Massacre" that occurred at "Superstition Mountain," in a place called "Bloody Cave," where Burns said he was "captured" just like Montezuma.[45] Burns confided to his cousin that he wanted to correct the one-sided narrative that the Whites were telling about the "bad Apaches." He wanted white readers to know that, to the contrary, "the Apaches were forced to be so: and they tried to protect themselves. their families. their homes and their land: and who would not [do] the same thing?"[46] Then, on March 28, Burns described his arduous move as an adult from the San Carlos Agency, where he was more positively regarded, to Fort McDowell, where he was poorly thought of by community members: "Most all those Indians are living at McDowell were used to be very kind and had tenderly feelings toward me: But since they have lived at McDowell so long. and are living independently: and now they think hardly worthy of me."[47]

Speaking of unpleasant relations, Burns told Montezuma on May 28 that he was at an "old post," possibly the original site of the 1865 Camp Verde, later called Camp Lincoln,[48] where the Yavapai once made peace with the American soldiers, in addition to being a place where they were often mistreated.

At this point Burns made an enigmatic reference to "only some Pimas and Maricopas."[49] In light of the historic rivalry between the Pimas and Mohave Apache, it was likely that Burns alluded to the Pima scouts, which were Akimel O'odham from Gila River, that worked for the U.S. Army as a part of their alliance with the United States.

> The Yavapai word for Pima is jo'go ha'na, which means "first enemy" or "primary enemy." Many of our stories refer to warfare with the Pimas, as well as raiding carried out on, or by, them. . . . Anglo Americans took advantage of traditional antagonisms as early as 1865, when hundreds of Pimas were enlisted in the Arizona Volunteers to fight Yavapais and Dilzh'es.[50]

A month later, Burns referred to the "old Camp Grant Messacre [sic]"[51] in quotation marks signifying that this was what the Whites called this crime against Apache humanity:

> I remembered at one time several hundred came here, but got away in a night to the hills and other younger men stolen 3 soldiers' horses. I could see from here. the hill sides and the four Peaks. on that place, where I was taken by the Soldiers. in that night of about the 22nd of December 1872. About 4 days afterwards the Soldiers went into our Main Camp: and killed all of My relatives: an about 30 some were captured and brought here: boy cousin of mine was taken and kept by an Officer who was under Capt Burns Named ED Thomas: but the boy escaped and went with the parties taken to Fort Grant: on San Pedro River. If I had known anything about that the prisoners were going to be taken away that, I Might have gone with the party too: But I thank God, that I did not. because all have died since only afew [sic] ones when I came to San Carlos Agency, but all gone Now. Only Hiram: who is my cousin on our Mother's (or your father's) side: and you are our cousin on our (uncle's side).[52]

No doubt Montezuma was moved by the family history not to mention deeply distressed by the tragedy shared. What Burns referred to as the Camp Grant massacre, which led to his forced adoption by Army Captain James Burns, was in fact the 1872 Skeleton or Skull Cave Massacre. However, the Yavapai who miraculously survived were rounded up as prisoners and taken to Camp Grant.

The Kwevkepaya [Yavapai] women and children who survived the cave slaughter went, as prisoners, to Camp Grant [northeast of Tucson, south of Winkelman] and, like most Yavapai refugees and prisoners, ended up on the San Carlos Apache Reservation, in eastern Arizona, in 1875. U.S. officers, however, stole the orphaned Hoomothya [Mike Burns] from his people. Captain Burns . . . named him Mickey Burns, or Mike. . . . As a Carlisle student Burns was still regarded as an "Indian," and in 1885 he was sent back to Arizona, to the San Carlos Reservation.[53]

As for the letter, Burns was anxious for his cousin's reply, which may have had to do with wanting to know what effect this tragedy in Yavapai history had on Montezuma, who had been called upon to play a role in the Fort McDowell battle against the Indian Bureau.

In regard to his ulterior motives for sharing the Yavapai account of the Skeleton Cave Massacre, Burns stated in a subsequent letter:

[Your] letter has given me much satisfaction in towards the much kind feelings of the Indian people. But you had ought not try to do much feelings in helping the Pima and Maricopa Indians. Just because them are the people who had made [you] fatherless and motherless. And they have slaughtered more of our people than any other people. No telling how many hundred of our people at different other places. They came upon them in nights: while our people were sleeping. At one and the first place: was at near the foot hills of the superstition Mountains: where they were called to council: and were told to come there without any weapon. There came over hundred: there must have been nearly 500 Pimas and Maricopas and some soldiers. The soldiers fired upon the Indians. When seating in two rows: and Pimas and Maricopas were on their ponies. Who were to chase after the Indians who tries to run for life. Only a few escaped alive. But all were wounded. Some miles from there several hundred were killed in a night: and more were again: some distance from there: a few years before your capture: where many were killed and several taken with you: and many other places: such occurrences of slaughters to our people. More so to our near relatives were killed in those ridge of a [mountain] . . . where our people used to room . . . I want to find time to write something about, how our people were treated: including your capture: also: but I want to make it to book form.[54]

While Burns acknowledged the value of Montezuma's inter-tribal agenda in principle, the relationship between the Yavapai and the Akimel O'odham in reality was complicated by the Skeleton Cave Massacre—not to mention other instances in which O'odham scouts supported military campaigns against the Yavapai and Apache—which was still a living memory. Indeed, the Skeleton Cave Massacre was of singular distinction in the oral history of the Yavapai:

> In the course of forcing all Yavapais onto the reservation, the army wiped out a large band of Kewevkapaya in the Salt River Canyon on December 27, 1872. These people were killed by soldiers who shot into a cave in which they had taken refuge. Of all the massacres during the 1860s and 1870s (for example, at Bloody Basin, Skull Valley, and Date Creek) the one at "Skeleton Cave" is remembered as the most horrendous in Yavapai history.[55]

With respect to this tragic legacy in Yavapai-O'odham relations, Crandall observes:

> [Montezuma's, and by extension, Burns's] capture and early life must be examined and understood as part of a larger Yavapai historical narrative. The 1860s and 1870s were a truly terrifying time for Yavapais, and the young [boys'] capture is one episode linked to a larger chain of events.[56]

In light of which, Burns thought that his Yavapai cousin ought to be more concerned about the "Pimas and Maricopas" than the Indian Bureau when it came to the latter's plans to remove the Yavapai down to the Salt River Reservation. At the same time, Burns was certainly not as knowledgeable about Akimel O'odham history as he was of Yavapai; otherwise, he might have commented on how the Salt and Gila River Reservations were suffering as much as the Yavapai under Indian Bureau control.

According to DeJong, as of 1913, the Akimel O'odham had been imploring the federal government to take action in protecting their water rights for more than four decades:

> The Pima [Akimel O'odham] initially requested federal support for their water rights in 1871, and the owners of the Florence Canal Company prepared for such litigation in 1886, although in neither instance did the U.S.

Government prosecute Pima water rights. In 1904, the Indian Service again rejected federal action, believing the cost of protecting Pima water rights unworthy of the expense. Not until 1913 did the Indian Service initiate action, recognizing that if federal action were not taken, Pima rights to water might be irretrievably lost.[57]

As for the other letters received throughout 1913, Charles Dickens continued to be the most earnest about maintaining a friendly relationship with his cousin. Given the hardship that Dickens endured, especially financially, it was likely that he felt enriched by his connection to Montezuma, not just as a source of financial aid but also in terms of self-esteem. Indeed, Charles often took the lead in arranging Montezuma's annual hunting trips to Arizona, which Dickens mentioned in all but one of his 1913 letters. Incidentally, in a letter dated June 28, after asking Montezuma for a 30–30 Winchester, Dickens relayed, "I am working for Reclamation Service yet. We dont know where we through. I may work all this Summer."[58] Then, on July 11, in addition to asking for an "Army Trumpet," Dickens shared his delight at the news that "You [Montezuma] are bring a party to hunt with us and I am glad to hear that Geo[rge] Morgan Coming back to Arizona again on September 5th or 10th. also Dr. Gibson or Mrs Gibson."[59]

Charles, in spite of his obsequiousness, was not unconcerned about the issues confronting the Yavapai. On July 28, Dickens urgently inquired: "Have you heard anything new from Washington or have you heard [from] Latimer yet[?] Tell him write[.] I would like to hear from you."[60] As of 1913, Cato Sells was Indian Commissioner, who made it immediately clear from the outset that he wanted to relocate the Yavapai to Salt River. What support Montezuma and Latimer earned for the Yavapai cause during the previous administration soon vanished when Woodrow Wilson entered the White House. In his 1913 annual report as commissioner of Indian Affairs, Sells summarized his progressive and, one might say at a glance, humanitarian agenda for the reservation system:

I am also emphasizing the need of and doing everything possible to obtain for the Indians more sanitary homes, more adequate school facilities for Indian children, supplying sick Indians with medical attention and taking precautionary methods to prevent disease, adjusting more equitably the cost of irrigation projects constructed out of reimbursable funds, making larger use of the timber resources of the Indians for their industrial and social advancement, taking advantage of the valuable grazing lands of the Indians to build up tribal herds as well as promoting among individual Indians a larger and more profitable cattle, sheep, and horse industry, and utilizing in every practicable way the resources of the Indians, both tribal and individual, in promoting their more complete civilization and economic independence.[61]

Indian affairs–related news turned up intermittently. Montezuma heard about the arrest of Richard Dickens—Charles and George's brother—for making "tefist wand [sic] from a corn for drink," by which is meant tiswin, an Indigenous type of wine; in the same letter George also shared the distressing news about a community member being killed by a local missionary:

> But Cousin one thing I want to write a protest against one Geo[rge] H. Gebby the Missionary of this reservation who acted as police going about the camps and search for this drinks. that might be alright But it comes to pa[c]king a six shooter or deadly weapon Not only at that but and attempt made by him. Now we need a protection or we need you to have you look in to the Matter. One of our people had been killed here by the same manner by William Gill [another missionary]. Now I think you have away of better teaching and than with six shooter. I dont believe this said person had any right to carry six shooter. This is all I have to say[.] Let me hear from [you] at once.[62]

The vigilantism on the part of the missionary may have been instigated by the assumption that the Indian Bureau, from the commissioner to superintendents to field employees, were empowered to micromanage Indian behavior on the pretense of guiding them toward "civilized habits."

With respect to Yavapai "civilization," Charles E. Coe, who was known for becoming livid at the mere mention of Montezuma's name, was also well known for his opposition to any kind of Indian dancing. Much to the frustration of the Yavapai, Coe repeatedly rejected requests for even a single night of accommodation. The only one with the authority to override Coe was Commissioner Sells, who did so during Montezuma's 1913 visit. Montezuma attended without qualms a cultural event that Coe and the Indian Bureau officially regarded as morally depraved. Consequently, after a night of dancing that included Montezuma's hunting party guests, "the dance stirred angry re-

sponses directed to the commissioner from Charles E. Coe, the Superintendent of the Salt River and Fort McDowell Reservations, and a Presbyterian
missionary in Scottsdale, George H. Gebby." Because of Montezuma's role in
getting Sells's permission—in addition to a subsequent effort at organizing
another Indian dance, which failed—Montezuma acquired a reputation as
an unwanted proponent of the "old ways."[63]

As for William Gill, who was also mentioned in Dickens's letter, Iverson
identifies him as the "Rev. W.H. Gill, a local missionary who had assisted
the Yavapais, [who] gained charge of the Indians and was told to get them
settled on their new land," meaning their newly created 1903 Fort McDowell
Reservation. With regard to the shooting that led to a Yavapai death:

> Before they [Rev. Gill and his wife] had to leave the reservation in 1907 be-
> cause of an altercation over gambling during which the missionary [Gebby]
> had killed a Yavapai, the Gills (together with the Yavapais) had realized some
> success [at adapting the Yavapais to the reservation economy and its "civiliz-
> ing" efforts]. Montezuma recalled in 1911 that his people had been instructed
> to be ". . . bee raisers, to raise domestic fowls (chickens and turkeys), cattle
> and horses; gardeners raised all kinds of vegetables, and did general farming;
> and then these good people, Mr. and Mrs. Gill, told the 'good old story' to
> them on Sunday."[64]

Yuma Frank, in his letters dated August 9–13 and August 9, 1913, shared
an instance in which three Akimel O'odham suddenly appeared carrying
an American flag. Frank's letter included comments from Juan Andrews,
who was from Salt River. The letter is important because it is an instance
in which the Yavapai and O'odham defied the Indian Bureau's prohibition
against inter-tribal communication (see below). Most important, Juan Andrews, the "Pima Indian chief at Salt River," expressed a desire for "50 acre
of lands" from the U.S. allotting agent surveying Salt River. Frank and other
Yavapai were resisting the land allotment policy that was driving the Indian
Bureau's management of the reservation system. Consequently, "Juan [and]
some the Indians dont like me [Yuma Frank] to be chief I didnt want to take
10 acre of land. Juan Andrews came ask me to write a letter to you."[65] It is
unclear if Chief Andrews was a member of the visiting party carrying the flag
or if the three men served as his messengers. In the letter dated August 9, the
anecdote about the three men carrying the flag and the message from An-

drews was repeated word for word. However, in addition, there was a short paragraph in which Frank acknowledged the seven dollars that Montezuma sent him, along with news that Mike Burns and others had gone to work with Charles Dickens, presumably for the Bureau of Reclamation, on the "Arizona Canal." Dickens, appearing as the third voice in Frank's letter, asked Montezuma, "who is new commissioner[?] have you heard anythings news from Washington D.C. from the Ind[ian] Department[?] or have you heard how soon McDowell Indians allotment[?]"[66] As the Yavapai were being pressured into accepting small allotments at Salt River, not to mention the Indian Bureau's intransigence in refusing the Yavapai request for an irrigation dam, Fisher's reversal of opinion about Yavapai relocation must have felt like an episode from an earlier era. Yet it was merely a year earlier.

As 1913 drew into fall, Charles Dickens mentioned to Montezuma that "Chief Frank and Geo[rge] Dickens were here at my Camp to-day and I explain to tham about your coming and with party. and with General Pratt and others. from Chicago and from New York City. to visit Arizona and hunt." Dickens then asked his cousin to secure permission "from the Indian Department of Washington for One night Indian dance here McDowell Reservation. for you party to see the Mohave Apache dance. Once than let us know if you get permission from Indian Department. Mr. Coe & Mr. Shafer they dont let us permission to dance. We all poor. You know the peoples [everywhere] have dance. The same was as we gone to have dance."[67] The year ended with another letter from Charles, who shared news that "Max Pelcher" was ill. Moreover, the Yavapai wanted to take their grievances to Washington, D.C.: "Some days ago we Spoken about that we would like to go to Washington again and more talking thing at McDowell[.] And we like take 10. good men & 2 women go along and we talking to Commissioner or President. If you think the best for us to go again with 2 old women! write me & let me know."[68]

At the behest of Richard Pratt, Montezuma accepted Arthur C. Parker's invitation to speak at a February 1914 meeting in Philadelphia, at which Cato Sells attended. Montezuma did not hesitate to speak truth to power:

> His featured address, "The Reservation Is Fatal to the Development of Good Citizenship," earned high marks from Parker. "You hit the nail and the Commissioner listened with marked attention," he told Montezuma. "We are

deeply indebted to you and I thank you from the bottom of my heart." . . .
Montezuma used the analogy of American policy toward foreign immigrants throughout his talk, suggesting that Indians must learn to speak English, attend public schools, and, in general, be placed in surroundings of
civilization.[69]

Montezuma then directed Sells's attention to the crisis brewing in Arizona:

> He also criticized the federal government for irrigation projects and forestry
> projects that had taken away Indian lands and timber and for locking up
> four Pima Indians at an agent's request and keeping them in the Phoenix jail
> without specific charges. Montezuma informed the commissioner that the
> Indian was generally still "an outlawed creature, with no rights that protect
> the ordinary human being," and that he was governed "by a machine whose
> agents have most despotic powers and whose unscrupulous actions in many
> instances 'smell to heaven.'"[70]

Abundantly clear at this juncture was the fact that the Yavapai, not to mention other Indigenous nations, were invisible to the powers that be, namely
Commissioner Sells and President Wilson. What Montezuma was unable to
do, yet, was turn the Yavapai conflict with the Indian Bureau into a political
issue, compelling Congress to act. More exactly, what was not happening was
making the federal system, from local Indian agent to Indian Affairs commissioner to president of the United States, accountable for its disregard for
Indigenous rights. Instead, Sells focused on making Indian Affairs friendly
toward non-Indigenous economic development, such as the Arizona canal.
On August 10, 1913, five months before Montezuma's confrontation with
Sells in Philadelphia, the *Arizona Republican* ran a story titled "Gem Valley
of Them All," which touted the economic value of the "Arizona canal" that
put an end to the flooding problem in Paradise Valley, just north of Phoenix.
Secretary of the Interior Franklin D. Lane personally inspected the canal,
along with Project Engineer F. W. Hanna, who was quoted on what was then
a crowning achievement of the Bureau of Reclamation:

> I predict a great future of this section [of the Arizona canal] and a most pros-
> perous one. It seems to me that every favorable condition for heavy crops of

much wanted classes of produce can be met in [Paradise Valley]. The disadvantages are few and advantages are many. I shall look forward to another visit to Phoenix in the course of my duties, with a great deal of pleasure.[71]

In the sunny glow of statehood, Arizona was growing and there would be no turning back. What then was the future of Indian Affairs?

FIGURE 1 Unknown photographer. "Vintage photograph depicting Charles, Richard, and Sam Dickens, undated." Photograph. Courtesy Carlos Montezuma Photograph Collection, Greater Arizona Collection, Arizona State University Library.

FIGURE 2 Unknown photographer. "Dr. Carlos Montezuma, c 1889." Photograph.
Courtesy Carlos Montezuma Photograph Collection, Greater Arizona Collection,
Arizona State University Library.

CHAPTER TWO

At the Brink of War

Montezuma Battles the American Kaiser

In 1914 the winds of war blew across Europe, erupting in armed conflict on July 28, as the United States stood by maintaining a supposedly neutral position under President Wilson. Far away in Arizona, on the Fort McDowell Mohave Apache Reservation, a very different kind of conflict continued to wreak havoc. Documenting the toll of this conflict, which most Americans knew nothing about, Charles and George Dickens, Mike Burns, and Yuma Frank sent Montezuma eleven letters recounting how Fort McDowell and Salt River divided into factions in which Burns and Juan Andrews stood on one side of the issue of land allotment and the Dickens brothers and Yuma Frank stood on the other. Montezuma consequently found himself in the middle, struggling to mediate a compromise, which, if Montezuma had his way, would mean the abolishment of the Indian Bureau, which forbade, as things stood, any group of Indians from meeting for the purpose of organizing to defend their rights.

In a letter dated March 19, 1914, Andrews informed Montezuma about an alleged scammer, Francisco Hill, who reportedly made his way around "Sacaton: Lehi. and Salt River" reservations, asking people for money for a planned trip to Washington, D.C. Andrews was trying to arrange for a Salt River delegation at this time. Under false pretenses, Hill was charging his unsuspecting victims upwards of $25.00 to write letters in English, presumably to either submit their grievances to Andrews or to express interest in joining the delegation. Andrews did not approve of this. Consequently, Andrews, through Burns, asked Montezuma "to send me a letter in regards to Francisco Hill: Whether you have really told him: to go around and collect from the Indians Money: to come over to Washington himself: He wants to have that man to put stop to talking about you all the time: and to be punish[ed] for taking money on fauls pretense: and also saying: that he sends you some money all the time: Answer soon."[1]

Burns's subsequent letter shows that, perhaps because of Montezuma's cordial relationship with the Akimel O'odham, Burns's relationship with Andrews became friendlier, as they developed into unexpected allies. Burns was the one who had advised Montezuma to be cautious about supporting the O'odham in their contentions with the Indian Bureau. As an example of his change of heart, Burns described a pleasant social engagement at Salt River, in which Andrews asked permission to hold a dance, but was unsurprisingly declined. Nonetheless, Burns enjoyed his visit. Burns then informed Montezuma of instances in which Superintendent Coe not only threatened the O'odham under his charge but also became angry at the mere mention of Montezuma's name. Seeing Montezuma as a genuine threat to his authority, Coe gathered together O'odham who were agreeable to accepting ten-acre allotments at Salt River, in contradiction to what Montezuma was advising. Together, Coe and his O'odham collaborators met with Inspector Otis B. Goodall, the "supervisor of Indian schools, Riverside, California."

Goodall heard that John Shafer, the farmer employed by the Bureau to work with the Yavapais, had been absent too much and gained the unyielding antagonism of much of the tribe. While contending that the Yavapais were "hard to govern owing to the prevalent habits among them of indulging in 'tiswin' and gambling," Goodall concluded that Shafer had no more usefulness at the reservation and should be transferred. Following Goodall's report to Sells, Shafer responded angrily to the charges. The farmer argued that the petition and charges had not "originated in the mind of any of these Indians, but was conceived and born during the visit of Dr. Carlos Montezuma and his party of hunters (game vandals) to this reservation in October of last year." Shafer said he had told Montezuma of his opposition to Indian dances, gambling, medicine men, and the making and drinking of tiswin and would do all he could to suppress them. He also learned after the dance held in Montezuma's honor that the doctor promised to "kick Superintendent Coe and myself off the Reservation, of course, through his influence with the Indian Department." Montezuma's visits had promoted opposition to him.

For the Indians to advance, the Department must "successfully combat the effect of this outside influence."[2]

Implied in Shafer's alarm was the realization that there were many O'odham who were not amenable to Coe's agenda, and who were anxious to meet Montezuma about their rights. Unfortunately, because of Indian Bureau oppression of Indian rights, the Salt River coalition needed permission from the commissioner of Indian Affairs to meet, otherwise they could only expect trouble from Coe and the Indian police:

> I have learned that the Pimas are not allowed to come together and have some meetings or councils: unless they are arrested: Nor: they are not allowed to come over to McDowell to talk with these people: less they are suspected: You must tell me to be sure: to be here: on certain day: so I will tell Chief Juan [Andrews] to meet you: as he says: that the Agent told him that he is going to give 10 acres: to Indians in fall: as he cares not to accept that 10 acres with out seeing you first: lots of other things he wanted to see you about: More so than I can write and to tell you: about: I will be here until you come: then I may go back up north again. it is a very hard hole to be in: no house for work away from any civilized communities: or any news papers to read: so faraway to markets: I have never lived a harder life: as I have had since I came here: so goodbye.[3]

On July 22, Burns bemoaned how McDowell "is the loneliest place, I have ever lived. as there is no way to get work," by which he must have meant earning a livable income. Burns pointed out that he had periodically "been called to attend U.S. Courts: as to be interpreter. twice now. once: I was up to near my home: as it was at Prescott and once at Phoenix," for which he earned "$5.00 per day." As for affairs at Fort McDowell, Chief Yuma Frank had been ill, but fortunately was on the mend. Still, as Burns implored Montezuma: "This little band of ours: need much help here: and we are going to make a talk to some one: for claim on this state for settlement to the land of Arizona: which was taken away from us: with out treaty: I have not seen the Pimas near [nor?] Maricopas yet: So hoping to hear from you again."[4] Burns then wrote a few weeks later on behalf of Salt River Chief Andrews: "could you [Montezuma] come write the Commissioner Sells: As he needs your help very bad: and also wants me: to go down to Phoenix: to meet the

Commissioner and to have a talk with him there."[5] During September 1914, Assistant Indian Commissioner E. B. Merritt cautioned Cato Sells about expecting to move the Yavapai at Fort McDowell down to Salt River, making an unexpected recommendation: "all of McDowell should be allotted to the Yavapais; the reservation should be fenced to keep Anglo livestock from grazing on timberland and from destroying Yavapai crops." Ostensibly, this sounded like a plan that Montezuma would support, but for one thing. Merritt added: "It might be desirable to provide the Yavapais with additional allotments with irrigable acreage, 10 acres each, on Salt River."[6] Montezuma would see this as ploy, as the land at Fort McDowell would not include guaranteed water rights.

On September 12, Burns informed Montezuma that the dam was installed "on the Verde River . . . about 2 miles above the river the place." With regard to the structure's impact on Yavapai livelihood, Burns insisted that the dam would not do them any harm: "Not going to stop the water running down to the Indian ditch: When it be built they have to let the water go down just the same way as that of Roosevelt: there will be no canal to hurt the Indians. Only to store water when high water comes."[7] How Burns could feel so certain about this was unclear. On Christmas Day, Burns's account of events ended with a bang, as he warned his cousin that there were rumors circulating about him, that Montezuma's arrival was expected, and that dances planned in his honor were forbidden. Indeed, as Burns further recounted, a Fort McDowell teacher, "Mr Klingerberg" [sic],[8] read a letter from Commissioner Sells, in which he expressed grave concern for the Salt River Agency, mentioning the need to move the "Mohave Apaches."

> The new Indian Commissioner [Cato Sells] must be a hard man in treating the Indians desires: Geo[rge] Dickens, who is the head chief now, after Yuma Frank's death: he has been pretty sore: about the new orders: especially about the dances: The letter was read: at the last end: "From the troubles occurred at the last dance given at the time of Dr. Montezuma's visit": What troubles occurred I do not know. Also about chief Jaun Andrease, Pima of Saltriver: has wishing to see you: or could you come with the Commissioner if he should ever come? Since I have been among the Indians here: there has been no help given to these people: nor there has been nobody ever spoke to the Dept. at Washington for help here: so that they could be better situated, or could do much more.[9]

The Yavapai crisis was a classic case of a bureaucracy becoming completely out of touch with the people it was supposed to serve and protect, contrary to the intention of the trust relation between tribes and the federal government. The Indian Bureau was ostensibly responsible for every Indian in the reservation system, which, if handled responsibly, ought to mean that neither Congress nor the American people need be concerned. However, what was a given tribe supposed to do when that system, that bureaucracy, failed them? The Yavapai, insofar as they were considered "wards," were at the mercy of their trustee, the United States, which appointed the Indian Bureau as caretaker. Nevertheless, hidden behind the façade of normality—like a "happy family" hiding abuse—was a crisis that threatened lives.

On April 30, in a letter that must have challenged Montezuma's admiration for Indian education, George Dickens expressed his disdain for John Shafer, who was excoriated earlier for his abysmal job as Indian Bureau farmer. Similar to the gun-toting missionary mentioned earlier, Shafer was prone to abusing his power: "All he does is to go down to Phoenix two or three time a week and never go around among our farms and help us. . . . Also I told him that he separate for couples who has been married and sent them to Phoenix [Indian] school. I do not think it is right at all. Also when the Indians do any thing wrong Shafer always says to sent them to Phoenix for punished." In the same letter, growing animosity toward Mike Burns was on full display as Dickens shared his suspicion that Burns was an Indian Bureau collaborator: "Well after the inspector [Goodall?] was gone Two or three days after than, I heard and Mike Nelson the policeman[10] [that?] Mike Burns had a meeting and took all the names of the Yum[a]s and the old people and the little children and sent in."[11] Charles Dickens, in turn, corroborated his brother George's misgivings about Burns in a letter dated July 3, roughly two months after George's last letter: "The other day ago him [Burns] & others Yuma [Mohave Apache] tribes has signing a paper for something. & we dont know what they sign for. If anything you can hear from Washington what they sign. please let us know. We have heard Mike Burns pick up just Yuma tribes Indians signing apaper. to John W. Shafer Office without Mohave Apaches knowing. We Mohave tribes we dont sign any paper until we hear from you."[12]

On July 13 Richard Dickens, the third of the three brothers, added his concern about Burns spreading demeaning rumors about the Yavapai: "I want to know you had received any letter from Mike Burns saying that the

Indians were still drinking twiswine. and gamble yet. He is telling you a story. Because I am trying my very best to do what is right[.] I heard today that Mike Burns is against us." More urgently, "Geo[rge] Dickens, Cha[rle]s Dickens, Thomas Surramma, Harry Mott, [and] James Frank" were all worried that Burns had organized several Yavapai for the purpose of supporting Shafer's agenda, which included removing the Fort McDowell Yavapai down to Salt River.[13] Lastly, not long before he died, Yuma Frank wrote to Montezuma, stating, "Yes! I am willing to keep up what my father has said at the passe[past?]. We do not want to give up what he had done for the McDowell Indians. So please do still help us about the land and the dam building for the Indians."[14]

Throughout his adult life, Mike Burns was remembered for his youthful transgressions against his own people, which likely influenced the above concerns. Harrison and Williams recount that Burns was responsible for leading soldiers to a cave where many Kwevkepaya Yavapai were slaughtered. The cave in question was Skeleton Cave, as it was known in 1872 when Colonel George Crook led his soldiers, complete with O'odham and Aravaipa Apache scouts, on a campaign into Salt River Canyon. Burns was approximately seven years old. Nevertheless, despite his being a mere child, "After the soldiers killed my people in the cave, they take that boy away. Send him to school. Let him loose when he is a young man. But when he comes back to San Carlos, people are sure were pretty rough with him." Burns was spared when an elder, Wipukpa, saw value in the otherwise unwanted relative. Burns knew English, so he could serve as a translator. Still, anger continued to fester.

> Later Mike Burns come down here to Fort McDowell with his wife and kids. But people here are still rough with him. And they don't like his son. They don't like the son because the father showed the cave and all their relatives got killed. That time my [Williams's] father was boss for cleaning the irrigation ditches. He always send that man who showed the cave and his son the other way to clean ditches. Don't let them work with the rest of the people. If he do that, maybe someone hit them with a shovel.[15]

Among contemporary Yavapai, Crandall expresses compassion for Burns's ordeal: "Mike Burns, a Yavapai boy who had been taken captive by the army a few days before the Skeleton Cave Massacre, was dragged to the top of the canyon wall and forced to watch as the soldiers massacred his relatives and friends."[16] With respect to Burns's traumatic experience, Crandall argues that one can extrapolate from this how Montezuma, much more respected than Burns, went through a similarly distressing experience:

> [Montezuma's] early life was one of extreme violence and terror. He knew the constant fear of raids. He most likely had family members killed by settlers and soldiers. He probably lost members of his immediate circle to capture, or had captive members of other tribes incorporated into his own group. He knew the Pimas [Akimel O'odham] as the jo'go ha'na. He saw families broken up, with parents, aunties, cousins, and others killed, and kinship circles disrupted. He was literally born into a Yavapai world that was in complete chaos.[17]

On the one hand, it is easy to appreciate the cogency of Crandall's argument. After all, Montezuma did repeatedly refer to his storied abduction whenever he spoke of himself as an exemplar of Indian progress. On the other hand, one is hard pressed to find anything in Montezuma's writings—or the writings of anyone who knew him—in which he clearly exhibited his trauma. Which is not to say he did not suffer the long-term effects of the devastation he experienced. Rather it is to point out that, despite the parallels between Burns's and Montezuma's lives, they handled their trauma differently. Most important, Montezuma did not have to blame himself for leading soldiers to his people's hiding place.

Perhaps having poured out his heart the previous year, Burns only accounted for one of the thirteen letters that Montezuma received in 1915, which was a year that also saw Montezuma's historically important statement against the Indian Bureau, "Let My People Go." Burns was limited to being a cosigner to a letter dated January 22, along with "Geo[rge] Dickens (chief head), Frank Asif(?) chief, Cha[rle]s Dickens, Tom Suramma [*sic*], Harry Mott, Al Suber(?), Joe Bennett, Richard Dickens, [and] John Blake." The purpose of this joint missive was to inform Montezuma of their urgent concerns about the welfare of the Fort McDowell Reservation, specifically what they saw as the need to dam the Verde River. The Yavapai wanted an irrigation dam for the purpose of keeping their land, as opposed to diverting the water away from them to only benefit the whites. Toward this objective, the "head Men" wanted to go to Washington, D.C., to plead their case, as they had done in 1911.

This land is our Motherland: And for that reason: We desire no other land: We can remember: that our forefathers used to plant their crops: two places above here: on Verdi River: hundreds of years before Columbus: We can show any man: still can see some places the ditches: that some of our old people made: in those days even just with their hands: Because then, we were many Indians: and then no sickness nor deaths: occured so much: as it is now: So We care not to move to no other land: and We only wanted a dam to be built for us: and that is all we ask: the Government to help us now.

Burns concluded with a postscript about "Jaun Andrease [sic]," who wanted Montezuma "to write him a letter and advise him: concerning about the 10 acres allotment."[18]

Throughout 1915 the Dickens family provided Montezuma the clearest picture of what was happening on the Fort McDowell Reservation. Montezuma, of course, continued to hear from his cousin Charles above all others. However, the most urgent news arrived by way of George Dickens, now chief. In letters dated January 11, July 10, and August 28, Montezuma learned there was a dam planned for "horse shoe ranch"[19]—another major development in the Salt River Project—and that Shafer was finally transferred: "Well, I think we got the best farmer here Now; he seems to help the Indian's Alright on farming."[20] Chief Dickens also related that he had heard from "[Fayette] McKenzies," who said he would take the Yavapai grievances to Washington, D.C. In the meantime, construction of the previously proposed fence began, complete with 440 pounds of "Bob wire." Dickens further reported: "We work on now 2 miles from the Verde River at West side. and I think we work on other side Verde River east-side." Also, "Mr. Moore," the new farmer—Shafer's replacement—encouraged the Yavapai to build new houses, presumably to solidify their rightful claim to their land.[21] Whether or not the Yavapai owned water rights to their "rightful claim" was unclear. On the subject of Yavapai rights, Chief Dickens also asked Montezuma and his "friends" (a likely reference to attorney Latimer and the Society of American Indians) for help: "We all McDowell Indians[.] we all Stick togeather and to you yet. and also we dont want sign any papers as you told us. We alright now." Dickens's letter ended with a reminder of how little sovereignty the Yavapai had on their ancestral lands: "Dear Cousin I want you get permission to hunt more deer this year. and bring out here when you come."[22]

On August 28, Chief Dickens recounted Cato Sells's visit to Fort Mc-
Dowell, during which the chief appealed for support of the Yavapai's effort
to remain on their reservation. Coe and an unnamed engineer accompanied
Sells, who inspected the Horseshoe Ranch, which was on the Verde River
where the Bureau of Reclamation planned a dam for the benefit of non-
Indian residents and businesses. According to Dickens, Sells responded to
his entreaties with the kind of benign indifference that tribal leaders often
encountered when expecting their concerns to be taken seriously:

Commissioner [Sells] say if I move down to Salt River I can race more Crops
and he said I am Commissioner if I move he said he going to help me a gread
deal. and I said I dont want move. and I said I better stay here my old home.
I said to him you can see from here to the mountain belong when I was a
child. & I said all this Mohave Apache they home here. As I told you before
and Commissioner say to much money Cost to build adam by the ingneer
said. and I Answer back to him if you Cannot do anything for me adam &
I said let that go and I said it is alright for to stay on here and build me the
brush dam. and Commissioner said if You help me and I will help you. and I
said about you that You are my Cousin. and he said he know you very well.
and he said when he return to east he will see you and told you about what I
said to him. And Commissioner say he didnt mean he want me to move but
he dont know him self. and he said he will see the matter when he return to
Washington he want me to stay here without dam. he said he want me to
thing about lader. I said I don't . . . want to move. I better stay here. and he
never say anything as I said I dont want move. and it seems to me he will
help me after while. when he come to you you try to ask him adam again
also allots here.

Clearly anxious about Sells's promise to look into the Yavapai situation
upon his return to Washington, Chief Dickens confided in Montezuma that
they would benefit from a better translator. Was this a criticism of Burns?
Also, as usual, the Yavapai headmen were worried about sending a delegation
to Washington, D.C.:

I lāke Harry Mott & Richard Dickens[,] Alsiebri & Tom Surrama[,] Dock
Dogka, & Sam Jack[,] Frank Osif & Chicken Neck[,] Charles Dickens & Mike
Burns[.] this the Names I send to you we wants to go to Washington and

talked more things to Committee. if you things or if Mr. Latimer things be
alright for us to go again please let me know. or if you can write to James M.
Graham to washington about going over. to Washington.[23]

Among the potential delegates, Surrama and Chicken Neck are both recalled
in *Oral History of the Yavapai*: "My [Williams's] father's name is Surrama,
Thomas Surrama (1865–1939). Surrama, that means 'green spilt over.' I didn't
know they used that as his last name." Surrama is also remembered as "a
headman that tries to lead you guys."[24] As for Chicken Neck, or "Koleonoteh,"
he is remembered as one of the old men who "tell people how to live right,"
which is to say, an elder. As Williams clarifies this community role: "We call
them bakwau. Bakwau, that means 'talking.' Bakwau, that's an adviser. The
chief would choose somebody to do that." Chicken Neck was also one of
the Yavapai who wanted to kill Mike Burns for his role in the Skeleton Cave
Massacre.[25]

During 1915, Montezuma heard from two prominent figures, one from
the Maricopa, or Piipaash, community on the Gila River Reservation, the
other from Crow Nation. On April 22, Grace N. Stewart wrote to Montezuma on behalf of her father, William Stewart, whose brother was the chief
of the Maricopas. According to the chief's niece, it was "Christian people"
who deposed her uncle from his position in the Piipaash community on the
basis that he was too old to lead, which likely meant that he was too traditional and not assimilated enough to meet the satisfaction of the local white
community. Nevertheless, insofar as the upkeep of the reservation was a
concern, even the whites had to acknowledge that the elderly chief was the
best resource for tending the irrigation ditches. As with Fort McDowell, the
Indian Bureau was determined to assign ten-acre allotments against the will
of the people at Gila River.[26] Obviously, when dealing with a largely noncitizen, not to mention non-white, population, the Indian Bureau did not feel
obliged to get anyone's consent. In the meantime, the Piipaash at Gila River
were alarmed about the impact of being forced onto ten-acre allotments:

I think its Not right, to take away any body's land, after its been fixed all in
nice shape, and have worked hard with their lands, then these people went
and took it[.] what will the people do[?] They'll be all starving[,] especially
the . . . school children[.] They can't support them with clothes and food. if
this thing keeps up they'll have to close the school. on account of that they

don't like it a bit, and are fighting for their land to let them have it back. and we are anxiously waiting for, The Hon[orable] Cato sells to come and help them. out of their troubles and want to know when he is coming? Please answer [t]his soon as you can.[27]

Grace Stewart and her family were hopeful that the Indian commissioner would be more sympathetic, if not helpful, than were the local superintendents. What the Piipaash were unaware of was the fact that Commissioner Sells, more so than the men working under him, was responsible for carrying out these unfair policies against them.

The Indian Bureau, of course, thought the work it was doing at the Gila River Reservation, which included the Maricopa, or Piipaash, was making major strides at redressing the Indians' water-rights issues. In his annual reports for the fiscal years ending in 1915 and 1916, Sells highlighted what he thought were the Bureau's achievements. In 1915, Sells touted the development of "Egyptian cotton," which soon acquired the local sobriquet of "Pima cotton," which was "scientifically grown" and produced a substantial and lucrative crop. As for the allotment of Gila River land, contrary to the Akimel O'odham and Piipaash, who regarded the situation as a crisis, Sells portrayed the situation as one in which the Bureau could be more efficient. Noting that only one allotment agent was working at the Pima Agency, Sells observed: "A comparatively limited number of allotments have been made on various reservations by the respective superintendents in charge, but as a general rule activity along this line has been much lessened."[28] Then, with regard to two diversion dams approved for meeting the water needs of both the Gila River Reservation and local white communities, namely at Florence, Sells stated: "These appropriations are the first important steps to rectify the injustice which has been done these Pima Indians for the 30 or 40 years that their water supply has been encroached upon by the whites." As for allotments, in 1916 Sells highlighted what he thought was an impressive amount of progress over the previous year:

The important work of allotting irrigable land on the Gila River Reservation, Ariz., was continued during the year. In addition to the irrigable allotments, instructions have been issued to the allotting agent to allot the grazing lands pro rata. The area of irrigable land to be allotted is. estimated at 50,000 acres and grazing land 315,000 acres.[29]

Needless to say, in spite of the years of grievances that Gila River Reservation leaders brought to the Indian Bureau, from the local superintendents to the commissioner of Indian Affairs, Akimel O'odham and Piipaash were never consulted about the Bureau implementation of the 1887 General Allotment Act on its lands. Consequently, Sells did not acknowledge the crises he created across the reservation system.

As for the other tribal leader who reached out to Montezuma during 1915, Robert Yellowtail, whom Charles Vollan regarded as the "dominant political voice on the Crow Reservation in the mid-twentieth century," made a dramatic appearance late in the year.[30] On November 20, Yellowtail spoke as a friend, notifying Montezuma that he and his delegation would pass through Chicago on their way to Washington, D.C. Crow Nation was organizing against local efforts in Montana to open up their reservation to white settlers, in violation of their 1868 treaty with the United States. In the aftermath of *Lone Wolf v. Hitchcock* (1904), which affirmed Congress's plenary power, including its legal authority to abrogate treaty obligations unilaterally, the Crow found themselves at a disadvantage, which they hoped to convince Congress to correct. Frederick E. Hoxie, in *Parading Through History*, notes that Henry L. Myers, Montana's Democratic senator, sought on behalf of his constituents the acquisition of Crow Nation's unallotted lands. In collaboration with Thomas J. Walsh, Montana's other Democratic senator, they introduced a bill that instigated a firm response from the Crow:

> In December 1915, the two senators introduced a proposal to open all of the unallotted land west of the Bighorn and east of the Little Bighorn to homesteaders. Even though the sponsors promised that the tribe would retain the unallotted lands between the two rivers as a communal grazing area, the reactions to his [Myers's] bill were an echo [of] the struggle of 1908–10. A general council of the tribe met to "vigorously protest" Myers's efforts; Charles Kappler appeared at the Senate hearing on the bill to argue the tribe's position; and the Indian Rights Association issued a special pamphlet condemning this attempted "raid on the Crow Indian lands."[31]

Hoxie added in a footnote: "The Myers bill, S 2378 (64th Congress, 1st Session), was filed on December 16, 1915, but the [Crow] tribal council knew in advance of the proposal and met in November to condemn it."[32] Consequently, in an effort to forestall Myers and Walsh's legislative agenda, Yellowtail hoped to solicit Montezuma's advice on the matter: "It occurs to me in this connection that you may be a great help through the influence that you have with the Indian Member of Congress, Gen[eral] R.H. Pratt[.] The Society of American Indians, and any other agencies at your command. We will expect to visit with you a day a[nd] have a heart to heart talk."[33]

> In 1913 Yellowtail traveled to Washington, D.C.[,] as a translator for elders defending Crow lands. With support from Crow leader Plenty Coups, Yellowtail developed as a leader in his own right and quickly made a name as an eloquent speaker. He returned to Washington in 1915, 1916, and 1917, making alliances with non-Indian politicians and lawyers. When Senate leaders asked the Crows to compromise, Yellowtail sided with the young leadership, which favored dividing the entire Crow lands among the tribe, with limits on non-Indian landholdings and outright fee simple land ownership for Indians without a trust period. The Crow Act became law in 1920.[34]

Ultimately, what Yellowtail sought was Crow Nation control over its own lands, including those lands leased to whites and otherwise designated for economic development. Equally important was the drive to sustain traditional Crow religion, above all its Sun Dance ceremony. Insofar as Yellowtail saw the Indian Bureau as an obstacle to these objectives, he naturally regarded Montezuma as a trusted ally.

Yellowtail's reference to Pratt as the "Indian Member of Congress" sounds prima facie naïve, as Pratt was neither Indian nor a congressman. Yet the distinction symbolized the status Pratt held in the minds of many Indigenous leaders, that of a true friend and a strong advocate for Indian rights. Pratt believed that Indians were not only educable but also worthy of the rights and privileges of any white man in America. As for the abuses associated with the Indian boarding school experiment, which today are the topic of much criticism, during the early twentieth century these were blamed on the nefarious men who forced Pratt into retirement in 1904 in retaliation for his harsh criticisms of the Indian Bureau. The corporal punishment that Pratt sanctioned while still in charge at Carlisle, most notoriously for punishing students who dared to speak their Indigenous languages, was regarded as normal classroom management. In fact, not once did Montezuma ever claim that Pratt did anything wrong or immoral with respect to his treatment of Indians. If anything, Montezuma exhibited a cult-like devotion to the "Pratt ideal." Thus Pratt remained an exemplary figure, particularly in the pages of *Wassaja*, an exception to the rule in Indian Affairs, in which technocrats prioritized maintaining the Indian Bureau machine over the well-being, education, and prosperity of its "wards." Pratt sincerely believed, in Montezuma's estimation, in the potential of Indians to equal their white brothers in terms of ability and accomplishment. Toward that end, the Carlisle Indian School and the boarding school system it represented stood as a monument to Pratt's commitment to Indian welfare. Thus, "Pratt's dismissal [from Carlisle in 1904] served as a reminder to Montezuma that the Indian Bureau was incorrigible."[35]

As for the remaining letters received in 1915, Montezuma heard from his most devoted cousin, Charles, twice that year. First, Charles was one of six Yavapai men who signed a letter that was a word-for-word duplicate of the letter cited above, dated July 10, referring to Fayette Mckenzie and Farmer Moore, which was signed only by Chief George Dickens. In the duplicated version, both George and Charles Dickens were signatories, along with "Tom Surrama, Harry Mott, Alsibir(?), [and] Dick Dugka(?)."[36] Second, on December 14, Charles Dickens wrote to ask Montezuma if he knew "Em Witter," who was at Fort McDowell from California. Described enigmatically as a "founder boy," Dickens observed that Witter was well liked by the Yavapai.[37]

Montezuma also heard from two additional family members, Dwight Campbell and Thurma Dickens. Campbell identified as Montezuma's nephew in a letter dated June 23, in which he asked his uncle if he knew about the fence that had gone up on the "north side." Sounding worried, Campbell added: "do you heard that from the Government to fence Mc Dowell is it right—or not if you know about that why let me known and we are all not known that. And we Indians are wanted give us little more room before fence Mc Dowell that—what we also for."[38] As noted above, the fence was for the purported objective of keeping off-reservation cattle from wandering onto Yavapai land. Unsurprisingly, the Indian Bureau appears to have not done an efficient job of spreading word. According to Harrison and Williams, the stockman assigned to Fort McDowell was responsible for supervising the fence construction:

> In 1912, I was here at Fort McDowell and we camped at Yuma Frank's place. I was just a boy then. That time a stockman was superintendent. The stockman wanted the people to fence in a place here for cattle. He gathered the

people for a meeting there where my father's house used to be. He asked them, "I want you to fence this place here up. Just a little. I'm going to put cattle in here. And when the cattle has calves in the spring and fall we give it to you guys. To you people, all of you. You say, 'all right,' and it's all right."

When Yuma Frank was chief, he resisted the proposed fence, but to no avail. Three years later, "the cattle fence was made. . . . They got through with it in 1916 and brought the cattle in all right. Lots of cattle. It has the government brand ID. No Indian brand."[39]

Campbell wrote again September 4 and 11, in which he repeated asking for any news from Washington, D.C., then mentioned the ongoing construction of the fence. Campbell added that he was a part of the crew that was installing the controversial structure.[40] In the second letter, the news from Fort McDowell was much more significant: "I am going to let You Know This white people come from Phoenix get drinking water and run the water to Phoenix in pipe[.] they talk about put pump water weather you know this are not[.]"[41] Insofar as the letters were from "McDowell, Arizona," Campbell likely knew the Dickens Brothers and other Yavapai leaders. However, what his role was in the Yavapai community's affairs is undetermined. Campbell was never mentioned by any of the others in their letters. As for the reclamation project to provide the City of Phoenix with Yavapai water:

> The water supply continued to be unreliable [during the 1910s and 1920s] as water was controlled by the Salt River Project in reservoirs upstream.
>
> The city of Phoenix water plant built on the reservation in the middle 1940s [when the Horseshoe Dam was completed] provided local employment. The city has been diverting water for domestic use from the Verde River at McDowell through a pipeline since 1920 [which, as documented in the correspondence to Montezuma, was a project that began years earlier].[42]

It is important to acknowledge, before turning to Thurma Dickens, that Montezuma delivered his seminal speech, "Let My People Go," on September 30, 1915, at the annual meeting of the SAI, which took place in Lawrence, Kansas. In addition to excoriating the society for its ineffective response to the Indian Bureau's mismanagement of the reservation system, Montezuma advocated passionately for the liberation of all Indians from a "bureauism" that treated Indians inhumanely, incompetently, and yet with a condescending attitude that belittled Indian people's ability to take care of their own affairs.

> The reservation is a hot-house, the wrong "melting-pot," a demoralizing prison of idleness, beggary, gambling, pauperism and ruin,—where the Indians remain as Indians, a barrier against enlightenment and knowledge. There is not one redeeming feature on the Indian reservations for the Indians. The Indians condemn it; anyone who knows the reservation, condemns it, and those who have thought seriously to ascertain its redeeming qualities have condemned [it]; even the Indian Department condemns it, but does not dare to say so, or it would be without a job. The one feeds the other.[43]

While Montezuma certainly had other reservations in mind—indeed the system as a whole is implicated—one can easily see Montezuma's personal experience with his own community back at Fort McDowell influencing his indictment of the Indian Bureau. More than anything else, Montezuma wanted to liberate his family along the Verde River from the clutches of Indian Bureau oppression. In a chapter inspired by Montezuma's seminal speech, Thomas C. Maroukis makes clear in *We Are Not a Vanishing People: The Society of American Indians, 1911–1923*, contrary to Hertzberg, that Montezuma's skepticism of the SAI was shared by others:

> Both [Fayette] McKenzie and John Hewitt expressed serious concern about the reputation of the Society as an arm of the Indian Office. . . . McKenzie . . . pointed out [to Arthur C. Parker] that the 1914 Philadelphia banquet [where Montezuma confronted Sells] gave the impression that Indian Office officials were the chief figures in the eyes of the Society.[44]

Parker denied complicity with the Indian Office yet could not deny the problem with the SAI's reputation. To his defense, Parker claimed that the SAI's issues stemmed from a profound lack of resources: "Parker complained to [Thomas] Sloan and Montezuma about his workload. . . . [T]here were not enough hours in the day. . . . Many appeals for help came into the office, but there were no available attorneys, no funds to hire any, and a legal aid department that never functioned."[45] The last point is likely the reason Montezuma had to retain Latimer himself. As for "Let My People Go" as a political statement:

The response to Montezuma's speech was mixed. Some supported his attack on the Indian Office, but others wondered what would happen to the legal claims, the trust funds, the treaties, and the tribal lands. . . . Montezuma offered no follow-up plan. . . . Overall, Montezuma was disappointed with the response. . . . Parker [supported] the idea of abolishing the Indian Office, but not without a plan for the future.[46]

In fact, Parker criticized the indiscriminate use of the word *abolish*, which he felt led to the declining support for the SAI. Montezuma would have much to say in rebuttal, once the issue came up in the pages of *Wassaja*. Clearly, Parker was not as worried for his family and community as was Montezuma.

As for Thurma Dickens, whose father was Chief George Dickens, she appears three times in the correspondence, beginning with a letter dated November 27, 1915. In an exception to the letters in general, Thurma did not contact Montezuma with any urgency but wrote to share her memorable experiences at the Phoenix Indian School, where she was a student, as were her two brothers. Among the highlights was what she and her peers did for Thanksgiving: "Our big dinner was held in the evening at six Oclock. [W]e also have a football game at Riverside Park. between Indian School and Phoenix High School[.] Indian[s] win the game. The score is Fourteen to Nothing. We all very glad because Indian win the last game in the season. after we came back from Park We eat our meal. after when we came out from Dinning Hall we parade around between Boys Quarter and Grils [*sic*] Building about two times and stop. we sing our joyful tiperrerry."[47] If Dickens experienced any hardship under school officials, she did not feel obliged to share this with Montezuma.[48] On the contrary, given Montezuma's respectful relation with Chief George Dickens, Thurma's experience may have informed the author of "Let My People Go" in his opinion about Indian segregation and the need to free Indians from the reservation system so that they might attend school wherever they thought best. Thurma thrived at Phoenix Indian School, which Montezuma likely attributed to her opportunities to interact with local whites.[49] Nevertheless, it was not improbable Thurma was maintaining a brave face. Although the "education" that girls received may have been different from that given to boys, particularly the vocational training, insofar as the girls were "Indians," they were regarded by school officials as being of an inferior race and treated accordingly.[50]

What the letters to Montezuma from family and friends at Fort McDowell illustrate is the way in which crises, be they political, social, or environmental, become normalized over time, which is not to say that the Yavapai accepted Indian Bureau oppression as a fait accompli. On the contrary, they were adamant about agitating for change and reform in Indian Bureau policy, such that the Yavapai wanted to, without equivocation, remain on their lands, not move to Salt River. So, then, what was being clarified here? The Indian Bureau's threat to remove the Yavapai to Salt River was being carried out in incremental and what looked like irreversible stages. As Sells summarized in his annual reports, the allotment of Indian lands was proceeding, albeit slowly, as there was only one allotting agent working at the Pima Agency, which during this time covered the Gila and Salt River Reservations, plus Fort McDowell. Yet allotments were happening. At Fort McDowell, fencing appeared and over a period of years was completed. The Yavapai and O'odham-Piipaash economies were compelled to change as more white settlements developed into towns, cities, and farms. The Salt River Project, which would take decades to complete, rose to the top of Arizona's economic plans. Yavapai and O'odham-Piipaash children were obligated to go to Bureau-approved schools, such as Phoenix Indian School. Since these were long-range developments, the impact on Indigenous peoples was undoubtedly real but was often invisible to people not directly affected by Indian Bureau policy. Supposedly, the purpose of the SAI was to organize Indians and their progressive allies into a political movement that would give Indians a louder voice in American politics, but that did not seem to be happening. In fact, as far as Montezuma was concerned, the SAI was deaf to other Indians. In light of the situation, Montezuma determined that there was only one thing left to do, and that was take the bull by the proverbial horns and create his own political movement. Enter *Wassaja*.

CHAPTER THREE

The Rebirth of Wassaja

The Crisis at Fort McDowell Worsens

In the year 1916 Montezuma launched his eponymous newsletter, one of the most important developments in Progressive Era Indian affairs. The first issue was released in April and bore its iconic masthead: *Wassaja, Freedom's Signal for the Indian*, illustrated with an Indian man crushed under a heavy log labeled "Indian Bureau." There would be subsequent mastheads, but the first one, evoking the oppressive weight of the Indian Bureau, shocked readers into paying attention. Unlike his peers in the SAI, be it his good friend Charles Eastman (Mdewakanton Dakota), his intellectual rival Arthur C. Parker (Seneca), or his unrequited love interest Gertrude Bonnin, a.k.a. Zitkala-Sa (Lakota), Montezuma did not publish anything in any mainstream venue, be it book, journal, or magazine. Eastman, for example, published regularly with Little, Brown and Company, while Parker published frequently in archaeological and historical journals. Bonnin, for her part, saw her articles appear in *Harper's Weekly*. In the case of *Wassaja*, Montezuma became legendary for writing, editing, printing, and distributing his newsletter to his subscribers almost entirely by himself. Thus Montezuma's *Wassaja* has rightly earned its place in the history of American Indian journalism that extends from Elias Boudinot and *The Cherokee Phoenix* to Montezuma's peer Gus H. Beaulieu and *The Tomahawk* to Paul DeMain and *News from Indian Country* and Mark Trahant and *Indian Country Today*. Indeed, Iverson recounts the *Wassaja* that emerged during the Red Power movement, under the aegis of Rupert Costo (Cahuilla), as a fitting legacy:

When Indian editors Rupert Costo and Jeanette Henry [Cherokee] decided to publish a national Native American newspaper in the early 1970s, they turned to Montezuma's Wassaja as a name for their journal and as a model. "Let My People Know" replaced "Let My People Go" on the new Wassaja's masthead. Costo and Henry admired the combative Yavapai who showed the world "that Indians can become doctors, engineers, scholars, and who demanded self-determination for the Native Americans." Their newspaper became an important source for news about Indian America and a forum for Native American viewpoints.[1]

As for Wassaja's historical value, Julianne Newmark stated in her article "A Prescription for Freedom: Carlos Montezuma, Wassaja, and the Society of American Indians," in which she corroborated Iverson appraisal of Montezuma's journalistic work:

As [Iverson's] comments on Wassaja reveal, it is a publication noteworthy not only because Montezuma was its editor and principal author, but also because it serves current scholars as a valuable resource in the study of pan-Indian community formation, activist Native journalism, and Indigenous polemical rhetoric.[2]

As for the personal correspondence that Montezuma saw in 1916—as opposed to the letters that readers sent to Wassaja—these documented the increased pressure on the Yavapai to move to Salt River. Teachers and farmers assigned to Fort McDowell promoted Indian Bureau policy, as did Indian agents serving the area. Only Montezuma and Latimer were reliable allies against Indian Bureau aggression. At the same time, Montezuma continued to negotiate between Fort McDowell community members who were at odds with each other over how to handle the crisis. Noteworthy were the alliances that shifted from the previous year. In 1916, Mike Burns and George Dickens, who were earlier opposed to each other, became more in concurrence, leaving Charles Dickens and others on the other side of the allotment fence. (Salt River Chief Juan Andrews vanished from any further reference after 1915.) In fact, intratribal relations became heated when Burns and Chief Dickens arranged to sell land and water rights to Howard Hughes, a local white cattleman.[3] Burns saw this as an assertion of tribal sovereignty, even though he pursued this without a clear consensus from other Yavapai. Unsurprisingly, many at Fort McDowell regarded Burns's actions as another act of betrayal. All of these issues informed the political discourse that Montezuma railed about in the first volume of *Wassaja*.

During this eventful year, even nature seemed aligned against the Yavapai, as a flood hit the Fort McDowell community, causing much damage and distress. Adding insult to injury, the Indian Bureau exploited the natural disaster as an opportunity to further pressure the Yavapai into moving to Salt River, specifically by refusing to offer aid unless they agreed to Indian Bureau terms. In spite of ongoing grievances, several Yavapai continued to help build a fence around their reservation, if only because it was one of the few sources of personal income. The year 1916 ended with Burns asking Montezuma for help with getting his Yavapai stories, the tribe's history, published. Highlighted in Burns's account of the Yavapai experience was the promise that General George Crook—who was promoted from Colonel in the aftermath of the campaign against the Apache and the Skeleton Cave Massacre—made to them about never being removed from their land after the Skeleton Cave Massacre.

With regard to Crook's "promise," which the Yavapai regarded as tantamount to a treaty with the United States, Timothy Braatz has documented the agreement's origin in *Surviving Conquest*. In his effort at rounding up Yavapai into the reservation system during the 1870s, Crook, the commanding officer during the Skeleton Cave Massacre, utilized a practice common among field officers across Indian Country by arbitrarily appointing Yavapai headmen, complete with titles and uniforms symbolizing their position as political representatives of the Yavapai. Among these was a man named Motha.

> When the crisis of removal [from where they were being held at San Carlos] arose in 1875, other headmen moved to the fore. Motha's most important responsibility was as caretaker of certain papers signed by Crook. The general gave a written document to each of several prominent headmen, acknowledging their position, but Motha, as his official Yavapai spokesman, received special papers supposedly guaranteeing a lasting peace between the Rio Verde Yavapais and U.S. forces. The papers were a promise of survival in the midst of a hostile foreign invasion—survival as opposed to extermination—and their possessor was, in some way, guarding the Yavapai future.[4]

Alas, because these papers were eventually lost, their content—remembered in Yavapai oral tradition, referenced in the letters to Montezuma—proved to be ineffective in the ongoing battle against the Indian Bureau.[5] More bluntly, Crook's promise was no more pertinent than Fisher's 1912 reversal of the Indian Bureau's plans to remove the Yavapai to Salt River. Historically, Crook's promise symbolized the dramatic turn in events once the Yavapai accepted the promise's terms. As Braatz further recalls: "General Crook and other officers . . . were relentless, brutal, and cruel in their conquest of Yavapai territory. . . . However, once Yavapais surrendered and accepted Rio Verde boundaries, the officers won their trust by fulfilling promises and working to improve reservation conditions."[6] Unfortunately for the Yavapai, comparable to promises made to other Indigenous nations by other commanding officers, once that officer was ordered to leave his post, or else retired, any promises made were subject to review—which typically occurred as a consequence of a change in either Congress or the office of the president.

With regard to Yavapai factionalism, George Dickens's 1916 letters expressed aggravation with what other Yavapai said about Mike Burns and him. At the same time, Dickens was grateful for all that Montezuma had done for their community, especially the effort to help them remain on their reservation. Otherwise, as Dickens admitted, "We might be down on the deserts with Pimas: who are our dead enemies." As for the rumors about Burns and him:

> Some one has written to you: about that Mike Burns has wrote to you: about these Indians have always been making tizwin: an gambling: that you must stop helping them: who ever wrote you: about Mike has even said something bad about these Indians: I wish you will send me that letter: you had received: and tell me who were the parties that written a letter to you: about Mike Burns: because I do not like to have other believe that Mike is a bad Man. And who will always tells bad things about other persons. he is the only one whom I depend on: for help and advises: and wanted him to stay for me here.[7]

About a month later, Chief Dickens reported that Yavapai affairs had taken a turn for the worse when "Moore," the much-liked farmer, was relieved of his duties, to which the Yavapai responded with a petition addressed to Commissioner Sells. Dickens added an alarming accusation that the teacher assigned to them had used up rations that were supposed to go to their children and the elderly: "Much stuffs were seen brought here by the Indians [fighters] but the children never were given. We wish that Matter will soon be looked into."[8] The accused was likely Hans B. Klingenberger, who was named as the Camp McDowell day school teacher in a 1916 Congressional appropriation.[9] Much to their frustration, all that the Yavapai ever heard from the Indian Bureau was the plan for their removal to Salt River, which came up in Dickens's March 28 letter: "I am just now received a letter from [Arizona] Governor George W. P. Hunt[10] in Phoenix and he received a letter from Commissioner Cato Sells and Governor forward to me and I readed it make me pretty bad. and Commissioner alway talking about my peoples here at Camp McDowell Indians he alway says he want us to move to Salt River reservation all the time." Once again, the Yavapai headmen agitated for a delegation to Washington, D.C. More than anything, it seemed, the Yavapai wanted to remind the Indian Bureau about General Crook's promise: "So we come here Since 16 years ago [1900]. and the Government is giving us this land to live on. long as we live here. But Commissioner alway wants us to move down Salt River reservation. and I say no and no. As you told us not to move to any other place. I dont wanted take two places. I rather stay here my old home. The first man giving us this place by General Crook and we alie [?] him yet. if we go to Washington we show this on Commissioner."[11] What Chief Dickens meant by "showing" Crook's promise to Sells was ambiguous at best, though he may have meant that all the Yavapai leaders would testify to its veracity, including its significance to the Yavapai.

Lastly, on September 18, Chief Dickens was one of three signatories, along with Charles Dickens and Tom Surrama, who reported that the resident teacher and farmer demanded once again that the Yavapai move to Salt River. Several Yavapai families, alas, gave in and agreed to move. Among these was Nellie Davis, who was earlier described as a translator assisting Chief Dickens and whose letters appear in chapter 5. She was also referred to in poignant terms in a letter that Montezuma sent to Burns, cited in chapter 6. She and her husband Gilbert Davis were known for speaking English well and may have been the object of government favoritism.[12] Consistent with Sells's economic development agenda, in which land allotment was key to integrating Indians into the mainstream economy, the Indian Bureau promoted relocation as an opportunity for Yavapai prosperity. By accepting an allotment at Salt River, complete with water rights, while retaining grazing rights, but no water rights, at Fort McDowell, the Indian Bureau claimed that the Yavapai could have the best of both worlds. As for how the Indian Bureau reacted to Yavapai complaints at Fort McDowell:

> When the Commissioner himself here last fall he said something about mov-
> ing to Saltriver : Under that canal: but he only said that he was not going to
> force me to go down there: After I told him: that the desert land country I
> could not make a home: because the water was poor: No shade trees: that
> desert land was good only for the Papagoes and Pimas: So Dear Cousin
> urge your friends to fight for us afew Mohaves: And we can not see there is
> Any . . . this land . . . old Fort McDowell which the Government did: and then
> told us to live here: and make the most on it: as Much as We can: Because
> close by here: where our Fathers and Mothers buried: and that Gen[eral]
> Crook told our people: at Camp Verde on near the year 1873: that in course
> of 5 or 7 years: after Moving to San Carlos Arizona: that we will be back to
> our old homes: Some will come back on the Valleys Near Camp Verde: and
> some will come in the neighborhood of McDowell: This we Must queaten
> [quit?] down the rest of the Apaches on San Carlos: Agency: and that we
> did as we agreed to do: But on account of the death of Gen[eral] Crook [in
> 1890] that there was no one help us to get us back to our country: But I am
> not going to say all about what has been said in olden times by Gen[eral]
> Geo[rge] Crook: promised: And we were told at often time: to have all the
> reservation fenced in: and as soon as we have all done: there be cattle given
> us to raises: but now: After we fenced the whole reservation: The teacher and
> the new farmer tells us to move down to salt river: and then cattle be given us
> to put on this reservation: We ask nothing from the Government: only to be
> let alone and to live here: for the rest of our lives: because the surroundings
> is our fathers and mothers homes: So advise us further.[13]

As for Mike Burns, his letters arrived on Montezuma's desk on three occasions, dated May 12, August 11, and November 6. In the first missive, Burns asked Montezuma if he remembered the delegation sent to Washington, D.C., in 1870 to meet President Grant—a group that also transported the young Wassaja away from his homeland. Burns reminded Montezuma that he had traveled with a white man and "3 Yuma Apaches" from "Camp Wate [White?]." After summarizing the group's itinerary Burns mentioned "3 Pimas" who were with a "Mr. Cooke," a possible reference to Charles Cook. Whatever operation was underway, "Gen[eral] Howard was in charge" and everyone was loaded into an ambulance and wagons. As the journey proceeded, the wagons were lost in the Rio Grande, after which the party continued to Santa Fe, New Mexico, then on to Denver, Colorado, ultimately making their way to Washington, D.C.[14] One can only imagine what Montezuma thought as he read this account of his journey back East after his legendary abduction. Did Burns's version of events match what Montezuma remembered or shed light on his experience to show him things that had otherwise become foggy with time? Montezuma's reaction is not in the archival record and has likely been lost to posterity.

Burns further informed his cousin that only one person from that 1870 delegation was still alive in 1916. The unnamed source told Burns that Montezuma was left in Chicago, mentioning "the Man" (Carlo Gentile?) that took Montezuma, who shook everyone's hand. Altogether the delegation was gone for seven months, which caused many people to believe they had perished. In addition to surviving to tell the tale, the elder possessed a medal he received from President Grant. Burns's timeline then became ambiguous as he recalled a "conspiracy" instigated by "a Mohave chief named Nahah dav-vali: ah pu jul tah." The Mohave chief was "from Fort Mohave: Colorado River."[15] The "Party of Indians: and soldiers: came to the Yuma Apache Camp and took these men: over to the Garrison. and were shot down in presents of many other Indians and soldiers: For what cause nothing been found out til today." The Army took other men prisoners and executed them. Burns did not, or could not, clarify the source of the conflict.

Turning back to current events, Burns told Montezuma that he had sent a letter to Commissioner Sells for permission to lease a water hole to a local cattleman, Howard Hughes. Unsurprisingly, this generated criticism from other Yavapai. Burns claimed that he convinced his peers that they ought to have the right to lease land to whomever they chose. Concurrent with this controversy, Burns observed that the Verde River was overflowing: "This last Winter: we have had much water: and the Verde River: has washed lands although the Valley: and washed the bottom land just below our dam: to that bend: to its banks." Meanwhile, Superintendent Coe and the Fort McDowell school teacher continued to pressure the Yavapai into moving to Salt River. Burns ended his letter with praise for Tom Surrama, who worked diligently at maintaining the community ditch, even without pay. Others worked hard as well. Nonetheless, people were starving. Some tried to make extra money by cutting down mesquite trees, a much-desired resource.[16] Otherwise, the only other source of income came from building the fence around the reservation.[17] Because of the severe contraction in the Fort McDowell economy, Burns was one of several who chose to see what he wanted to see in the Indian Bureau's land allotment policy, which relocated Yavapai water rights to Salt River. Burns thought he saw freedom, when in fact he was walking into an Indian Bureau trap.

On August 11, Burns acknowledged Montezuma's advice to not "rent or give" land to "outsiders." Nevertheless, Burns pointed out that the cattleman in question, "Howard Hughes," had already purchased the land for $40.00, the receipt for which was sent to Commissioner Sells. Burns assured Montezuma that the transaction was completed without any objection from "any of the Indians out this reservation." Clearly feeling defensive about what he had done, Burns spent the rest of his letter making his case:

> Is it right way: to treat any communities:? where the people lived on land. or has not a right to say what should be done on their homes? Not even to doctor: any of our sick people: by any one of our Indian doctors: Nor: let us have any social dances. If the Government. or any one man is doing those things: in not allowing Indians. to have thing to say about their lands: or to arrange their own affairs: is not doing the same as he does to other Indians: If the Government is so strict about not allowing Indians to have their own style sociable Meetings: Why is it: some Indians having all kinds of Indian style shows and dance all they want: if they treat all Indians a like: why do the Government let us do things as sociable ways: as the same as any other communities? We want to deal our own affairs at homes: here: just the same as any corparated towns in the country: I can not see: where we are wards of the Government of the United States: We lived here: a long time with out any aid from the Government: any thing the Government have spent Money here: just having a white man as an expert farmer: Most all the Indians: Knows just as much about farming than any farmers were here. Just drawing salaries from the Government.[18]

Burns's position was problematic because his status as a Yavapai community member remained tainted from his role in the Skeleton Cave Massacre. There was no getting around this. Burns's leasing or sale—what type of transaction Burns thought he had made is ambiguous—of Yavapai land to a white man symbolized his conflicted tendencies. On the one hand, Burns argued that the Yavapai needed to assert their sovereignty and stand up to Indian Bureau abuses. Toward that end, Burns's land transaction was done in the name of all Yavapai and their land rights. On the other hand, Burns handed over Yavapai land to a white man at a time when all Yavapai were under pressure to abandon their land for the Salt River Reservation. Granted, the Yavapai were not in a position to reacquire lost land, which would have been a greater act of tribal sovereignty. Still, it was easy to see how Montezuma must have been alarmed by Burns's land deal, specifically as hastening Indian Bureau objectives.

At the same time, insofar as Montezuma was well known for advocating an assimilationist agenda, which included abolishing the Indian Bureau, ending the reservation system, and enabling all Indians to enter the American mainstream, be it for work or school, one cannot overlook the possibility that what Burns did was one way of interpreting what Montezuma preached. After all, when one preaches freedom, as did Montezuma on behalf of all American Indians, then one was advocating for the right to do as one wished, whether or not it coincided with what one imagined ought to be done. Put another way, Burns took the initiative of filling in the gap that Parker and others, noted above, saw in Montezuma's campaign to abolish the Indian Bureau—Burns acted as if there was no Indian Bureau to tell him what to do. He acted on his freedom.

The pale-face boys and girls are kept at home and sent to public schools and sent away to colleges. When they finish school, these same boys and girls go away from home and make their own way in the busy, active life of the country,—to succeed or fail; survive or perish. They know not what may befall them, they only take their chance away from home. For in this journey of life God's decree is that we cannot see the path all the way,—only from day to day; nor the hereafter, only by faith. The start is hard, we [Indians] know it is hard and killing, but it fits us to compete with the world.

The Indian boys and girls are schooled on reservations near their Indian homes. By promotion they go into non-reservation Indian boarding-schools. To go higher, they enter Carlisle, Haskell or other government Indian boarding-schools, and when these same boys and girls finish the eighth grade, they are carefully sent back to their homes on the reservations. That end[s] his or her school chapter, and what has been the outcome of such method of Indian schooling? Back, back in everything, of course.[19]

What this said about Burns's land deal was that he wanted to engage the white man as an equal, complete with the same individual right to buy, sell, and lease land. Of course, what Burns did not appreciate were the implications of selling land that, despite what federal law claimed per the provisions of the 1887 General Allotment Act, was still considered to be Yavapai land, in the collective sense of that term, not Burns's alone to dispose of as he saw fit. What Montezuma, in turn, did not stop to consider was why when white American boys and girls went out into the world so many of them were ignorant about Indians, were prejudiced against them, and even worked for the Indian Bureau.

In "Let My People Go" Montezuma asserted that racial prejudice was a chronic problem, which he confronted personally as one of the rare Indians in the medical profession. In a much-cited story about his return to Chicago after serving as an Indian Service physician, Montezuma shared his outrage at the suggestion from a friend that he would be better off staying with his reservation job, stating: "even though you may be the best physician—you are an Indian."

> When I read these words, my Apache blood rushed into my head, and I said, "God helping me, I will resign the government service and go back to Chicago and fight prejudice." I was willing to sacrifice everything for my race, so I took the choice of coming in contact with prejudice and going against the current of life and defying the world for the rights with which God has endowed the Indian, as one of His creatures, and I assure you I am not discouraged or dismayed.[20]

Montezuma found himself dealing with financial difficulties, which may be an inevitable consequence of confronting an unjust society, noble intentions notwithstanding. What this implied for Burns's land deal was that he too might wind up with the proverbial short end of the stick. When it comes to being Indian in America, simply being given your freedom is not enough if you expect to succeed, which was to say acquire the status and lifestyle of your white peers. Montezuma, for example, returned to Chicago, confronted prejudice, and wound up less distinguished than his white peers in the medical profession. A similar fate awaited Charles Eastman when he returned to Minneapolis. How Montezuma and Eastman are remembered today is due to the work they did on behalf of American Indians, including their respective nations.

Three months after Burns's letter defending his land deal, the short end of the stick appeared. Burns recounted the legal dispute that had developed over the leased waterhole. Specifically, when Hughes paid Burns $40.00, a year's rent, he assumed he had leased 42 acres, whereas Burns and other Yavapai asserted that the deal was for only 4 acres. Even more frustrating was the fact that Hughes had been charging Yavapai a fee for using his presumed 42 acres to graze their cattle and access the waterhole. In spite of how proud Burns was of his deal-making in previous messages, he and other Yavapai were now angry at the government for approving Hughes's arrangement. Burns's account seems to be missing some facts of the case. What is evident is that most Yavapai assumed, even under adversarial conditions, that the Indian Bureau would fulfill its trust responsibilities and protect them from nefarious businessmen like Hughes. Unfortunately, what the Yavapai encountered was a "New Agent" whose only interest, like that of the others, was getting them to move to Salt River. Their grievance against Hughes went unresolved.

That was not the only grievance. The Yavapai wanted their schoolhouse repaired, as well as help with their farming and ditch maintenance. Their resident farmer was reassigned to Salt River, leaving them without recourse. However, after an extended account of Yavapai complaints against the Indian Bureau, Burns asked for help once again with getting his manuscript published. Perhaps he thought this was his way out of this reservation life:

I have nearly 300 pages: and that is not half yet: I have only got as far or as near as I can make just coming into Camp Verde: in the year about 1873 The Men were claimed in twos: by the arms: and were kept under guards: by the soldiers for 6 months I have asked some Men: who are supposed a great friend to Me: and said that they will see it through but it is going on 5 years now: and at least they say: it would cost lots of money: No Matter how Much it May cost: to have it published in book forms: it will pay back for itself. in short time: I have got the original copies and also have the typewritten form too: I would like to have this little stories: about the troubles have been between the Indians and white people: especially in Arizona: among the Apaches: The soldiers killed the Indians when they were gathered in: when having pretence treaties: shooting them down while seating down on the ground.[21]

Burns clearly felt a moral imperative at getting his Yavapai history published. Undoubtedly, Burns possessed a version of American Indian history that was

radically different from the Progressive Era histories of the American republic that lauded the settling of the continent, the closing of the frontier, and the
triumph of progress, such as those by Frederick Jackson Turner, Charles A.
Beard, or, most notoriously, Theodore Roosevelt and Joseph K. Dixon. Moreover, Burns's work made him a part of a small but significant community of
Indigenous historians who took on the difficult task of bringing the Indian's
point of view to the story of how the American nation was built, such as William Apess (Pequot), George Copway (Ojibwe), William Whipple Warren
(Ojibwe), Elias Johnson (Tuscarora), Sarah Winnemucca Hopkins (Paiute),
Richard C. Adams (Delaware), Andrew Blackbird (Odawa), and Charles A.
Eastman (Dakota). Still, the exact nature of the problem with getting his
work published is not clear. While Burns managed to get people, including
Montezuma, interested in his project, there was no evidence that he sent it to
a publishing house. In which case, while the race factor and the presumption
of incompetence should not be underestimated here, it was equally likely
that Burns was a victim of his own naivety; in particular he did not know
how books were published, did not know anyone who had published a book,
and asked all the wrong people for help.

Now, lest we forget the other letters Montezuma received during 1916,
Charles Dickens added to a developing picture of Yavapai affairs with six letters, dated January 6, 25, 30, June 9, July 21, and September 9. As the new year
began, Dickens updated Montezuma on "Witter Em," who was interested in
the "Romo ranch 2 miles east from old Fort":

> He [Witter Em] say if he buy that ranch and he say he going to Give me a
> work and stay with him long as I live with him. . . . I said to him when he
> buy that place he can make lots of money and make a Station there for the
> Cattles men comes to that place every time and stay there over nights get
> about 5 or 6 dollars for putting a horses for one night beside that if they
> putting Cattles in pasture for one night he can get 25 or 30 Dollars a night.
> also meal 50c a person.[22]

Witter Em was likely the Em Witter identified in Charles Dickens's 1915 letter as someone who visited Fort McDowell from California. If Dickens was
aware of what he did to facilitate the further expropriation of Yavapai land,
he did not express it in his letters. Instead, Dickens assured his cousin that

the Yavapai were hard at work, mostly farming; also they wanted to remain on their reservation. At the same time, Dickens alluded to the fence under construction like it was an abstraction and did not acknowledge that there were Yavapai working on this project, which would likely be finished during the upcoming summer. As recounted above when Yuma Frank expressed opposition to building a fence, the cattle eventually brought in only had "the government brand ID. No Indian brand."[23]

In a way, Charles Dickens represented the point of view of the average inhabitant of the reservation system, someone who knew a great deal about his community, but was bereft of any sense of the big picture. Did he read Montezuma's newsletter, *Wassaja*? Dickens was salt of the earth, which is evident in his letters to his cousin. He simply knew what he knew and did not pretend to possess any expertise on the federal Indian law and policy that shaped Yavapai lives. On January 25, Dickens thanked Montezuma for a winter coat he requested because of the cold weather. Unfortunately, it was too small, so he gave it to his daughter, Dorothy. As for Yavapai affairs, Dickens relayed a common concern for the dismissal of their resident farmer, Moore, complete with a reference to the letter that a group of them sent to Commissioner Sells. Speaking again of grievances, of which there was never a shortage, Dickens briefed Montezuma on the complaints about "Klinger," Fort McDowell's teacher. Klinger—or Hans B. Klingenberger, identified above—had been derelict in his duties to the community, as he did not appear to spend much time instructing Yavapai children as he should. Could Montezuma help with getting him removed from his post? Perhaps "Clark"[24] could return? Lastly, "If you [Montezuma] hear from anything from Washington please let us Know right away. So remembmber us and we all follow you. and is anything wrong here we will write you and let you know[,] so you forward to the Indian Office at Washington."[25]

On January 30 urgent news arrived. The Verde River flooded. Unlike George Dickens's letter, which seemed to minimize the danger, Charles's account was much more honest. The people at Fort McDowell had to flee for safety. As for Charles, he was at his "Nephew Camps Captain Jim now; raining five days and nights, railroad bridge wiped out; waters have overflown." Despite the devastation, Dickens made plans for when the flood subsided, complete with inviting Montezuma and his wife, Marie, to stay with him for a month when he next visited Arizona.

Still now rainning Yet last night. May be more water rasing. Those peoples camp here told me Arizona Canal & Granite Reef dam is the waters run over the dam is about 16 or 17 feets hie. and they say the Phoenix peoples farid [afraid?] gone brick [break?] the dam.

Our ditches and our dams wash out and just as soon as the river down we gone fixed. and I am Moving up here to my old place. near my land. and I am going to plants lots of melons and corns and Musk Melons for You to eat when You coming this Summer in June or July crops.

In the meantime, George Dickens and Tom Surrama asked Montezuma to contact Latimer, whom they had yet to hear from regarding some undisclosed business. Charles added that he had not heard from "George Morgan."[26] Lastly, as always, had Montezuma heard anything from Washington?[27]

On June 9 Charles Dickens sent Montezuma news of his distress over the Mike Burns land deal, in which his brother George and Tom Surrama were partners. The land leased was a "4 acre land near romo(?) at the spring and giving to cattles men. for cattles water to drink." Burns and company, moreover, had been to the Salt River Agency, where they completed their transaction. "He [Mike] have no right only this 3 men do them self and talking them the Supt giving McDowell water with out letting know You first. What you think of that spring[?] you think it will be alright for them to have that our spring[?] 2 miles east the others side the river. If you think be alright or not right You fine out from Commissioner Cato Sells or Assistant Commissioner." Dickens asked Montezuma to also obtain permission to hold a "1 night" social dance on July 4.[28] Charles Dickens's last letter of the year was July 21, in which he again expressed his frustration with his brother George and the others for allowing white cattlemen to acquire land and water rights on Yavapai land. This time, however, Dickens threatened to write to the "Indian Department" himself, seemingly ignorant of who had made his brother's land deal possible in the first place. In the meantime, Dickens hoped that Montezuma would contact his two cousins, George and Mike, about this.[29]

The last batch of letters that arrived in 1916 were from Montezuma's nephew and niece, Dwight Campbell and Thurma Dickens. In both cases, the news was light and reflective of young people more interested in maintaining friendly contact with their uncle than as participants in Yavapai political issues. On February 8, Campbell asked if Montezuma had heard anything from Washington, D.C., lately, then mentioned the flood and the repair work on the community's ditch. Thurma Dickens, for her part, sent Montezuma two letters, both from the Phoenix Indian School. In the first, March 27, Dickens shared her "Spring Vacation" experience. Among the highlights was a baseball game with McDowell, in which the Phoenix Indian School team prevailed 11–1. Other students played "field Sport," which may have been a reference to track and field. Also typical of the high school experience was news about classmates and an account of socializing on a Saturday night. Dickens closed with an update on her family: "I'm very sorry that my father Chief George Dickens was not here. If it is here I might tell you the news From McDowell But it was not here. I and my father an Steps Brother were getting along nice here for a long time."[30] On a dramatically different note, in a letter dated August 2 she wrote on behalf of her father, Chief Dickens, Montezuma's niece relayed her father's concern about his brother "Charlie," who allegedly kept from George the letters that Montezuma sent to him. Consequently, Chief Dickens asked Montezuma "don't sent letter to Charlie, Charlie always don't went let George know What you write to George." Given Charles's opinion about his brother George's land lease deal, it was not surprising that the former wanted to hide his correspondence from the latter. George, in turn, likely suspected that his brother wanted to interfere with his business transactions. Symptomatic of the Dickens's sibling rivalry, Chief Dickens accused his brother of keeping the $30.00 that Montezuma had sent for him through Charles. The remainder of Thurma's letter consisted of a brief reference to her summer break and another to her mother's need for an overcoat.[31]

As for how Montezuma synthesized all of this into his political thought, the first issue of *Wassaja* was launched in April 1916 for all the world to read. Interestingly, Montezuma did not mention Fort McDowell or any aspect of Yavapai affairs. In fact, the inaugural issue did not name any tribes or individuals in its diatribe against the Indian Bureau. On the contrary, Montezuma issued what may be described as a declaration of war against the federal government's Indian policy. Using rhetoric that characterized him as the "fiery Apache," Montezuma set the tone for his campaign against "bureauism:"[32]

> Had the Indian been treated as a man, without discrimination, in the beginning of the pale-face invasion, today there would be no Indian Bureau and the word "Indian" would be only an obsolete name.
> The Indian problem is a problem because the country has taken it and nursed it as a problem; otherwise it is not a problem at all.

It is worth pointing out that aside from being an example of Montezuma's polemical style of writing, his observations about the nature of the so-called Indian problem made it a reflection of white attitudes toward Indians, as opposed to being an accurate portrayal of Indians themselves, which aligned him with other historically important American Indian intellectuals. In regard to the word "Indian" becoming obsolete as a term of racialized discrimination, such sentiment goes as far back as Elias Boudinot's "An Address to the Whites" (1826), in which Boudinot, the founder of *The Cherokee Phoenix*, stated:

> Some there are, perhaps even in this enlightened assembly, who at the bare sight of an Indian, or at the mention of the name, would throw back their imaginations to ancient times, to the savages of savage warfare, to the yells pronounced over the mangled bodies of women and children, thus creating an opinion, inapplicable and highly injurious to those for whose temporal interest and eternal welfare, I come to plead.[33]

Comparable to Montezuma, Boudinot affirmed that he too was an Indian, though far from the savage stereotypes that were commonplace in the thinking of the whites he hoped to convince to support the Cherokee Nation cause against forced removal. In fact, there were multiple instances throughout *Wassaja*'s eight volumes in which Montezuma enjoyed pointing out to his readers that he too was an Indian, the same as the ones that joined SAI and that dwelled under Indian Bureau tyranny on the reservation.

As for Montezuma's criticism that the Indian problem was the product of the white American imagination, Vine Deloria Jr. echoed this opinion in *Custer Died for Your Sins: An Indian Manifesto* (1969), in which he stated with obvious frustration, after observing the absence of Indians in Michael Harrington's influential book *The Other America* (1962):

> Indians are probably invisible because of the tremendous amount of misinformation about them. Most books about Indians cover some abstract and esoteric topic of the last century [meaning the nineteenth]. Contemporary books are predominantly by whites trying to solve the "Indian problem."[34] Between the two extremes [namely, the esoteric and the so-called Indian problem] lives a dynamic people [Indigenous nations] in a social structure of their own [tribalism], asking only to be freed from cultural oppression [what Montezuma called bureauism].[35]

The future, though, as of 1969—let alone 1916—did not look bright for Indian freedom, for the simple reason that "the white does not understand the Indian and the Indian does not wish to understand the white."[36] As for the "Indian problem's" influence on federal Indian law and policy: "Congress always wants to do away with paternalism. So it has a policy [which during the 1960s was termination] designed to do away with Indians. If there are no Indians, there cannot be any paternalism."[37]

From 1906 to 1921, the Indian Bureau wanted to do away with the Yavapai problem, something the U.S. Army failed to do at Skeleton Cave but could be accomplished through the attrition of an oppressive, not to mention capricious, reservation system. Unless the Yavapai and their allies resisted. *Wassaja* was the loudest voice of this rebellion. In the subsequent 1916 issues, Montezuma established his political agenda against the Indian Bureau and, as Newmark argued, SAI. In the May 1916 issue, Montezuma asserted that contrary to claims from the federal government, the Indian Bureau was serving not the Indians' interests but its own. In "The Repression of the Indian" Montezuma observed sardonically that the Indian Bureau was ostensibly established "to protect the outnumbered Indians from the ravages of the pale faces." Of course, all the Indian Bureau accomplished was asserting federal control, as opposed to local tribal control, over Indian affairs, complete with plenary power over Indian land and lives: "It [the Indian Bureau] has become a formidable branch of the government and it is going to be a difficult thing to get it out of the way."[38]

In the June 1916 issue, Montezuma added to his critical analysis of Indian affairs an article titled "Error Dominates the Indian Bureau and Indian Bureau Dominates the Indian." Basically, what Montezuma argued was that the Indian Bureau was guilty of institutional racism. However, he wrote at a time before critics of institutional bias had developed the technical language to describe the nature of the problem. Marxism had yet to develop into Critical Theory, let alone Critical Race Theory. Consequently, *Wassaja* expressed the dilemma polemically:

> The great and powerful United States of America remains as clouded and blighted in its method of dealing with the Indian as it was fifty years ago—dominated by error.
>
> With a proper conception of the Indian in his place as one of the races of men among men, in the beginning, together with a possession of a spirit of

justice, this nation could have saved itself millions of treasure and countless horrors of war and strife; and at the same time the distinctiveness of the American Indian, as such, would now be a thing of the remote past; but as the ivy clings to the walls of an ancient ruin, so error, having once been embraced, remains to propagate itself to the exclusion of anything else.[39]

The "error" in question, of course, was the assumption on the part of the Indian Bureau that the Indian by nature was too "primitive" in his thinking to adjust to modern society without the tutelage of Indian agents, missionaries, and other so-called experts on the "Indian problem." Unfortunately, as Montezuma observed elsewhere, the Indian Bureau was benefitting politically and financially from maintaining this fallacious status quo. In fact, in another article from the same issue, titled "More Scare-Crows to Keep the Indian Dependent," Montezuma made efficient work of dispelling the three dominant "myths" that grounded Indian Bureau policy: (1) Indians will lose everything to conniving whites because of their naivety in business; (2) Indian elderly will starve because younger Indians are listless and unproductive; and (3) without Indian Bureau charity, Indians will inevitably find themselves in the proverbial poor house, unable to fend for themselves.[40] Montezuma may also have had Parker and other gradualists in the SAI in mind. With respect to these racial stereotypes, one can see Montezuma thinking about his family and friends at Fort McDowell, who worked hard and struggled in good faith to protect their land and water rights, who labored long hours at maintaining their farms and ranches—even helping to fence themselves in—and who willingly shared what little they had with one another. And what was their reward? To have their water rights transferred to Salt River while they faced utter destitution and civil rights abuses at Fort McDowell.

In a little-discussed aspect of Montezuma's radical politics, in the July 1916 issue Montezuma excoriated churches' complicity in the oppression of Indians. More specifically, in an argument that presaged the one that Vine Deloria Jr. made against missionaries in *Custer Died for Your Sins* (1969) and Christianity in general in *God Is Red* (1973), Montezuma inveighed in "The Church and the Indian" that the churches ministering to the reservation system were just as guilty as the Indian Bureau of violating Indian rights:

It is regrettable that the churches have laid too much faith in the Indian Bureau of the Interior Department of the Government. The churches' method of aiding the Indians with the Indian Bureau, has been brother loving, in a soothing and smoothing fashion, because they did not want to hurt the Indian Bureau, they did not want to hurt the Indians, and they did not want to express themselves. They wanted to be neutral and peaceable. They entertained the mistaken idea that they must work hand in hand with the Indian Bureau in order to do the most good for the Indians. Had they worked against the Indian Bureau, the Indian Bureau would have ignored them, cut off their share of money appropriation or not favored them in many ways. Financially there is no hope for the churches from the Indians, but all their hope for money comes from the Indian Bureau, and so the churches have traveled in the wrong, glittering path and left the Indians to travel in another and unknown direction.[41]

Montezuma, like Deloria, was gravely disappointed that church leaders did not speak out against the inequities of the Indian Bureau's treatment of Indians. Although the Reverend Charles Cook, missionary to the Gila River Reservation, sent Montezuma some much-needed moral support in his letter dated June 10, 1911, Cook failed to become for the Yavapai or the Akimel O'odham what, say, Bishop Henry Whipple was for the Mdewakanton Dakota during the 1862 United States–Dakota War, someone who spoke out against the abuses heaped upon the Indians on the reservation, which brought them to near starvation. Nor was Cook anything like Samuel Worcester, the missionary to Cherokee Nation, who risked imprisonment and hard labor for defying the State of Georgia's illegal effort at abolishing Cherokee sovereignty from the face of the earth. Instead, white church leaders and the institutions they led had "fattened and gone after other gods, thinking they are doing the will of the true God."[42] One wonders at which point Montezuma thought about the missionary at Fort McDowell who appointed himself sheriff, complete with a six-shooter, and gunned a Yavapai man down with impunity.

From August to December 1916, the subsequent five issues of *Wassaja* maintained a steady flow of criticism for the Indian Bureau and its racial bias against Indians, complemented with critiques of Indian rights organizations, both white (Mohonk Conference) and Indian (SAI), which were counter-balanced with examples of Indian perseverance and success. The Fort McDowell Mohave Apache and their particular battle against the Indian Bureau, however, remained out of the picture—for the time being. They appeared with a vengeance in later issues. At this point, only if one was familiar with the crisis at Fort McDowell and the correspondence that Montezuma received might one perceive indirect references to this situation in the first volume of *Wassaja*.

In "Indians and Indians," Montezuma claimed that the Indian's racial pride had been summarily killed by the Indian Bureau with Pavlovian efficiency in its management of the reservation system, consequently preventing Indians from successfully entering American society. They were in a state of learned helplessness. Thus, the Indian Bureau proved to be hypocritical in its advocacy for Indian assimilation into American society. If this was the Indian Bureau's objective, then why did it do everything to prevent this from succeeding? With his own experience in mind, Montezuma referred to himself in the third person, using his Yavapai name: "Wassaja is not writing a thesis, is not writing for rhetorical affect. He is retracing his own steps from the most primitive grass hut of Arizona to a civilized life in a great city. It is not a dead message that he is writing about but the most vital for his people," by which one can only assume that the Yavapai were included in this aspiration.[43] As for *Wassaja*'s example, anyone familiar with his story knew that he avoided the stifling effects of the reservation system only because of his abduction by "Pima raiders" from his Mohave Apache home and his subsequent adoption by Carlo Gentile. Only if Indians were wrenched free from the clutches of the Indian Bureau could Indians be expected to fulfill their potential as American citizens. Otherwise, Indians would be forever imprisoned behind the walls of the reservation, where the Bureau's never-ending promise to raise them into civilized life would play in their ears like a siren song beckoning them to their destruction. In response, Montezuma stated emphatically: "That is what ails us Indians; we have relied too much on promises. Let promises go; GET MAD AND FIGHT YOUR WAY IN LIFE. Let us not be monkeyed with any longer."[44] The stage was set. Let the battle against bureauism begin! The "Kaiserism" of the Indian Bureau was of far greater concern to Indians than the German Kaiser and all the problems of Europe combined. Could anyone make America safe for Indian democracy?

As the United States inched closer to entering the war in Europe despite President Wilson's claims to neutrality, Montezuma was confronted with the pressure placed on American Indians to demonstrate their loyalty to the United States by offering themselves for the ultimate sacrifice, even though they did not enjoy the rights and privileges of citizenship. Montezuma may have been clear that he wanted to eliminate the Indian Bureau, but what would fill in the void? Can one criticize the Indian Bureau, which was an agency of the federal government, without looking, at the very least, ungrateful or, at worst, like a threat to the political order? Given the imminent disaster that threatened the Yavapai, there was no time to waste on appeasing anyone, least of all the Indian Bureau. In which case, asking about what comes after liberation from the Indian Bureau is the wrong question. In Montezuma's estimation, Indians and their allies needed to be asking the more immediate question about how to end Indian Bureau abuses, such as those occurring at Fort McDowell. *Wassaja* sought to lead the way to an answer.

CHAPTER FOUR

The Unknown Indian Soldier

America Goes to War While Another
Battle Is Waged at Home

The year 1917 is when the United States relented on its neutrality and declared war on Germany. It was also a time in which thousands of American Indians volunteered to join the war effort, and their sacrifices became the basis on which Progressive Indian leaders like Montezuma, Eastman, Zitkala-Sa, and Parker argued for Indian citizenship rights.[1] With regard to correspondence during America's war years, 1917–1918, the Carlos Montezuma Collection holds only three letters. Nevertheless, Montezuma continued his campaign in *Wassaja* against the Indian Bureau, while the Society of American Indians persevered with its agenda of a gradualist approach to Indian Bureau reform. As for the three letters, these were from Chief George Dickens and Joseph Latimer, in addition to an unsigned letter from Santan, Arizona, on the Gila River Pima reservation. The three letters documented further difficult times for the Yavapai and Akimel O'odham, as the Indian Bureau kept pressure on the Yavapai to move to Salt River. Because of this, Montezuma maintained Indian rights issues in his readers' minds, using the bully pulpit of *Wassaja* to criticize the federal government despite its war effort. Between his disdain for the Indian Bureau and his criticism of the draft, since it affected noncitizen Indians, Montezuma added to his notoriety as an Indian rights activist. Indians on the reservation, however, often saw Montezuma in a dramatically different light. In the case of the unsigned letter from Santan, dated January 11, 1917:

> Your letter was handed to me for sometime To day[.] I am going to answer
> Your letter. You said that everything is to be done is not truth at all. We ask

40 acres each men. You tell us something in your letter is not true every thing is wrong[.] We want our right stand for our land[.] The Agent was here telling the Indians built their New allotment right way[.] The Agent said I[?] will stand right when the Indian will built their allotment. We do not want to built fence around our new allotment. because it is to small land[,] everything will die. It is about 2 Miles from our farming. It is just same Indians that gather at the Agent house. All the time. It is just same Indian that built the fence around us. We want the Government to give large land or put right homes[,] that is what we want[.][2]

It is evident that the Indian Bureau was implementing an allotment and fencing policy at Santan, and across the Gila River Indian Community, that paralleled the one up at Fort McDowell. What was meant when the letter claimed that "You [Montezuma] said that everything to be done is not truth at all" was not entirely clear. Did Montezuma alert the people at Santan about Indian Bureau deception that proved accurate or was Montezuma being apprised of some mistake he had made in his assessment of the situation? What is abundantly obvious was that there was a major dispute between Indian Bureau objectives, which included land allotments, and the demand on the part of the Santan community for larger parcels of land, if they were to sustain their agricultural economy.[3] The meagre five- and ten-acre allotments that the Indian Bureau was trying to impose on the Fort McDowell and Salt River Indians were simply not enough.

Corroborating the account from Santan, in the February 1917 issue of *Wassaja* Montezuma made his first candid reference to Arizona. In "Fear Rules the Indians," Montezuma informed his readers about the situation at "the Pima Agency at Sacaton, Arizona":

There are several leaders who are rebelling against allotments of 5 and 10 acres. Because from time immemorial they cultivated 75 or 100 acres and it was their own land. The Agent orders the Indian police to arrest these Indians for standing up for their rights. They are put in jail and, it may be, they are tried by Indian judges (of course they are in with the Indian Agent) and the fate of these Indians is to stay in jail until they are ready to take the allotments of 5 or 10 acres.[4]

According to DeJong, in *Stealing the Gila*, the above crisis was the result of the "Sacaton Project," which was intended to resolve O'odham water rights at Gila River. Instead, it created an uproar. Sometimes called the "Santan Project," in 1905 "[Superintendent] Code sought to irrigate 10,000 acres on the north side of the [Gila] river at Santan." Frederick Newell, the geologist assigned to this project, insisted that the O'odham only needed "an 'average of 4 or 5 acres of good irrigated land' to support their families." White farmers, on the other hand, under the Homestead Act, could acquire as much as 160 acres; while under the Desert Land Act, upwards of 320 acres was possible. By 1911, "despite irrigating this land . . . water shortages were still acute." Needless to say, the O'odham grew increasingly wary of the allotment process. "The allotments were simply drawn up on paper."[5]

A few months later, on May 14, Chief George Dickens sent Montezuma the first typed letter in the collection under analysis. Unfortunately, Dickens did not acknowledge his typist. Was it Burns? What he recounted was an anecdote about "Mr Gibby," an Indian Bureau policeman, who was concerned about the Yavapai making "tis-wine."[6] Dickens assured Gibby that no one was engaged in any bootlegging, certainly not since the Indian Bureau made it illegal. Nevertheless, Gibby asked him and Mike Burns to sign a document—perhaps an affidavit—recording their testimony. Dickens and Burns complied. However, other Yavapai refused, not because the request violated their right to make "tis-wine" but because they were afraid that Gibby wanted to trick them into signing an agreement to move to Salt River, which was a reasonable concern.

What happened next was the arrival of "Supt. Mr. [C. T.] Coggeshall," whom Gibby notified about the Yavapai who had refused to sign the document about not making "tis-wine." Coggeshall took it upon himself to confront the dissenting Yavapai. Once again, they refused. Coggeshall became angry. The resistant Yavapai asserted that they would not sign anything until they heard from Montezuma about it. Coggeshall was well known for his staunch support of the Indian Bureau's plans to move them to Salt River. In fact, Coggeshall had recently impressed upon the Yavapai that "$30,000" was requested for their relocation, which was a considerable sum in 1917 dollars ($677,599.22 in 2022).[7] "And he say that money for working on that [Salt River land] and building houses for school agency also. A Mr. Coggeshall say he wanted us to move very bad when the money come, and he say if we don't want move down there he say he is going to Soldiers to make us to move." Dickens confided that he became aggravated when Coggeshall attempted to shame them by referring to America's war effort and the Yavapai's lack of interest: "and we say we have nothing to do that war there in the leg. The Supt. Coggeshall he have no right to talk that." The question of Indian loyalty, as noted above, was a major issue—another obstacle—to the pursuit of Indian rights, which Montezuma had to confront. This was an example of what it looked like on the ground.

With the above issues in mind, Chief Dickens asked Montezuma to consult with Latimer and to contact Commissioner Sells about Coggeshall, who was also accused of abducting Yavapai children to place them "in Phoenix [Indian] School without anybody known." In regard to this atrocity, Dickens confronted Indian School Superintendent John B. Brown, who confirmed that Coggeshall was behind these abductions. More than anything else, Dickens argued, Fort McDowell needed a day school dedicated to serving their community. Interestingly, Dickens did not mention Thurma, whose letters expressed appreciation for her Phoenix Indian School experience—she at least enjoyed the social aspect of being away from home. Was Thurma an exception to the rule? What Dickens was clear about was his contempt for Coggeshall: "Here is our day school closed three months [ago]. And our children running away [from Phoenix] two or three times and come home and Mr. Coggeshall say he is going to send off to east school [Carlisle?] or Calif School [Sherman?]. He got no right to say that. If they running away too much, I got to have my own day school here too, not close[d]. You can tell Commissioner this too for me."[8] Dickens concluded with a brief account of "Mr. [Thomas Little] Bison," a cattleman who threatened to have people arrested for violating his made-up rules. Otherwise, as always, the Yavapai worked hard at maintaining their community.[9]

During 1917, March through December, in *Wassaja* Montezuma generated a steady stream of condemnations of the Indian Bureau. Intermittently, *Wassaja* complemented its campaign against "bureauism" with articles and correspondence from sympathizers, among which were multiple pieces republished from *The Tomahawk*, the White Earth Reservation newspaper founded by Gus H. Beaulieu.[10] Other fellow travelers included Congressman Edwin S. Johnson (D-S.Dak.), Joseph K. Dixon (author of *The Vanishing Race*), Senator Harry Lane (D-Ore.), and, of course, General Richard H. Pratt (founder of the Carlisle Indian Industrial School). *Wassaja*, however, did not acknowledge all of its contributors. Montezuma regularly omitted the letter writer's name, most notably from his rank-and-file followers, Indians on the reservation. The reasons for this editorial practice, Montezuma did

not clarify. His complaints about Indian Bureau abuses of civil rights suggest
that he wanted to protect his Indian readers from retaliation. For example, in
November 1917 *Wassaja* shared a disturbing account of "D.W.," whose Lakota
name was "Tateiyangmani," a "full blood Sioux Indian" and member of the
"Sisseton and Wahpeton tribe," who sought assistance from the Indian agent.
Specifically, Tateiyangmani wanted to access funds from a "$3,400" account
that was kept in his name in an off-reservation bank. Frail and blind, Tateiyangmani needed the funds to sustain himself. The Indian agent, however,
offered a mere "$20.00," which Tateiyangmani made clear was insufficient
for his needs. "That said agent then became furiously angry," which resulted
in Tateiyangmani being beaten in the agent's office, in front of a roomful of
witnesses. Needless to say, the Indian agent did not face any charges, and
might have gone without being held accountable at all if not for the unnamed
law office that took up his case and brought it to the Fifth Circuit Federal
Court in South Dakota.[11]

As for the campaign to liberate Indians from Indian Bureau tyranny, probably the most radical argument that Montezuma made on behalf of Indian
rights was his opposition to drafting American Indians into the U.S. military
during World War I. While Montezuma was focused on the national issue of
Indian conscription, it was not improbable that he had in mind Coggeshall's
condescending attitude toward the Yavapai for not caring about America's
war effort more. In the October issue, Montezuma published "Drafting Indians and Justice." The article was illustrated with a political cartoon bearing
the caption "A Voice from the Happy Hunting Grounds," in which Sitting Bull
was quoted as saying "And they called us savages!" The image depicted the
renowned Hunkpapa leader startled by the mayhem of an ongoing battle,
waged on the terrain behind and below him, in which cannon and airplanes
appeared with explosions. Sitting Bull, standing atop a high ledge, cast his
eyes back to look with alarm at a ship that had just been hit, engulfed in
smoke and sinking. Based on the poignant premise that Indians ought not
to be drafted into the U.S. military while they were not citizens and did
not have any rights under the Constitution, Montezuma argued: "They [the
Indians] have fewer privileges than have foreigners." He made clear that he
was not against the war effort or its justification, which was, according to
President Wilson, to guard the United States against German aggression,[12]
but rather the exploitation of Indian lives by a federal government that cared
little for their humanity. After all, one need only look at the humanitarian

crises raging across the reservation system, including Fort McDowell and the Salt and Gila River Reservations, to understand what Montezuma was talking about here.

> We Indians are ready to defend the country of our forefathers as we have been doing these five hundred years against all odds, but what have we and what are we? We are nothing but wards; we are not citizens and we are without a country in this wide world. It is a sad picture that haunts America's conscience, and now worse than ever we are forced into the army, as though we were citizens or at least aliens. The wards are called upon to protect their Protectors! Has God given us Indians to the world to be used as tools, without justice? It is damnable to be an Indian![13]

The reference to the lack of citizenship was a criticism of the ineffective job the Indian Bureau and Congress had done in implementing the provision for citizenship mandated in the 1887 General Allotment Act, which had been hobbled by the 1906 Burke Act and the institution of competency commissions, which Commissioner Cato Sells employed more for the sake of robbing Indians of their land than for according them the right to manage their own affairs.[14] The jibe about Indians protecting their protectors was a coded reference to the numerous treaties in which the United States pledged to protect its Indian allies against foreign aggressors.[15]

Another common provision in Indian treaties was the cession of land in exchange for goods and annuities, not to mention the aforementioned protection, for the purpose of compensating tribes for their substantial losses due to westward expansion. The Yavapai—Crook's promise notwithstanding— did not have a treaty with the United States, as each of the three Yavapai reservations, including Fort McDowell, was established by executive order. Nonetheless, the treaty-making tradition went a long way in shaping federal Indian policy, most importantly the nation-to-nation relation between tribes and the United States. Ostensibly, treaty-making was a way for the United States to obtain legal title, recognized by international law (specifically, the Doctrine of Discovery), to Indian land. This developed into the "trust relation" that defined Indian-white relations in modern times. To put it succinctly, the trust relation affirmed that the United States promised to protect Indian fiduciary interests, namely land and resources, in honor of the special political status that tribes maintained within the federal system.

In more colloquial terms, the trust relation was based on the fact that the United States owed a never-ending debt to Indians for all the land they took.

With the trust relation in mind, Montezuma shared an anecdote about Crow Nation Chief Plenty Coups, who visited Washington, D.C., to protest the drafting of Crow Indians. Through an interpreter—who may have been Robert Yellowtail—Plenty Coups said to "the Washington Father":

> "If you give us everything, you can take my young men across the water to fight the Germans." By "give us everything" he clearly meant freedom from the oppression of the Indian Office and citizenship—that they might enjoy the rights and privileges thereof. That strikes the keynote of the Indian's contention. He wants "everything" that you have for himself—meaning citizenship. The Indian Office keeps us Indians from our rights. It tells the co[u]ntry that we are competent to be soldiers, but are not competent to be citizens.[16]

Certainly, the rights enshrined in the Fourteenth Amendment were high on the Progressive Indian rights movement's agenda. Nevertheless, it is probable that Plenty Coups thought first and foremost that the United States ought to honor its 1868 treaty with Crow Nation, which, in addition to defining the boundaries of the Crow Reservation and protecting it from "bad men," asserted in Article XI:

> No treaty for the cession of any portion of the reservations herein described, which may be held in common, shall be of any force or validity as against the said Indians, unless executed and signed by at least a majority of all the adult male Indians, occupying or interested in the same; and no cession by the tribe shall be understood or construed in such a manner as to deprive, without his consent, any individual member of the tribe of his right to any tract of land selected by him, as provided in Article VI [the allotment of farmland] of this treaty.[17]

With respect to any interest the Crow had in acquiring the rights and privileges of U.S. citizenship, that may have been on the minds of Robert Yellowtail and his peers, who were highlighted in a separate article in the October 1917 issue, titled "The Crow Indians." In this piece, Yellowtail, James Hill, Russell White Bear, and Yellow Brow were admired for bringing a more informed and focused generation to the bargaining table: "Generation after generation, the Crows are growing wiser. They are now in a position to take care of themselves and look after their own interests without the Indian Office, and they will assert that contention until Congress shall grant them the rights that are given to everybody except Indians."[18]

In 1918 the year's only letter arrived from Montezuma's comrade-in-arms, Joseph W. Latimer. In a letter dated September 23, Latimer apprised Montezuma of the tension between George and Charles Dickens, who had earlier developed conflicting opinions about Mike Burns, and what this entailed with respect to the allotment of Fort McDowell. Though details are lacking, Chief Dickens complained about another letter that Charles had sent to Latimer, allegedly offering the attorney $500 to go to Washington, D.C., "and take care of the McDowell Indian interests." In response, Latimer stated that he planned to reply to George and Charles Dickens that he did not think it was proper of him, as a representative of Montezuma—not of the "McDowell Indians"—to represent their grievances before the Secretary of the Interior Franklin Knight Lane and Commissioner Sells: "Now, my dear Doctor and friend, I wish that you would be kind enough to criticize adversely every position that I am taking in reference to the situation that does not in every way, shape and form meet with your approval, be kind enough to advise me accordingly."[19] Because of the rules governing tribal representation, Latimer knew that he could not legally represent Fort McDowell without Indian Bureau approval. He could, as affirmed in his letter, represent Montezuma as a private citizen. What was unclear, in the absence of additional correspondence, is what exactly Charles Dickens expected for $500. One can only speculate on this point. Also, if Charles did make this offer to Latimer, what did this imply about his opinion of Montezuma's work representing "McDowell Indians"? Given how slowly government acts on anything, this may be no more than Charles having become anxious about the lack of progress on Yavapai interests. After all, how many times had Montezuma's correspondents asked him for any news from Washington, D.C.?

Meanwhile, Montezuma's activity as editor and opinion writer for *Wassaja* continued without fail. During 1918–1919, he maintained his monthly output of criticism of the Indian Bureau, complete with a range of related issues in Indian affairs. Of particular interest during this time is Montezuma's willingness to endure criticism from Indians and non-Indians alike for repeatedly raising the issue of Indian rights and the inequities of the Indian Bureau during a time of global crisis. The United States had troops on the ground supporting the allied effort against the German Kaiser. Among these troops were some six, nearly seven, thousand Indian volunteers. How dare *Wassaja* keep reminding America that these same brave souls were not free at home on the reservation? In addition, Montezuma did not relent in his disappointment with the Society of American Indians, not to mention its allies in the Indian Rights Association and the Lake Mohonk Conference. The SAI, above all others, was guilty of being complicit with the Indian Bureau in its suppression of Indian freedom on the reservation. As Julianne Newmark observed in her analysis of Montezuma's critique of the SAI: "In Montezuma's assessment, the SAI came to figure as an organization that could only 'meet and discuss.' As *Wassaja*'s issues of 1916–1919 show, Montezuma saw the SAI's inaction impeding, rather than facilitating, his multifaceted goal of Indian emancipation."[20]

With the foregoing agenda Montezuma began 1918 with an appeal in the January issue for Indians to cease working for the Indian Bureau, as they were only supporting their own oppression.[21] In February, the Carter Bill was criticized for taking a gradualist approach to Indian citizenship rights in a feature complemented by remarks about Indian schools as a form of racial segregation.[22] Then in March 1918 an extraordinary panel of correspondence appeared in the back pages of *Wassaja*. Arriving from Lehi, Arizona, James Rhoades wrote on behalf of Salt River Pima Chief Sam Eldridge about the issues frustrating them with their superintendent's obstruction of their water rights. Eldridge blamed Commissioner Sells for reneging on his admission that the Pima ought to have more water and be able to plow all of their land, by which he meant the land that O'odham had historically farmed, not the meagre allotments they were being assigned. Factionalism exacerbated the situation, which arose between the "allotted boys," who were angry with Montezuma's commentary about the American war effort, and those like Eldridge who resisted allotment and the reduced water rights that this entailed. However, the problems besetting the Akimel O'odham did not end there.

There were two more letters from Pima readers. One, from Mesa, on a rare positive note, expressed his appreciation for *Wassaja*, along with a brief account of sharing his enthusiasm with Chief Eldridge. Such mundane pleasures as reading a newsletter, however, came with a heavy price. The unnamed Pima claimed that he was threatened with arrest for subscribing to *Wassaja* and supporting Montezuma's campaign against the Indian bureau. Second, from Santan, another reader recounted asserting he did not want his land taken from him, only to find himself and others arrested because they resisted the Indian Bureau's land allotment policy. The letter was signed by eight men, whose stories were not referred to in the letter but who may have signed as witnesses to the letter writer's ordeal. Complementing the urgent news coming from the Salt and Gila River Reservations were letters from Rosebud, South Dakota, which recounted a nagging issue with leased lands, and Pit River, California, which dealt with the consequences of not having a reservation.[23] Obviously, the allotment policy that was once the hallmark of Progressive Indian politics was making an "Indian problem" go from bad to worse.

Later, in September 1918, Montezuma at long last gave an account of his activist work in Arizona. Instead of simply denouncing Indian Bureau mismanagement of the reservation system, not to mention America's hypocritical espousal of democratic ideals—as occurred in the April through August issues—Montezuma summarized his experience fighting on behalf of the Yavapai community. Typical of his editing style, Montezuma wrote in the third person. In "The Indian Bureau Is Autocracy," Montezuma observed that until Cato Sells took the reins at the Indian Bureau, he was treated well by this federal agency, meaning the time of Secretary Fisher and Commissioner Valentine. However, things took a dramatic turn as he continued to make his annual trips to Arizona. In 1910 Montezuma accepted the request to aid with grievances that the "McDowell Indians" had with the Indian Bureau, subsequently taking an equally serious concern with the Salt and Gila River Reservations. More exactly, Montezuma visited these communities on the assumption that he could mediate a solution with the Indian Bureau, as opposed to fomenting a confrontation.

Unsurprisingly, given Montezuma's heated rhetoric denouncing the Indian Bureau, not to mention the animosity he incurred from the local superintendent, he did not get a warm welcome: "Indian policemen . . . informed him that Superintendent [Frank A.] Thackery wished to see him," at which point Montezuma was escorted to the Pima Agency at Sacaton. Thackery asked Montezuma to state his business, to which he replied, "for the justice of the Indians." Apparently, this was not what Thackery wanted to hear.

> The doctor was made to understand that he could not hold any meeting with the Indians without a permission from the Hon. Commissioner of Indian Affairs [Cato Sells]. He tried to explain that his mission was philanthropic, no contracts with the Indians involving mercenary consideration.[24] Dr. Mon-

tezuma tried to explain to Superintendent Thackery that the Indian Office regulations referring to contracts with the Indians, are for those who make contracts with the Indians for mercenary purposes, which did not involve the doctor. But Superintendent Thackery insisted that Dr. Montezuma had no right on the reservation to hold meetings, with the Indians, without the approval of the Indian Commissioner. Wassaja left the tyrannical agent (and the questions come: "Why should he be questioned as to his motive? Has he not been working for his race going on nearly forty-four years?["] He has been on nearly all reservations and this was the first time he has ever been questioned and not allowed to open his mouth,) with the understanding that his wishes would be complied with he went back to the meeting of the Indians and explained to them that Superintendent Thackery will not permit him to speak to them, and for them to make no trouble in the matter.

Montezuma reported that a message from Sells awaited him upon his return to Chicago, in which he was advised not to pursue accepting the power of attorney on behalf of the "Pimas," and that he must comply with "Indian Office Circular four ninety-seven."[25] Montezuma launched into a diatribe. However, in order to understand Montezuma's rebuttal, one needs to know the content of Indian Office Circular 497.

Published by Sells's predecessor Robert G. Valentine on December 23, 1910, the circular instructed Indian agents and tribal members about "Attorney's Contracts with Indians." Obviously, Montezuma was not an attorney, although he possessed a 1910 memorandum of understanding from the Fort McDowell community that expressed their consensus that he represented them in their business with the Indian Bureau. With regard to the Akimel O'odham at the Salt and Gila River Reservations, Montezuma's visit appeared to be for the purpose of obtaining a similar memorandum. As for the circular, typical of legal documents the language was ambiguous, giving those charged with upholding the policy latitude in its interpretation. More to the point, the circular stipulated that "no agreement shall be made by any person with any tribe of Indians or individual Indians not citizens of the United States for certain purposes, except that it be executed in a certain manner and receive the approval of the Secretary of the Interior and the Commissioner of Indian Affairs." Noteworthy was the fact that the statement was not limited to licensed attorneys but to "any person" pursuing an "agreement," which meant any manifestation of mutual assent, such as a contract. Consequently, this implied to Thackery that anyone, including Montezuma, seeking any kind of formal arrangement with the Indians under his charge had to first acquire permission from the Indian commissioner. Here the significance of the circular's reference to "Indians not citizens" became important. As noncitizens, the Indians at the Salt and Gila River Reservations, not to mention Fort McDowell, were considered wards of the federal government. In which case, insofar as contracts required consideration, meaning "something bargained for and received by a promisor from a promisee,"[26] as the Indians' trustee the federal government—represented by the Indian Bureau—must give its consent or approval to any proposed agreement. Furthermore, the circular asserted "there are important considerations necessarily connected with such transactions affecting the welfare and material interests of the Indians that should be considered by the Department [of the Interior] and the Indian Office prior to the presentation of the subject to the Indians concerned."[27] However, what happened when the threat to "the welfare and material interests of the Indians" came from the Indians' so-called trustee, the federal government? Superintendent Thackery was a classic case of the fox guarding the hen house.

Montezuma criticized Sells's hypocrisy at presuming to protect the Indians' welfare as justification for denying him the opportunity to represent the Akimel O'odham in their grievance with the Indian Bureau. In the spirit of political satire, Montezuma conjured a scenario in which Sells showed visitors his "power of attorney papers" and claimed he was "too much of a friend to those Indians" to give away their rights to Montezuma. Speaking of papers, Montezuma reminded his reader that he was from the "Mohave Apache" community that Sells presumed to protect and that they had a "promise" from General Crook stating that they may "live there [on their Verde Valley homeland] forever." Unfortunately, because of its location along the Verde River and its proximity to Phoenix, developers began coveting Yavapai resources, instigating a drive to remove them from their homeland.[28] Consequently, the Yavapai were to be extricated in contravention to the promise they had, not only from Crook, but also in President Wilson's executive order. Where then was the Indians' protector and trustee? Montezuma answered: "Cato Sells is weak where he should stand up for the Indians."

The McDowell Indians were ordered to be allotted, a small diversion dam constructed for their use. Commissioner Cato Sells has allotted or con-

structed a small dam for the McDowell Indians. He has used coercing methods to have the McDowell Indians move. He tries to starve the Indians into
moving. He has not allowed the farmer in charge to improve McDowell or
encourage the Indians to work. He has not asked a cent of appropriation
for McDowell Indians. He has driven 250 head of cattle into the reservation against the protest of the McDowell Indians. He has taken away their
schools. Ft. McDowell agency is in ashes of ruin. Cato Sells has tried to
smoke those McDowell Indians out and please his friends and the "nigger
in the wood-pile" is sicking him on, but the Indians will not "smoke out"
worth a cent.[29]

The N-word has never not been offensive. Yet Montezuma's unfortunate
choice of phrase was a commonplace figure of speech meant to denote something problematic, annoying, or embarrassing. Currier & Ives published an
infamous 1860 image of Abraham Lincoln, in which this racist trope was
used as its title. According to the summary provided by the Library of Congress, the image depicted "A racist parody of Republican efforts to play down
the antislavery plank in their 1860 platform."[30] In the case of Montezuma's
editorial, the Yavapai were the Indians in the woodpile spoiling Sells's plans
to open up reservation land to the above-mentioned commercial developers
constructing the Arizona Canal.

The remainder of 1918 was filled with now familiar diatribes against the
Indian Bureau, appeals for citizenship rights, and scolding remarks for the
Society of American Indians. Between October and December, the most
significant topic that appeared in *Wassaja* was the closure of the Carlisle
Indian Industrial School. In a brief article titled "Carlisle Misunderstood,"
Montezuma defended the institution's historical importance. More to the
point, Montezuma praised Pratt for his bravery in standing up to the intense
prejudice that Indians faced in the years after the 1876 Battle of the Little
Bighorn, which—at the risk of sounding glib—was the Pearl Harbor of its
day. Hardly anyone believed that Indians should be accorded the access to
American society that education could provide them. Indeed, as Montezuma
asserted: "Carlisle, in Gen. R. H. Pratt's time, single handed, stood against the
sentimentalists, the faddists, the churches, the scientists and interested par-
ties on Indian matters. Gen. Pratt stood for the highest and nobles and best
for the Indian race, so stood Carlisle before the world—and it is no more!"[31]
In a lengthier harangue, published in November, titled "Carlisle U.S. Indian

School," Montezuma took the opportunity to express his deep disappointment with President Theodore Roosevelt, whom many in the Indian rights
movement expected to support a more Indian-friendly progressive agenda:
"Roosevelt writes a whole lot about Indians, but he does not know anything
about Indians." Thus, Carlisle's closure was symptomatic of America's in-
sincere claim that it was a democratic society. Whereas Carlisle symbolized
America's commitment to the Indian and produced distinguished alumni
such as Luther Standing Bear (Lakota), Dennison Wheelock (Oneida), and
Albert Bender (Ojibwe), the closure of the school—a place that Montezuma
anointed as "sacred"—signified America's disregard for its original people:
"When the German army destroyed cathedrals wrought by masters, art
paintings that can never be replaced and other ruthless destructions, America protested with righteous indignation at such outrage and it was a grand
stand taken by the American people."[32] But where was the outrage for Carlisle's termination?

Fortunately, all was not bad news. *Wassaja* expressed enthusiasm for the
election of Charles A. Eastman as SAI president and for the upcoming 1919
October meeting in Minneapolis, Minnesota. In January and February, *Wassaja* published two letters from Eastman acknowledging his ambition to get
the SAI out from the under the "clutches of a Bureau Machine," as well as
the need for "patriotic citizenship," which was his way of asserting the need
for U.S. citizenship rights for all American Indians. In the aftermath of the
annual SAI meeting, *Wassaja* heralded in its November issue the dawn of
a new era in the SAI, which was no longer ambivalent about its relation to
the Indian Bureau and was now openly calling for its abolition. In terms of
the political agenda, Montezuma urged American Indian veterans to fight
for their rights at home with the same fortitude they displayed on the European battlefield on behalf of European freedom. After all, if Indians were
good enough to fight as soldiers, then they were good enough to be treated
equally as Americans. And shame on President Wilson if he believed it was
appropriate for the United States to purport to make the world safe for democracy but keep Indians on the reservation under the Kaiser-like control
of Cato Sells and the Indian Bureau.[33]

In regard to the issues that drove Montezuma's pen during 1919, selecting attorneys to represent tribes and Indian mineral rights were frequently
under scrutiny. In the January, February, and November issues, Montezuma criticized the Indian Bureau's policy, as a part of the Department of

the Interior, of asserting the right of approval of any attorneys interested in representing any of the reservations under its supervision, even if said attorney was specifically chosen by the tribe in question. In "In Regard to Attorneys for Indians," Montezuma referred to his frustration at representing, at their behest, the Salt River "Pima and Maricopa Indians," which was "DISAPPROVED BY HON. CATO SELLS."[34] Then, in November, the paper excerpted at length Robert Yellowtail's testimony before the Senate Committee on Indian Affairs, in which he stated: "Mr. Chairman, to accord them [the Crow] the right to select and employ such legal assistance, without any foreign interference whatsoever, is an inalienable right of every American Indian." Worth mentioning was the fact that Senator Charles Curtis (R-Kans.) was the chair of the committee before which Yellowtail spoke.[35] In addition to being a prominent Republican senator and the future vice president under Herbert Hoover, Curtis was remembered as the infamous sponsor of the 1898 Curtis Act, which "helped weaken and dissolve Indian Territory tribal governments by abolishing tribal courts and subjecting all persons in the territory to federal law."[36] Indeed, in the February 1919 issue, Montezuma reported: "They [the Crow Indian delegation] say, 'Senator Charles Curtis of Kansas, is an Indian, but he is not a friend of the Indians.'"[37]

As for the equally serious issue of Indian mineral rights, this appeared in the March, June, July, and August 1919 issues. In March, Montezuma focused his criticism on the Indian Bureau's policy, under the provisions of the 1887 General Allotment Act, to sell so-called surplus land once a reservation had undergone allotment: "It appears to us that if the surplus land belongs to the Indians . . . the Indians ought to have something to say as to whether they want the land sold or not." Montezuma underscored his point with reference to the economic and social justice impact of allotment in "the Salt River Valley."[38] In June, in "Is It Legal?" Montezuma challenged the legality of the Indian Bureau's regulations for carrying out the statute authorizing the allotment of Indian land: "The fact that Indians are wards of the United States Government may have some weight, but it does not follow that the Indians can be ruled without law."[39] Then in July, with respect to subsurface rights, Montezuma stated in "Bleeding the Indians More": "The Indians own the mineral lands. If they want to lease or sell the land, let the Indians say so or not. The land, mineral and riches of the soil are as good to the Indians as to capitalists."[40] Finally, in August, in "Gold Against the Indians' Rights and Justice," Montezuma emphasized the federal government's bla-

tant plan to extort wealth from the wards for whom it was legally responsible: "THE RIDER that gives all power to the Secretary of the Interior to
lease 30,000,000 acres of Indian mining lands that accompanied the Indian
appropriation of $15,000,000 is another great steal from the Indians. We
notice that the Indian has no voice in the matter."[41] The presumption on the
part of Congress that it could unilaterally invest such power in the secretary
of the interior stemmed not only from the 1887 General Allotment Act but
also from Congress's plenary power over Indian affairs, as held in *Lone Wolf
v. Hitchcock* (1903).

The years 1919–1920, falling between World War I and Montezuma's death
in early 1923, marked the high point in the correspondence that the Yavapai
doctor and activist received. Now in his early fifties, Montezuma was at the
pinnacle of his status as a revered elder in the struggle for Indian rights. In
1919 Montezuma received twenty-one letters, mostly, as in previous years,
from his cousins, the Dickens brothers and Mike Burns. In 1920, Montezuma received fifteen letters. Finally, in 1921 there were only two letters, the
last of which was written by Montezuma to Mike Burns. Now that America
had won the war in Europe, Montezuma challenged President Woodrow
Wilson to do for Indians what the United States had done for its foreign allies, namely protect their freedom. Toward that end, 1919 saw some progress
when Congress passed "An Act Granting Citizenship to Certain Indians,"
which gave honorably discharged American Indian veterans the right to ap-
ply for citizenship.[42] Not quite the universal citizenship that Montezuma
demanded, but a clear step in the right direction.

As for the struggle for Indian rights, 1919 was also the year, as noted above,
that Mdewakanton Dakota writer and activist Charles A. Eastman, author
of *Soul of the Indian* (1911) and *From the Deep Woods to Civilization* (1916),
was elected president of the Society of American Indians, which held its annual conference in Minneapolis, Minnesota.[43] Montezuma enthusiastically
reported this event on the front page of the November 1919 issue of *Wassaja*.
Eastman's ascent to the apex of the Indian rights movement signaled that
the organization was at long last amenable to Montezuma's political agenda:

> With regard to the SAI's agenda, Montezuma is important because of his
> influence on Eastman. Despite their vastly different personalities, Eastman
> and Montezuma became fast friends. They were united, perhaps, by their
> common criticism of federal bureaucracy—what Montezuma called "bu-

reauism." Equally important was their dismay over the rise in popularity of "peyotism," which included proponents in the SAI's rank and file. Together with Zitkala-Sa, Arthur Parker, and other Christian Indians, they lobbied hard to repress what they thought of as a "menace" to the Indian community.[44]

Eastman, as Iverson observes, admired all that Montezuma had accomplished on behalf of American Indians and their struggle for citizenship rights:

> "You have been a strong warrior for our race," wrote Charles Eastman to Carlos Montezuma. In his book, *The Indian To-day*, published in 1915, Eastman acknowledged the stature Montezuma had achieved. Chapter 8, "The Indian in College and the Professions," included a section on "Some Noted Indians of To-day." "Perhaps the foremost of these," wrote Eastman, "is Dr. Carlos Montezuma of Chicago. . . . He stands uncompromisingly for the total abolition of the reservation system and of the Indian Bureau, holding that the red man must be allowed to work out his own salvation."[45]

Unfortunately for both Montezuma and Eastman, the latter's election as SAI president marked the climax of the organization's influence over Indian affairs. The SAI soon faded into oblivion after the 1919 Minneapolis meeting.[46] In the interim, Montezuma tried rallying interest in the subsequent meetings, in particular the 1920 meeting held at Saint Louis, Missouri, where Thomas Sloan (Omaha) served as SAI president. Indeed, in the November 1919 issue of *Wassaja*, Montezuma touted the election of "Tommy Sloan" as a worthy successor to Eastman: "If there was ever a man that made the Indian Bureau feel uneasy, it was Tommy Sloan. . . . Mr. Sloan is a self-made Indian man; he worked and made his way from a reservation [Omaha] to the highest profession, that of attorney-at-law."[47]

Perhaps likewise making the Indian Bureau feel uneasy, Montezuma increased his advocacy for Akimel O'odham land and water rights during 1919, as the Salt and Gila River communities appeared more prominently in his correspondence, complementing their appearances in *Wassaja* both as editorial topics and in the letters to the editor he received. The situation on the Gila River Reservation in particular was due to developments in Florence and Casa Grande, which came under the auspices of Secretary of the Interior John Barton Payne, whose commissioner of Indian Affairs remained Cato Sells.

Payne sent Indian Service Superintendent of Irrigation John R.T. Reeves to reach an agreement with off-reservation landowners, who had to convince the secretary as to the merit of their land and priority of their water rights. By May 1919, Reeves had contracts for more than 80,000 acres of land, with parcels ranging in size from 5 to 4,145 acres. By late summer, Reeves hammered out an agreement between the landowners and the Department of the Interior, with more than 85 percent of the eligible land under contract. In determining eligibility, Reeves gave priority to previously irrigated and cultivated land, as well as irrigated lands protected under the Lockwood Decree.[48]

Further complicating life for everyone was the "Spanish Influenza," which had begun the previous year and was taking a toll on the Yavapai community.[49] Nevertheless, this did not stop the Indian Bureau from pressuring the Yavapai to move to Salt River. Similar to how it handled the damage done by the flood recounted in chapter 3, the Indian Bureau used the influenza as evidence that the Yavapai would be better off moving to Salt River. On January 1, 1919, Charles Dickens informed Montezuma about a relative who died from the influenza, one of about fifteen community members lost to the pandemic. Among the casualties were Dwight Campbell, who identified earlier (June 23, 1915) as Montezuma's nephew, along with Campbell's wife, mother, and sister. In addition, Dickens named as casualties Jose Rice,[50] George Norton's wife,[51] Joe Jose's wife, Polly Vuilta's mother and her baby, Jim Johnson's mother,[52] and Mike Burns's mother-in-law. As may be apparent, the pandemic was especially hard on the female members of the community. However, Dickens's list of the deceased continued, naming his nephew Dock Dogka and his wife and baby.[53] In spite of the tragedy, Dickens assured Montezuma that others were well, such as his brothers George and Richard, who, along with other survivors, worked as hard as ever at keeping up their community. Dickens concluded by asking Montezuma if he had received "my Picture," which he had sent some time ago.[54]

Mike Burns also wrote to Montezuma on February 1. However, Burns did not send an account of the pandemic's impact. Instead, he bemoaned the fact that it had been more than a year since his cousin's last visit. Burns then recounted the trouble with Thomas Little Bison, an unexpected interloper. Little Bison was the resident stockman at Fort McDowell, where he lived with his wife.[55]

And he always says, if you Apaches do not move down there: there will be 4 or 5 hundred soldiers to drive you down there: But he is discharged now. and expected to stand before the U.S. Grand Jury: at Phoenix: for larceny: But Mrs. Bison: still comes up here: and wants to keep on doctoring the sick: I am going to copy the papers: she has made: such reports: about on the McDowell: and says: Greatly about us: Cousin: It does not so nice: but the papers have been returned back to Mr. Sharpe: the present Supt.: at Salt river Agency: And some of the reports: that Mr. Bison has sent to Washington: Where Bison has said something about Mr. Sharpe: as being too easy with the Apaches.

After earning the Yavapai's confidence, Little Bison turned on his friends, becoming defensive and threatening them if they did not move to Salt River. Perhaps Little Bison felt threatened himself if he did not toe the Indian Bureau line. Or perhaps he was just another scoundrel hoping to benefit personally from Yavapai hardship. What was reported to Montezuma was the accusation that Little Bison was scheming with Phoenix Indian School Superintendent John Brown to abduct Yavapai children.

As a result of Little Bison's improprieties, "Mr. [L. C.] Bennett," whom Burns regarded as a friend, replaced Little Bison as the Fort McDowell stockman. Bennett said he would ask the government, meaning the Indian Bureau, for a new day school, which was something that the Yavapai had long wanted as an alternative to Phoenix Indian School. Burns concluded his updates with a promise to send Montezuma a copy of Little Bison's wife's "Field Matrons" report.[56] As for Little Bison's legal troubles, his conviction or acquittal was unclear. However, an update of a sort did appear in a 1921 issue of *Adventure*. In an article titled "Three Countries to Get Rich In," readers learned:

Thomas Little Bison, a Sioux Indian who was formerly Indian agent [*sic*] for the U.S. Government, has a ranch near Tegucigalpa [Honduras] and has options on several other large ranches. He wrote me he would sell one for $10,000 with all houses and plantations. There was some coffee and some general farm products. I am not in the land game, but have found Bison a good scout.[57]

On February 19 and 20, Montezuma heard from Thurma Dickens and Dwight Campbell, respectively. Both addressed Montezuma as their "nephew," which was symptomatic of ongoing challenges with English grammar and its kinship terms. Campbell, perplexingly, was named in Charles Dickens's January 1 letter as among the victims of the recent influenza pandemic. As for Thurma Dickens, she told her uncle the distressing news that "here at Reservation Many are dieing with 'Flue.'" However, her father, George Dickens, and his two brothers, Charles and Richard, were thankfully well. Then, in a departure from her youthful accounts of attending the Phoenix Indian School, Thurma shared her observations of the new Fort McDowell stockman, the one who replaced the nefarious Little Bison: "So I may say that the stockman L.O. [*sic*] Bennett trying hard to help us to keep the Indian to Cultivate their farms this Year. And I think nothing wrong to hime. Geo[rge] is also trying to keep Mr. Bennett to do the right way not to lisen with other Indian, that is telling him untruth story."[58] As for Campbell, in addition to expressing his continued concern for the Indian Bureau's plans to move the Yavapai to Salt River, he alerted Montezuma to claims that "some white people" were making about him, namely that he was in favor of the Indian Bureau's plans. Campbell asked his uncle to set the record straight. He did not, however, name any of the white people in question.[59] Montezuma was on record as stating that the Indian Bureau ought to allot land to the Yavapai at Fort McDowell, not at Salt River. Consequently, the confusion that Campbell reported may have been caused by the Indian Bureau and Montezuma both proposing allotments, albeit toward different ends.

As a sign of Montezuma's elevated status as an Indian rights leader he received what can only be described as a fan letter. Dated February 21, 1919, and signed by "Brother Ben," the letter arrived from White Swan, Washington, from the heart of the Yakama Nation. It may be worth mentioning that Nipo T. Strongheart (1891–1966) was Brother Ben's contemporary. Strongheart, a respected member of Yakama Nation, was well-known during his time as a performer and lecturer, which included advocating for Indian rights, even playing a role in the passage of the 1924 Indian Citizenship Act.[60] Ben, however, did not name Strongheart in this letter. On the other hand, Ben pointed out that he had written Montezuma at least six letters before. In this letter Ben was frustrated with many of the social and legal issues burdening his community. He credited *Wassaja*, however, for teaching him about the prominent Indian rights proponents of the day, with whom, Ben confided, he felt intellectual camaraderie: "My Ideas ran in the same way yours but couldnt express my self in Language and after I did read the message from you to your people." At this point, Ben started evoking the rhetoric he learned from "Let My People Go," excitedly telling Montezuma that he was sharing these ideas with others in his community. One might say that Ben was proselytizing on behalf of Montezuma. Whether or not a Yakama chapter of the "Montezumas" was formed (see the discussion in chapter 7 on Spicer) Brother Ben did not say. Instead, he expressed gratitude for having been able to clean up his life, denouncing the whites for introducing whiskey and immorality:

> Doctor I am talking because I . . . been down the sames as my brothers are now, and was helpless tell, white brothers [missionaries?] came to my rescue, and told the agent to let me up, That I was a Man, My Indian people never done eny thing to degrade my character it has all ways been the best of advice from Grandma. Whiskey and emortalaty is not the Indians, teachings, That is what our White brother has introduced, and we all know is the Hell & damnation to our week people.

In a postscript signed "Confidentially Yours, Buffalo," Ben reiterated his gratitude to Montezuma for waking him to what was going on outside of White Swan.[61] In spite of how frequently Ben wrote to Montezuma, none of his letters were ever published in *Wassaja*.

During February 1919, the Dickens family sent missives dated the twenty-third and twenty-sixth. Charles Dickens, for his part, updated his recovery from some back pain, along with naming a variety of mutual acquaintances who were doing well since he last wrote, assuring his long-distance cousin, "No one of us die." Also, in an indication of the distrust that had emerged between cousins, Charles asked Montezuma to tell him what he had written to Mike Burns: "my brother Geo[rge] Dickens Just he told me Mike Burns got letter from you. but he never tell me about your message yet. what did you tell him[?] Please write me and let me know in your letter written to Mike Burns." Like so many letters before, Charles asked Montezuma about his plans to visit Arizona. Yuma Dick hoped that Montezuma could give him an "old hat," while Dickens's mother inquired about getting fifteen yards of calico. As for Charles, he wanted shoes for his children, including coats for his sons.[62] When Richard and Pauline Dickens wrote a few days later, it was to inform him that his gifts to them had arrived, that they were well, and that there was a new baby in the house, "Bertille," who was the child of their son John and the woman he had married, whom he had met at the Phoenix Indian School. All three were now living with them.[63]

Mike Burns wrote the next three letters, all of which were dated in March. In the first of the three, which had the return address of Superior Magna Mining Company, Thomas Little Bison and his wife surfaced again. According to Burns, Superintendent Sharp asked Little Bison's wife to resign from her field matron's post. She simply laughed at Sharp and refused his request. Apparently, Matron Little Bison made regular trips to Fort McDowell, accompanied by Phoenix Indian School superintendent John B. Brown, on the pretense of caring for the sick. Their ulterior motive was, as in previous complaints, to abduct Yavapai children and force them to attend Phoenix Indian School. Naturally, Little Bison and Brown did not bother to get the parents' consent. Burns wondered why Thomas Little Bison, who was regarded as the worst of the three, a "Big Theaf," had not been sent to prison. Little Bison was notorious for concocting money-making schemes that cheated Yavapai out of what little money they possessed:

> He [Little Bison] has kept all the money given in here for prespass [trespass?] fees the money he charges: 1^{00} a head for every one come here to hunt: on the Indian reservation: and charges 1^{00} for passes: he and his wife gave out to parties: On every Sunday there comes Not less than 40 or 50 cars: and contains 5 and 6 men in them: and each men given 1^{00} to Bison: and he never Made any record of the amount given to him and states what purposes: So he Must have Made hundreds of dollars besides his wages: and all these facts never been known: about it: only we went to Mr. Sharpe and asked whether Mr. Bison had turn in to him: that 15^{00} that were left over: at last "Labor Day Celebration." As we put in Most of it: for to pay for the events: and after was over: that day: Mr. Bison held out to the crowd: saying "boys here is 15^{00} I have in My hand[,] it is yours: and that Much for you to put in some more: on next holidays: Such as Thankgiven Day. or on christmas Day: So you may rest assured that you have that much already for you to start on making Much more": and have agood [sic] time.[64]

Regarding another form of cheating the Yavapai, Burns griped about the whites who coveted their land and water, comparing this to the situation of the Osage in Oklahoma, who were targeted by crooks after their oil revenue.[65] Burns asked Montezuma if he thought the Yavapai would ever be compensated for any of their land lost. Feeling fed up with white attitudes toward the Yavapai, Burns changed the subject, mentioning that he was staying with his son, hence the unusual return address of "Superior Magma Mining Company." He pointed out that he was staying not far from where Montezuma was abducted by the "Pimas." "It is about 25 Miles North of Florence: To where my son Solomon has been working a little over 2 years." Then, in a series of random thoughts, Burns asked Montezuma to contact a "Mr. [Roy E.?] Ayers," who was "One of the Indian Commissioners." Also, Burns asked for medicine, presumably to share with others at Fort McDowell. Specifically, Burns requested the "brown greasy substance [castor oil?]" that helped Tom Surrama recover from influenza.[66]

In the next two letters, both dated March 17, Burns thanked Montezuma for his offer to help him with getting his manuscript published, a work that included anecdotes about "old chiefs," such as "Oha-waw-cha-cum ma: Mojave Charlie," also known as "Motha," whom, as may be recalled, General Crook made a chief of the Yavapai. Burns connected him to Skull Valley, west of Prescott, Arizona, and the site of multiple violent incidents: "being the head man lead the party into a Soldier Camp: at Skull Valley: where he [Mojave Charlie] was seen shot down by an Officer: and was seen his clothing was on fire: but still he came to: and join his people in the mountain in near the vicinities of Prescott: or in the range mountain of Granite Mountain." Burns signed off as Montezuma's "Co-worker of the Indian troubles."[67]

As a reminder that Yavapai troubles were ongoing, and not just historical, Burns took his turn at alerting Montezuma about Phoenix Indian School superintendent John B. Brown. Specifically, several students had run away, only to be caught and returned against their will. They were harshly punished without anyone asking them why they had run away in the first place:

> while in prison life only of small pieces of bread: and . . . water for some children be in that confinement for 2 to 3 weeks: and when they let out: they looked like as skeleton: so weak: can hardly walk: and they be also sent to work on hard labors: and finally: some of them get sick: and there has been so many death caues: I believe that is the mean cause to sickness: and many has been beaten up so: there be no strength in them: and some other be punished for not cared to eat the meals in the dining rooms: and also he sent to hard labors: The employees of that School under Brown's Supt's has always beaten boys with heavy clubs: or something baseball bats: Many have been

kept in the School when others are out on their vacations: that is the cause
of so many derestions [desertions?].

Burns bemoaned a community bereft of any children. Could Montezuma
help? Burns was worried about his own children, stating that this sort of
thing did not happen during "Gen. Pratt's time." Superintendent Brown, in
Burns's estimation, was "too cruel himself."[68]

Of the remaining twelve letters of 1919, Charles Dickens wrote eight, received between May 2 and December 28. The four additional letters were
written by Joshua Russell of Santan, Arizona, and Chief George Dickens.
Russell, a rare exception in the Yavapai-centric narrative, regarded Montezuma as a friend and acknowledged receipt of his subscription to *Wassaja* in
a June 3 letter. Russell promised to send the required fee and also promised
to send Juan Narisco's subscription money. Russell then brought up a much
more urgent concern, the allotment of Santan land:

> Your Friends Indians are well but the[y] do not understand what you mean
> by 10 aces to work on now. But I try to explain them what you said[.] We
> had no water now the river is all [dry] now. The Wells is ran now again[.]
> The Indians are very Busy harvesting their wheat now also making hay. I
> plant some Water Melon the[y] come up very Nicely Now also corn. I did
> not fence my allotment Now because I have No wire to built it. That is the
> only trouble for Indians to built their allotments. That is the only trouble
> for the Indians.[69]

If Russell sounded optimistic, it was due to the economic opportunity that
a Bureau of Plant Industry experimental station at Sacaton, installed for the
purpose of developing "Pima cotton," was creating for local Akimel O'odham
farmers like Russell. Those farmers who were willing to integrate themselves
into the economic agenda set by the Indian Bureau, as a subagency of Interior, could see a personal return on their investment.[70] As for O'odham
sovereignty, it was unlikely that many on the reservation had read the 1887
General Allotment Act, let alone understood the implications of reducing
their farms to ten-acre allotments. What they were quite aware of was the
fact that ten-acre allotments were too small to sustain them as an indepen-
dent community. Montezuma likely advised Santan farmers to take the ten-
acre allotments, nonetheless, complete with the water rights, lest the Indian

Bureau take their land and water from them altogether, as they were trying to do at Fort McDowell.

During the last days of summer, Chief Dickens asked Montezuma if he knew anything about the land surveyor that visited Fort McDowell.[71] Typical of Indian Bureau disregard for community leadership, Dickens was left completely in the dark as to what was being done on Yavapai land.[72] Three months later, Chief Dickens wrote to Montezuma again, saying nothing about the surveyor, but assuring his cousin that he would send him the promised "Oyah" basket. Did Dickens give up on finding out more about the surveying of Yavapai land or did he receive an unpreserved reply from Montezuma? As for other news, Dickens shared with his cousin that "Lowell Mason"[73] had been around: "I guess you remember the boy that was with you while you was here. He is still with us and helpe right along." No urgent news was shared.[74] At least, not until three days before New Year's Eve, when Dickens expressed concern about the ongoing issue of Yavapai land allotment: "remember I,am /asking my Allotment McDowell still I,am looking for that yet. I told you when you out here I would not take any lands to Salt River Vally. and remember I told you I would not sign any papers until I hear from you. So now I rather stay my old home McDowell."[75]

On May 2, Charles Dickens reported that Sam and Jimiy Kill were causing trouble, often getting the Indian agent and the stockman involved. Apparently, they were snitching on community members. Consequently, Dickens asked Montezuma to contact the Kills and ask them to stop. Dickens also expressed worry about land allotments, and of course water rights. Moreover, "George Dickens say Mike Burns is not help us. and he say allway Mike is Report about some things to our Stockman Louis Bennett he is in charge McDowell. He is good man if you want write to him and ask him how is Mike Burns and ask him did he is good to Help his Peoples. Mohave Apache."[76] Three weeks later, Dickens expressed delight that Montezuma would visit soon, offering to make plans and advising his cousin to get a "good pass from the Indian Office." It was not legal for Indians to hunt off of the reservation. Dickens then added a passing observation about how Montezuma was regarded back home: "You know every time when you come out here McDowell Peoples Against you but you will alright. Because you belong here McDowell and you relation here[,] your home here."[77]

On July 10, Dickens informed Montezuma that there were plenty of horses and multiple options for his upcoming hunting trip. As was characteristic of

Charles, he asked for a .30–30 Winchester, in addition to getting Superintendent Brown's permission for his daughter Dorothy to stay with them, after which she would return to the Phoenix Indian School.[78] Nearly a month later, Dickens sent the usual mix of personal and community updates:

> Did you peoples there who they coming out with you did they have hunting License or buying here in Arizona. When you arrive at Phoenix you better see our good friends Lawyer P.H. Hayes.[79] he may go with us these tribes. his talking about hunting these coming Season. If you get him go with us If we get trouble by hunting he will help us and he will help you People to. He is a big Lawyer in Phoenix.[80]

The issue of hunting licenses was much more than a formality, as indicated by the reference to "trouble." In a 1917 article titled "State Game Laws," Montezuma raised the unfair restrictions placed on Indian hunters.

> Wassaja was down in Arizona and had a strange experience, and on his account the Indians on reservations cannot hunt or kill deer with a State license, but must take out alien (not citizen of the State) license.
>
> Reservation Indians are not considered State citizens. A citizen of a State is one who resides within that State. These Indians as wards are not citizens of the United States, but they reside within the State of Arizona; as such they are entitled to the rights and privileges of the State law when they wish to hunt outside of the reservation.[81]
>
> It would be unjust to claim them as living outside of the State of Arizona. . . . He was in Arizona before the game law existed and yet he is not a citizen of Arizona nor is he an alien.
>
> Indians who procured license to hunt and kill deer in past years were refused the same privileges this year, because they were not citizens and yet they gave licenses to other Indians who are wards of the Government.[82]

In late August, Charles acknowledged receipt of some packages, then expressed disappointment that not everyone expected would join Montezuma on his upcoming trip. Still, there was good news to be celebrated. Dickens announced his daughter Dorothy's marriage to "George Norton." Also, L. C. Bennett, their current stockman, was trying to open a day school. Toward that end, Dickens said he had contacted Commissioner Sells, asserting:

We want send our childrens to School here at day school. So we want you
see these . . . to Commissioner about our day [sc]hool here McDowell reservation [th]ese coming year. Please . . . these to . . . Mr Sells . . . him we
want Commissioner [S]ells our friends Please open our day School here
McDowell.

Dickens then made another plea for a .30–30 Winchester, as well as to "Please
send $10⁰⁰ and I will pay my spring wagon. I had there in the Shop ever since
May."[83]

On September 20, Montezuma learned about a surveyor who worked for
the City of Phoenix. Likely this was the same surveyor that Chief Dickens
asked about earlier. Charles, however, was unable to learn who had given
him permission to survey Yavapai land. Montezuma would have known, of
course, that this was approved by Cato Sells, regardless of what the Yavapai
thought. In any case, Dickens hoped that Montezuma could learn more on
the community's behalf. Otherwise, as usual, Dickens was more interested
about making plans for another hunting trip:

Now Cousin[,] from to-day only 18 or 19th days more, you arrive at Mesa.,
and I will be there at Mesa Oct 8th in the morning to meet you. be sure you
come on Oct 8th we may bring 2 wagons down if you bring any Parly along.
Wish you wife come along. dear Cousin I,am down here near Scottsdale
Picking cotton with McDowell Indians and we get 4 cts. albs., we make little
money on Cotton Picking. Ill tell you what I am going to say right now. if you
come to Tempe[.] short way from here my Camps I will meet there at Tempe
will bring you out here to my Camps and then to McDowell. You can see our
Picking Cotton. Just think over where is the best for me to meet you with 2
wagons. Mesa and Tempe. Only 3 miles we camps clos to Tempe. I think not
very far from here to Tempe 3 miles. I had everything down here my camps,
Write me before Oct 8th and let me know where is I can meet you as I say
in this letter I am down here near Tempe.[84]

The growing city of Phoenix was changing the tribal economy. Yavapai like
Charles Dickens were now relying less on farming their own land and more
on off-reservation day labor, which included working on what was the
Akimel O'odham *jeved*, or ancestral homeland, namely Tempe and Mesa.[85]

One might regard this as the first sign of urbanization in Indian life, which would accelerate in the generations ahead.

As a reflection of the changes in the Northeast Valley, between the Verde and Salt rivers, on December 2 Charles Dickens moved to Mesa, Arizona, where he was "Picking Cotton for Isaac Dana." Dickens admitted: "We like here better and down there to near Scottsdale." Yavapai were consistently adamant that they did not want to be removed to the Salt River reservation, yet some, like Charles Dickens, found living "near Scottsdale" quite appealing. With respect to news from Fort McDowell, Dickens heard his brother George had been ill but was now recovering. As for Charles, he wanted to go into the cattle business and, as expected, wanted his cousin's help:

> Now my Cousin Montezuma I'am now to-day while I'am writing these letter to you & I am thinking, and thinking over about you that I want you help me out this year. for my famileys. What I want you get for me I want you buy 3 or 4 cows for me and I want rase lots. my two Brothers did not give me anythings. They both got lots of Cattles now. I think there got about 50 or 60 cattles. If you can do these for me I thank you very much indeed.[86]

According to Khera and Mariella: "Many at McDowell . . . turned to cattle raising to make a partial living from the reservation land. As cattle raising developed, most farmers grew feed as supplement to open range grazing. However, the water supply continued to be unreliable as water was controlled by the Salt River Project in reservoirs upstream."[87] As with Dickens's earlier ambition to open a store, Montezuma proved to be uninterested in his cousin's latest risky venture. Consequently, Dickens was palpably upset:

> If I was you or if I got lots money in the bank and some boby came to me and talked to me about somethings they wanted me to do for him and I am welcome do it. now I,am sorry. We think of you you will ,do these and not say no money. I,am working out here to Picking Cotton and I never make any money yet. only I get afew dollars of cotton wieges and we buying something to eat. you know I had big family.[88]

One can only speculate about the damage that this altercation caused. Did Montezuma feel conned or even threatened by his cousin's behavior and hostile language? How aware was Dickens that his educated and affluent-looking cousin was often strapped for cash himself due to the generosity he regularly displayed to those around him, including his low-income patients who could not afford to pay? It probably went without saying that there was much about Montezuma's life that he could not adequately explain to his family and friends at Fort McDowell. While Montezuma distinguished himself as a medical physician, he was held back from achieving a career of "excellence," such as awards and recognition from his peers, simply because he was not white.

> No one ever thought Montezuma was a millionaire [though perhaps his family back in Fort McDowell did]. To the contrary, his financial records continually reflect monetary difficulties. His patients would often write expressing an inability to pay their overdue fees. Sometimes, of course, they would not write at all. Montezuma would write a delinquent patient, telling him that he badly needed the money, and urging him to "be a man" and pay. An old friend of Montezuma's recalled that he moved in high social circles and was invited to all the social events of importance in the city. She suggested that if he had not given highest priority to Indian rights, his life could have been far easier. While her testimony about Montezuma's standing in high society is suspect, she no doubt was correct in her assessment of his commitment to Native American well-being.[89]

America may have won the War in Europe and made the world safe for democracy, but it was still losing the battle at home for equal rights for all, in particular the nonwhite, nonmale, and typically impoverished populations that did not hesitate to answer the call-to-arms, but now wanted the respect that had long been due to them. In a sense, subaltern groups, second-class citizens, and colonized nations were responding to President Wilson's enumeration of his historic "Fourteen Points" (1918), among which was Point V, which many interpreted as a statement about "self-determination":

> A free, open-minded, and absolutely impartial adjustment of all colonial claims, based upon a strict observance of the principle that in determining all such questions of sovereignty the interests of the populations concerned must have equal weight with the equitable claims of the government whose title is to be determined.[90]

Insofar as Indigenous nations in the reservation system were colonized, then their claims against the U.S. government about infractions of their sovereignty ought to be treated equally under the law, contravening the Indian status as ward. Hence the resistance to land allotments without consent; the right to live, work, and prosper where they choose; the right to choose legal representation; and the demand for day schools on reservation land. These were not just the rights of the individual citizen, they were the sovereign rights of nations. Maurice Crandall argues that from the beginning of European contact, Indigenous peoples along what is today the U.S.–Mexico border have been reacting, adapting to, resisting, and subverting the colonial expansion of Spain, Mexico, and the United States. Moreover, these peoples were recognized as nations in the international sense of the term long before the U.S. Office of Indian Affairs intervened into Indigenous lives.

> While the colonizers brought their own forms of democratic town government, and attempted to incorporate Indigenous peoples into the political mainstream and to reorder political life, they neither destroyed nor replaced Indigenous forms of democracy traditionally rooted in concepts of consensus, dialogue, persuasion, and the power of words.[91]

In Montezuma's estimation, it was Indigenous peoples who taught Americans how to be free, which was a cultural—Montezuma would say racial—trait that all American Indians bring to the "Indian Question." More to the point, the Indian does not need the white man to teach him to be free—from his earliest ancestors, he was born free!

CHAPTER FIVE

Resistance, Survival, and the Approaching End of an Era

The year 1920 was exceptional in that Montezuma received noticeably fewer letters from his cousins than from strangers. In the wake of the 1919 Minneapolis meeting, the SAI began its steady decline, holding scaled-down meetings that failed to attract much attention.[1] Montezuma, nevertheless, continued to lambaste the Indian Bureau in the pages of *Wassaja*. Concurrently, the call for federal Indian policy reform persevered, gaining momentum with the 1919 Act Granting citizenship to certain Indians, namely "every American Indian who served in the Military or Naval Establishments of the United States during the war against the Imperial German Government."[2] Throughout 1920, letters arrived from Buffalo Ben, Wanda Shirt, John Hunter, Capt. R. D. Parker, and Nellie H. David (also known as Nellie Davis). From the Dickens Brothers and Mike Burns, plus the occasional letter from Salt River, the news was mostly mundane family affairs, people working hard, Burns's book manuscript, and upcoming hunting trips. There was little about the Fort McDowell–Salt River crisis, even though it was by no means settled. Indeed, the growing crisis at the Salt and Gila River Reservations was drawing Montezuma's attention much more, including his failed attempt at representing the Akimel O'odham.

Exemplary of Montezuma's stature as a renowned Indian rights activist was the letter received from Ben Buffalo, who previously appeared as Brother Ben, dated February 19, 1920. Buffalo wrote about the issue of alcohol in the Yakama community. Prior to 1917, when the Eighteenth Amendment was submitted to the states for ratification, Indians purchased their whiskey at twice the price that the whites paid. Three years hence, there was more drunkenness than before. As for the health and safety crisis, the Indian Bureau did nothing to help the people. Whether Buffalo was aware of the failure of Prohibition to curtail the scourge of alcoholism nationwide, as opposed to simply driving alcohol into the black market, is unclear.[3] Buffalo, like many in the reservation system, was primarily concerned with his own community's problems, never mind America. They can handle themselves. Consequently, Buffalo was especially frustrated by the illicit liquor trade that came in from neighboring white communities. Exacerbating the crisis was the Yakama selling their land to the whites for the purpose of supporting their addiction. With his alcohol-afflicted community in mind, Buffalo argued, emulating Montezuma's "Let My People Go," that he thought it was best for Indians to "look out for him self," pay taxes, and vote. Buffalo was frustrated that young people were being held back by Indian Bureau mismanagement of the reservation:

> If the Indian Beauro would say to the Indian here is your Money and land. take it and let them crooks beat you out of it. they would keep it longer yes 75% longer than under present conditions he would be 70% better man with in a reasonable time Nobody will go around feeling sorry for the Indian if he gets what belongs to him.
>
> [E]very Indian thats a ward of our Government now is to be pitied especially the young Indian . . . that is raring to go but has the hold back straps on him.[4]

Further regarding Indigenous wherewithal, Wanda Shirt wrote to the editor of *Wassaja* in a letter dated March 20 with a return address in Everett, Washington. Shirt informed Montezuma that she had sent him a poem she hoped would be published. She said her poem was for the "Sioux," whom she wanted to honor. If Shirt identified as Sioux, she did not say here. Instead, she mentioned that she had received several issues of *Wassaja* and expressed sincere interest in Montezuma's political agenda. As evidence that she had corresponded before, Shirt took a defensive tone when she referred to Montezuma having told her that her Indian readers—including him, perhaps—did not understand her work. Shirt retorted that the problem was not with her poetry but others' resentfulness of her. In Shirt's opinion, she was the target of "jealous hearted Squaws. . . . But like flies they are easily brushed aside." Shirt pitied her critics, blaming their alleged ignorance on the Indian Bureau: "It is all the fault of the Agents who keep them under their rule so close that they do not have a chance to broaden or grow."

> I'd like to help them [the Sioux?] if they would trust me. and some day they will for I am going home. I do not fear opposition. I expect it. But I mean to overcome it, by sheer strength of Will and determination I mean to say what I think. And to do what I ought to do. In Love of all. And I'll get through if I have to fight every one of them. I won't give up because there is opposition, that is when I fight best. I mean to show some of them that the fighting Souix are not yet dead. And that the spirit of Sitting Bull still lives.

By "them" Shirt primarily meant the women she derided as "jealous hearted Squaws." However, what was ambiguous was where these women were located. Was Shirt referring to the Sioux reservations in North and South Dakota or the reservations in Washington State? Or did Shirt have in mind all Indians who were trapped in the reservation system? As a person influenced by *Wassaja*, any and all of these were possible. Shirt's letter ended with the assertion that she did not care what people thought of her, but it was written in a way that clearly indicated that she cared quite a lot about others' opinions.[5] As for the poem dedicated to the Sioux, unfortunately the original was not preserved in the archival collection in hand. A poem by Wanda Short, however, titled "On, Straight On to Freedom" was published in the January 1920 issue. Written in heroic couplets, excerpted below, the poem did not mention the Sioux, but did passionately sing an ode to Indian freedom, complete with some swipes against Cato Sells and the Indian Bureau:

> This was once our father's land —
> > Let us fight till we have conquered
> Freedom for the Indian man;
> > Let us work and let us struggle
> Till we win throughout the land,
> > All that we have asked is freedom
> And equal rights on which to stand —
> > Freedom in a free man's land,
> Absolutely free from the Cato gang.[6]

Short's poem sat alongside an editorial against the expropriation of Indian mineral rights by the bill rider that empowered the secretary of the
interior to lease some thirty million acres without Indian consent (see
chapter 4).[7]

Closer to home, Joe Easchief sent a letter from Salt River dated June 15.[8]
He updated Montezuma on the situation on the Salt River Reservation,
which was described obliquely as "just same it was befor," which meant that
the Indian Bureau still expected them to take small allotments and prepare for the arrival of the Yavapai. In which case Montezuma "going stand
for our rights. and so we take care of ourself here on our reservation (Jose
King)." The injection of the name "Jose King" indicates that Easchief was
relaying what another community member had said. Easchief furthermore
bemoaned the fact that at one time they had plenty of water to sustain their
community, but now they had very little, which pushed the reservation to
the brink of extinction: "Now the water are very small head. and that small
head of water are use for the 3 to 5 acres of land (Jose Kisto)." According to
Easchief, the Akimel O'odham knew how to take care of themselves without
any intercession from the whites. Presently, though, the Whites, namely the
Indian Bureau, presumed that it was impossible for the Salt River Reservation to maintain itself without their direct control. Belying their arrogance,
the Indian Bureau, Easchief argued, had been grossly negligent in fulfilling its
trust obligations: "It seem that the Government are just govern the Money
for Nothings. Thats way look on. John [Juan?] Andrew." In closing, Easchief
shared the community's frustration with being kept in the dark about Indian
Bureau intrusions into their affairs, complete with making decisions on their
behalf at the highest level:

> I am going to tell you are that we are just the same. I had been press down
> here on the Salt river Ind[ian] reservation. like the rest are same I like to
> know how this things are going raise up. we held the Ind[ian] Meeting and
> try to talk over. We like to heard from You Sooner about that Some White
> Man had been here on our Ind[ian] reservation from Washington D.C. They
> say that were Congressman [Carl Hayden?]. And nobody knew what they
> were for on our reservation. The Indians are Trying ask about it and nobody
> knew it. That was very to find out all about it. I wishe that You could let us
> know what they here for.[9]

Two weeks later, Montezuma received a letter from a very different part of Indian Country, complete with its own perspective on Indian affairs. John Hunter asked for help with the "Indian department." He was responsible for his niece and nephew, both of whom were students at Haskell Indian School in Lawrence, Kansas. Hunter complained about what he considered to be the grossly inadequate education his niece and nephew were receiving at their Indian boarding school. By comparison, Hunter shared his son's educational experience in Winnebago, Nebraska. The public school in his opinion did a much better job. Wanting his niece and nephew to enjoy the same opportunity, Hunter contacted "Mr. [Charles F.] Pierce at Haskell" about returning them to his care: "every Indian boy and girl can do this if he is given the chance. but long as an Indian boy or girl is in a government school he is going to be held back like all that have been attended these schools[.] If it wasn't for this we would have more well educated Indians." Hunter closed his appeal by pointing out that Montezuma and he had met before "at the [Society of American Indians] conference at Madison Wis. 1914."[10] As with the 1901 letter from Manuel Ruiz that began this discourse, Montezuma's response to Hunter has not been preserved. Nonetheless, given that Montezuma was a financially struggling physician living in Chicago, complete with the thankless job of publishing *Wassaja*, it was unlikely that Montezuma could do much to address Hunter's concerns beyond sympathize.

Nellie H. David[11] referred to Montezuma on July 5, 1920, as "Friend & tribe," which signified a tribal relation between the two, but not a personal one. As may be recalled, David comes up in the story about Montezuma's confrontation with Superintendent Sharp. Referred to as "Nellie Davis," she served as Chief Dickens's interpreter. Consequently, David felt justified in bringing her grievance of arbitrary dismissal to Montezuma's attention. Specifically, David was let go from her post at the San Carlos Agency "by [Edgar B.] Merrit [*sic*]"[12] because she "was diseased as reported by San Carlos physician Ferrel [*sic*?]."[13] David claimed that what was done to her was a "dirty trick." According to David, the San Carlos Apache were upset about her dismissal: "The Apaches were angry because I was fired but it can not be helped I told them. We had our last meeting & told them of what you have said to them. They want you to help them in everything." In the meantime, David took pleasure from learning that one of her accusers—it is unclear which one—was killed in an automobile accident in California. Because of her connection to the Fort McDowell community, David also referred to developments there:

> I see trouble everywhere I go. The McDowell Indians are working on a wagon road & soon will lay pipe to draw water from here for the city.[14] That don't sound fair but they are doing it. I feel McDowell is not safe yet.
>
> I don't know what will turn up but I will wait & see. If you wish to say anything write to Cecil Hazzarner[15] at San Carlos & he will explain it to the Apaches.
>
> The McDowell Indians are having a good time, they had two nights of dancing & expect to have another one soon. One of Mike Burn's daughter died Saturday., the other Indians are well. I will close now.[16]

Captain R. D. Parker[17] sent Montezuma a letter, dated July 14, by way of Downers Grove, Illinois, which was the only time a fellow Illinoisan wrote. Addressing Montezuma as "Sir and Brother," Captain Parker briefed Montezuma about a plot he had been hatching to "capture and control our enemies." What Parker meant by "our," let alone "enemies," is undetermined. Unlike other correspondents, Parker did not indicate having written to Montezuma previously. Nonetheless, Parker invited Montezuma, along with "Miss Letta Meyers," to his home.[18] As an enticement, Parker said that "Dr. Wheeler of Aurora [Illinois]" would be at the Sunday meeting.[19] Parker then stated rather enigmatically, "I will go [to] the meeting friday night and take things in and observe and after may do some thinking then as thoughts proceeds actions I may do some action." For reasons that must have been utterly arbitrary, Parker highlighted the words "thoughts proceeds actions" and "action" in red. Whether Parker did this for dramatic effect or as coded language or because there was a flaw in his typewriter ribbon is unknown. As for Sunday, Parker advised Montezuma that Meyers might wish to travel with him. Whatever Parker was plotting he did not want to start "until we had sufficient Indians to back us up and help us through." Parker ended just as mysteriously as he had begun: "I am quite shure we have enough [Indians?] to control the situation without very much of a fight. Hoping to see you in the near future, and with good thoughts for your success I remain yours truly in AF & AM."[20] Finally, below Parker's signature, there was a postscript that made an incomprehensible reference to a "ticket with a time card."[21]

Chief George Dickens wrote three letters in 1920. The first, dated January 18, disclosed little about Yavapai affairs other than an obscure reference to a "strike" that Montezuma had asked him about and about which Dickens knew nothing. Dickens was more focused on informing Montezuma that he did "send the basket one day after christmas." Did Montezuma "get it or not?"[22] Another six months would pass before Dickens sent another short note. This time the news, arriving in the middle of July, was more urgent: "the agent of Salt River [Sharp?] look it up the Indian's their names & the tribes already so I don't understand this. The reason I write to you. I never get a news from you about this." In all likelihood, Sharp was conducting a census for the Indian Bureau, specifically in preparation for relocating the Yavapai to Salt River. Dickens was just as alarmed by developments at Fort McDowell, about which he felt he had been kept in the dark: "The stockman [Bennett?] here of McDowell told me that the Government to issue us money & the company going to gave us. How is that you know? or not. or you ever heard it any? So I don't want get this money if they ever do this. without your advise me. You must tell me about this. If you know." What Dickens did know and mentioned in passing was that "The Company worked on the pipe line already right below the reservation."[23] Chief Dickens's third and last letter of 1920 was dated September 14, and he assured Montezuma that his plans to visit were agreeable for what sounded like the usual hunting trip: "Im still working on the cord of wood for city as Ive waste [sic?] you before. I had nothing more to write so Goodbye."[24]

Montezuma's annual hunting trip was anything but casual, as recounted in the October 1920 issue of *Wassaja*. Chief Dickens was obliged to tell Montezuma that his presence was required at the Salt River Agency office. Superintendent Sharp wanted to see him. Two men, "a sub-game warden and an Indian police," soon arrived at the hunting party's camp at Four Peaks to accompany Montezuma. Montezuma's wife, Marie, Chief Dickens, and Nellie Davis went with Montezuma and the escort. Arriving at the Agency after dark, the sub-game warden spoke with Sharp, who wanted Montezuma and his wife taken down to Phoenix and jailed. The sub-warden advised against this, if only for the reason that they did not have a warrant for Montezuma's arrest. Eventually, Sharp spoke with Montezuma, at which point he accused the Yavapai physician of making trouble by speaking against the Indian Bureau, which was underscored with the accusation: "We think you have been an undesirable person. You have agitated these Indians contrary to the will of the Indian Bureau." As an example, Sharp brought up the fact that Indians were not allowed to hunt off of reservation land, whether or not they had a license. Montezuma emphatically rebutted Sharp's derisive comments about his work defending Indian rights: "I want you to know that I am unselfishly interested for the best interest of my people before you were born. I am an Indian, blood related to these Indians on the McDowell reservation. I was born here, and my heart is bound up with them." With respect to Montezuma's claim that he was working for his community's best interest, Dickens testified before Sharp: "Dr. Montezuma has always said the right things to us because he is one of us. He has done no wrong. We like him, and would like him to stay with us." The article goes on to summarize Montezuma's criticisms of Sharp's treatment of the Yavapai, which had never been fair or lawful. If there was any unwanted influence on the Yavapai, it was committed by Sharp, whom Montezuma accused of being more anxious about supporting Phoenix business interests than about addressing the well-being of the Indians. Montezuma then enumerated the ways in which the Indian Bureau had ruined the Yavapai economy by turning it from a self-sustaining agrarian community living off the Verde River to a failed stock-raising enterprise with uncertain land and water rights.[25]

As for Charles Dickens, he remained Montezuma's most devoted cousin and correspondent. Similar to Chief Dickens's, Charles's letters were brief, with the exception of the last one. On January 6 and 16, 1920, Dickens sent Montezuma two short letters filled with the mundanities that typically occupied his mind, beginning with a renewed effort at getting Montezuma interested in his ambition to go into the cattle business, complete with his characteristic assurances that Montezuma would see a great return on his investment. Despite Montezuma's opinion about stock-raising at Fort McDowell, as expressed in the article above, there were a number of Yavapai who attempted to succeed at the cattle industry. Dickens, wanting to be one of these cattlemen, ended his appeal by trying, as he had done before, to prick his cousin's conscience: "You know I, got big familey. and buying lots of things to eat and buying lots of Cloths for them. and Dear Cousin If you will do these buying Cattles for us I, and My wife we thank you very much. & Dont think you lose your money we will pay you back frist time we rase 3 Steers to sell."[26]

Dickens's subsequent letter was little more than a minor update, in which he noted that he had been picking cotton and that people at home in Fort McDowell were doing well. Also, as expected, "Dear Cousin Dont forget me about Cattles."[27] February 17 saw another update on the hard work being done at home, along with the customary remarks about everyone's well-being. Dickens's note may be regarded as his way of maintaining a healthy kinship relation with Montezuma. Though he had to deal with Cousin Charles's never-ending financial frustrations, Montezuma likely appreciated receiving these tidbits. Indeed, it is easy to imagine that Montezuma idealized his childhood home, where people knew his name, Wassaja, and where he did not have to explain being Indian in America: "Here the wheather getting little worm now. all McDowell Indians is looks, all well. No one sick, George & Richard & my mother & My Sister we all well. dear Cousin these is all the news here. When I hear from You again I will tell you more things at McDowell."[28]

Charles sent two more letters. In the second-to-last letter, August 30, Dickens asked about Montezuma's plans to visit Arizona: "all McDowell Indians expect you come again with your wife."[29] Two weeks later, September 13, Dickens expressed excitement that Montezuma would soon visit. In light of which, Dickens informed Montezuma that they would venture "to the Mountains where you was Captured and to Bloody Cave and to Sugar Coat ranch." According to the October 1920 issue of *Wassaja*, the hunting party camped "at the Devil's Hip Pocket, south-west of the Four Peak Mountain."[30] Also, aside from making plans for the hunting trip, Dickens told his cousin, "frist next month Oct. we go to Prescott for 10 days to see the best medison man there and Singing for my famileys and we leave here on 30th itis Month Sept to arrive Prescott on frist Oct on 2 Oclock train."[31] Dickens was likely worried about not just his family's physical health but also their spiritual lives. Did the medicine man mentioned include the same one that would see Montezuma during his final days? Only Anna Moore Shaw, the author of *A Pima Past* (1974), claimed that Montezuma saw a Yavapai traditional healer during his final return to Fort McDowell. Neither Iverson nor Speroff referred to any medicine man, nor, for that matter, did George Webb, who recounted seeing Montezuma on his death bed in *A Pima Remembers* (1959). (Webb and Shaw's works are analyzed for their portrayals of Montezuma in the final chapter.)

The only letter that arrived from Mike Burns during all of 1920 was dated February 19 and was considerably shorter than Burns's previous letters to Montezuma. Burns said that he had shown Montezuma's feedback on his book to "educated Men." He claimed moreover in rather ambiguous terms that parts of his manuscript had been published: "being afraid: to reprint:

some of my Manuscript[:] which some parts were published." Such phrasing is difficult to decipher. In any case, Burns segued into the more important development in his publishing pursuits, which had to do with the interest that a local historian took in his work:

> Mr. Thos. Harish [*sic*]:[32] who was the State Hostorian: of Arizona: to allow him to put it his history: about the doing of its people: and by putting that part: of what I had written: that will goes to show: that an Indian: can speak for himself and the wrongs has been done by the White people and others: as well as the whites: But he said: that I was the real Author: because I wrote it Myself: and he also said: that will Not hinder Me from My history: Whish I am working to Make a little history of my own.[33]

As documented previously, Burns did not publish his book during his lifetime (he died in 1934), in spite of multiple attempts through different contacts, including Montezuma, to shepherd his work into print.[34]

As the 1920s began, complete with a new president, Warren G. Harding, and a new commissioner of Indian Affairs, Charles H. Burke, the era of Indian rights history that Montezuma defined was drawing to a close. With citizenship on the horizon for all American Indians—it would be passed on June 2, 1924—the SAI, along with Montezuma, reached its twilight years. Except for anemic meetings in Saint Louis, Missouri (1920), and Detroit, Michigan (1921), the SAI became a relic of Progressive history and would soon be overshadowed by the Committee of One Hundred that Secretary of Commerce Herbert Hoover formed in 1922 to discuss Indian Affairs; the National Council of American Indians that Gertrude Bonnin organized in 1926; and the survey team that Lewis Meriam formed at the behest of Secretary of the Interior Hubert Work, which produced the comprehensive report titled *The Problem of Indian Administration* in 1928. As for Montezuma, his final years fighting for Yavapai land and water rights were marked by an effort to capitalize on the departure of Wilson and Sells, in hopes that a change in presidential administration, not to mention political affiliation, would enable the Yavapai to achieve their long-sought goal.

CHAPTER SIX

A New Dawn Breaks

Montezuma Completes His Journey

The year 1921 marked the final year of correspondence preserved in the Carlos Montezuma Collection. *Wassaja* continued with its regular monthly issues. A major highlight of the May, June, and July 1921 issues was the three-part account of the Fort McDowell Yavapai's twelve-year battle with the Indian Bureau. As for correspondence, there were only two letters to speak of: one from "Davis" (Nellie H. David), the other from Montezuma. Davis, in a letter dated February 12, addressed Montezuma as "friend" and informed him about a conversation she had had with "Mr. [John] Baum," the local "alloting Agent."[1] Baum, according to Davis, did "not know anything about water, but he say's for us to go ahead & get our allotment & that water question will come later." What Baum was likely not prepared to state was the class of water rights, per the Kent Decree, that went with allotments at Salt River. Naturally, the Yavapai were skeptical and took their concerns to Superintendent Sharp, who concurred with Baum, assuring them that they possessed water rights at Salt River. Whether or not he was any clearer than Baum was not recorded. Should the Yavapai decline their Salt River allotments, the land would go on the open market along with the attached water rights: "He [Sharp] also tell them [the Yavapai] that the President [Woodrow Wilson] have signed that we must be alloted at Saltriver as farming land & at[?] McDowell as grazing land." Davis wondered if Montezuma knew anything about this.

Davis went on to describe a stressful meeting at which community leaders were on the verge of giving in to Indian Bureau demands. Davis was particularly critical of Chief George Dickens. As may be recalled, Dickens began siding with Burns on the allotment issue, seeing the Indian Bureau plan as the Yavapai's best option for retaining land and water rights within the reservation system, albeit split between Fort McDowell and Salt River:

> The Indians are weak when it comes to strong & lying arguments so we are to alloted whether we want to or not at Saltriver & McDowell as it is an authority from the Interior as stated by Sharp & Baum. But as I have said we have no legal rights to water. I do not know whether to rely on "Sent [sic] Decree" or not. Your letter just came on time as we to have a meeting Sat[urday] evening as it was hard to have the Indians from getting an . . . allotment without water., it took some hard talking from both of us to make them understand. Geo[rge] Dickens is not bright when you come to know him personally., he was bound to except an allotment also have also Yuma Apache get what is left & live by themselves & you might guess how hard it was for us to make him see his mistake & he did see it before morning & so we ask him to apologize as most of the Indians were for water-rights as well as land., so we were of one mind.

The Yavapai confronted Baum and told him that they would not accept any kind of allotment without water rights to the Verde River. Baum, unsurprisingly, took umbrage. Like other Indian Bureau officials, Baum was adamant that what the Yavapai were resisting was policy set by the president of the United States, which he and Sharp were bound to carry out. Davis wrote: "So I burst out and said that is the old rule you [Baum] are going by as if we did not know for ourselves what is right or what we want but he did not ans[wer] me." By "old rule," Davis referred to the fact that the allotment policy that Baum was determined to carry out had been established by President Wilson. However, the United States now had a new president, Warren G. Harding, which also meant a new secretary of the interior and a new commissioner of Indian Affairs. Cato Sells was now out of office. Beyond asserting themselves, Davis did not point to anything in her letter that was evidence of the Yavapai's success at protecting their land and water rights. She merely reiterated Baum's threats, then shared the sympathy she felt for the San Carlos Apache, who were going through an equally distressing time.

Indeed, the April 1921 issue of *Wassaja* included a story titled "Horse Meat as Food for Man," which was about the attempt by the Indian agent at

San Carlos to compel the Apache to accept horse meat as a part of their rations: "Feeding its wards with horse flesh is a sign of starvation and of leading the Indians down to the lowest depths of life."[2]

Davis disclosed that she brought the Yavapai grievances to her superior:

> I got a letter from Commissioner Merrt [sic] offering me a . . . matrons place at Fort Mojave School [Bullhead City, Arizona].
>
> He only stated, "looking into the matter thoroughly & is willing to assign me another position Iam not human enough nor the Office is human enough to apologize to me. Of course you know I won't except it. I had enough of it[,] not the Indians[,] but the dirty employees of the Indian Bureau."

Finally, as an example of how out of touch the Indian Bureau was with the issues that confronted reservation communities like Fort McDowell, among Davis's anecdotes was a brief but unexpected reference to a visiting anthropologist: "A woman was here saying she was sent from the Office to get Indian songs but I told Geo[rge] Dickens, to say we under strict against singing & dancing & we cannot please one & not the rest so she left but expect to come in three weeks. I told the Indians, —see that is where our money spent & we are poor of it."[3]

The last letter in this two-decades long chain of correspondence was written by Carlos Montezuma, dated March 24, 1921, and addressed to Mike Burns. Montezuma began by assuring his cousin that he was not aware of anyone speaking against Burns, admonishing him to not do the same to others, as it would add to the community's troubles. Then, in a passage that would have likely riled Davis had she seen this out of context, Montezuma validated the work that Burns did on behalf of the Yavapai: "Mike, you are just the same as I am. If I were in your place I would do the same thing that you are doing now. I would think it was a great honor to be an interpreter for Mr. Baum, the allotting agent." Montezuma confided in Burns that he might even "tell the Indians to sign this paper, for the Government is good." At this point, anyone who knew anything about Montezuma's political principles would suspect that his advice was not going in the direction that it initially feigned. Montezuma continued: "See how good the Government is to us Indians; they will give us [an] extra five acres of irrigating lands on [the] Salt River reservation." Then, after stroking Burns's ego with compliments, Montezuma sprung his trap: "Why would I do this? Because I am paid as an interpreter and I feel big, and not because I know it is right or that it is in the best interest of my people."

Montezuma reminded Burns why he had fought so diligently for Yavapai rights all of these years, antagonizing the Indian Bureau every step of the way; it was because the Indian Bureau has never worked for them but only worked for personal profit. The Indian Bureau, from Cato Sells on down, were in the back pockets of "Land grabbers" and the "Phoenix Water Users Association," meaning the Salt River Project and the Arizona Canal. Together, the government and these businessmen conspired to strip the Yavapai of their land and water, coercing them to move to Salt River, because of greed, nothing more: "Mike, when you Indians move down to [the] Salt River reservation and sign papers, you Indians are gone," meaning that they will have lost everything that they once possessed at Fort McDowell, including their water rights to the Verde River. In fact, everything that the Indian Bureau had been saying, even those instances when they sounded sympathetic—Cato Sells always sounded sympathetic—was for the express purpose of tricking the Yavapai into relinquishing their rights at Fort McDowell. Even worse, Montezuma explained how Baum and Sharp regularly lied to the Yavapai about the possibility of retaining their Verde River water rights even after accepting land allotments at Salt River. On the contrary, all of their Verde River water rights would be transferred to the Roosevelt Dam—the Yavapai would never be allowed to use that water for their own farming. The Yavapai would be left with nothing but their meagre five acres apiece at Salt River:

> When I was there [Fort McDowell] last Fall engineers were sounding the Verde River East of the McDowell mountain. Do you know what that means? Some day a dam will be built and the McDowell land will be flooded and the water will be used for drinking water for the Salt River Valley people [SRP]. No wonder the McDowell Indians are hoodwinked and urged to move to Salt River reservation? White people's heads are long; they can see many years ahead, but you Indians are blind. You think five acres at Salt River reservation and grazing land is a great offer from the Indian Bureau, when in reality, it is only a bait to have you Indians move off the McDowell land, so that the Phoenix people will get that land for themselves by and by.

The Yavapai and the Akimel O'odham were being pressured into a deal they did not want or need, yet the Indian Bureau was trying to make it look

like accepting the five acres was their choice. The choice between two evils
is not a choice. "You are human beings," Montezuma affirmed, "and it is no
more than just and right that you should be considered and consulted in
the matter before allotting you McDowell Indians." As for what Montezuma
thought the Yavapai ought to do:

> Do not accept five acres of irrigation land on Salt River Reservation. Do
> not move off of the McDowell reservation. Accept allotment of pro-rata on
> McDowell reservation with all the rights intact, as when you were first given
> the McDowell reservation as your home for grazing, timber and farming
> lands. That includes Kent's decree of 390 miner's inches of continual flow of
> the Verde River water.[4]

Montezuma reminded Burns that the Yavapai possessed the right to negotiate. Whether or not Montezuma had in mind the 1887 General Allotment
Act, which required Indian consent or some other source, such as a statement from Commissioner Sells or his successor Charles H. Burke, is unclear.
Regardless, Montezuma wanted Burns to be aware that they did not have to
accept just anything that the Indian Bureau offered them.

As a cautionary tale, Montezuma shared what happened to Nellie and Gilbert Davis. This was the same Nellie who had written to Montezuma about
her travails at San Carlos and who had served as translator during the Superintendent Sharp affair. In this story the Davises suffered the consequences
of accepting their five acres at Salt River. In fact, the Davises, as Montezuma
recalled, were at one time true believers in the Indian Bureau's plans: "They
thought it would be a good thing for the Indians to have two places. They
could be like rich white people." What the Davises found out the hard way
was that the Indian Bureau was not offering them the opportunity to keep
their Fort McDowell land for grazing while acquiring five additional acres
at Salt River for farming: "Nellie and Gilbert and you and all of the Indians
know that the Verde River water is better than the water from Roosevelt
dam. Stay where you can get good water." Montezuma understood that without water rights, grazing rights alone at Fort McDowell would preclude them
from keeping that land. They would be pressured to sell.

> I want to tell you, Mike, that those Salt River Reservation Indians at Lehi are
> complaining for want of water to irrigate their lands. This is about the way

the Mohave-Apaches will be treated if they move to Salt River reservation. They will be crying for water, and water will not be given to them.

Again I urge the McDowell Indians to fix the brush dam and get to work to raise wheat, corn, barley and other things. Do not wait, but get to work for your lives. No one will do anything for you, you must do everything for yourselves.

Montezuma reiterated his advice to not sign anything from the Indian Bureau that obliged them to move or give up any of their rights at Fort McDowell. Lastly, Montezuma stated assuredly that he and his friends in the Indians Rights movement were working hard at protecting the Yavapai's right to remain on their land where they would "not be molested or annoyed." Montezuma signed his letter, "Sincerely your cousin, Carlos Montezuma, 'Wassaja.'"[5]

In the March 1921 issue of *Wassaja*, Montezuma editorialized about the profound lack of rights that Indians enjoyed as Americans. In particular, Montezuma complained about the almost unlimited discretionary power that the secretary of the interior had over Indian lives, against which protest was futile. For example, opposition arose when a pipeline cut through the McDowell Reservation, which got this reply from assistant commissioner of Indian Affairs Edgard B. Merritt:

> The Office is not aware of any infringement on the Indians' rights by reason of granting a pipe line through the McDowell Reservation. The Act of February 15, 1901 (31 Stats., 790), authorizes the Secretary of the Interior, under general regulations to be fixed by him, to permit the use of rights of way through the reservations of the United States, including Indian reservations, for canals, ditches, pipes and pipe lines, flumes, tunnels or other water conduits, and for water plants, dams and reservoirs used to promote irrigation or mining or quarrying or the manufacturing or cutting of timber or lumber or the supplying of water for domestic, public or any other beneficial uses.[6]

Final approval for these enumerated projects rested with the secretary of the interior, and affected Indian communities were omitted from any consideration, be it notification, consultation, or approval. Hence the instances throughout the correspondence to Montezuma in which fences, surveys, and pipelines were implemented without a word to the Yavapai. Insofar as

Indian reservations were considered part of the public lands that fell within
the jurisdiction of the Department of the Interior, similar to lands held in
trust by the federal government on behalf of the American people, any use or
development of said lands could only proceed with approval from the highest authority, namely the secretary of the interior, which "he" must find to be
in the "public interest," which is to say the country as a whole. Given that the
exploitation of public lands was regarded as of vital interest to the national
economy, the Indigenous nations that inhabited the reservation system were
constantly at a disadvantage, legally and politically.

After campaigning unsuccessfully for Thomas Sloan to be nominated as
President Harding's commissioner of Indian Affairs, *Wassaja* announced in
its April 1921 issue that Charles H. Burke would succeed Cato Sells. Despite
the fact that Burke was responsible for the 1906 Burke Act,[7] which established the much-reviled competency commissions, Montezuma refrained
from expressing any opinion about Burke. Nonetheless, Montezuma revealed
his suspicions that this was another political appointment that had nothing
whatsoever to do with the good of the Indians and everything to do with political favoritism: "To the Republican party belongs the spoils. . . . To reward
a brother Republican to the Commissionership of Indian Affairs, he does not
have to know anything about Indians. All he has to do is to take the oil can
and grease the Indian machine faithfully."[8]

In the ensuing three issues of *Wassaja*, after more than a decade of struggle against the Indian Bureau's arbitrary plans to forcibly remove the Yavapai
to the Salt River Reservation, Montezuma published his account of the effort
to protect Yavapai rights against the tyranny of the Indian Bureau. In May
1921, *Wassaja* bore three lengthy articles that took up all four pages: two
letters from Joseph W. Latimer and one from Edgar B. Merritt. In the first
of the two Latimer letters, dated April 2, 1921, Latimer addressed the newly
appointed commissioner of Indian Affairs Charles H. Burke, alerting him
about the urgent situation at "Camp McDowell, Arizona." The issue at hand,
as of 1910, was the Indian Bureau's plan to allot "irrigable land" to the Yavapai
"in the Salt River District" for the purpose of relocating them "against their
wishes." Montezuma and Latimer together took up the Yavapai cause and
sent letters of protest to Robert G. Valentine, commissioner of Indian Affairs,
and Walter L. Fisher, secretary of the interior, both of whom served under
President William Howard Taft. What the Yavapai sought was "full allotment
on McDowell and the building of an irrigation dam thereon." Toward this ob-

jective, Montezuma presented the Yavapai case before the House Committee on Expenditures, Interior Department, in June 1911. More than a year later, on August 10, 1912, Secretary Fisher notified Montezuma, after consulting with an irrigation engineer, W. H. Rosecrans, about the feasibility of a dam at Verde River, that the Yavapai would be granted their resolution, calling the plan to remove the Yavapai to Salt River "a mistake." (William H. Code, who had previously insisted that a dam on the Verde was impractical due to the river's turbulent waters, making an irrigation dam too costly, was out of the picture.) A few days later, on August 17, First Assistant Secretary Samuel Adams wrote to Montezuma about the need to prepare an enrollment roll for the purpose of allotting land at Camp McDowell. Unfortunately for the Yavapai, before the Indian Bureau's mistake could be corrected, Woodrow Wilson was elected president, and as commissioner of Indian Affairs he installed Cato Sells, who was unequivocal—contrary to Fisher—about relocating the "McDowell Indians" to Salt River. Montezuma, Latimer, and the Yavapai were suddenly back where they were in 1910. Naturally, with the 1920 election of a Republican president, who would appoint a new Indian commissioner, the Yavapai and their allies were hopeful, after eight years of Wilson and Sells, that the new administration would finish what Fisher and Valentine had begun. Meanwhile, the situation at Fort McDowell and Salt River grew worrisome:

> We have . . . just learned that an agent [Baum] is now on McDowell allotting these Indians in the Salt River District . . . [and] is endeavoring to obtain the Indians' written consent thereto. It is further alleged that the Indians in signing the papers . . . do not know they are signing a consent to move. . . . Therefore, we urge your immediate suspension of further activities of your Department Agent at McDowell until you can give this matter a full and complete hearing.

Latimer pleaded to Burke for his informed opinion about this pressing issue, complete with reminding him that the Fort McDowell Reservation was in compensation, meaning General Crook's promise, for the loyalty that the Yavapai showed the United States in its campaign against Geronimo.[9]

The same issue included a second missive from Latimer to Burke regarding John Baum, in addition to a letter from Assistant Commissioner Edgar B. Merritt to Baum. Both letters were about Baum's allotment work. In Latimer's second letter, dated April 22, Burke was made aware that the Yavapai and their representatives, Montezuma and Latimer, did know that the allotting agent accused of deliberately tricking the Yavapai into signing agreements was Baum. Secondly, that the Yavapai were aware that the Indian Bureau's ulterior motive for removing them to Salt River was the seizure of the Verde River with the construction of a pipeline from McDowell to Phoenix as part of the growing Salt River Project—a major development backed by Arizona Representative Carl Hayden. Obviously, Latimer was greatly concerned that Yavapai rights would be swept aside for the sake of accommodating what was regarded by the new State of Arizona as a much-needed addition to the infrastructure of its burgeoning economy and increasing population. As for the letter from Merritt to Baum, dated June 22, 1920, it preceded chronologically the two letters from Latimer to Burke. The purpose of printing Merritt's 1920 letter was to document the working orders under which Baum was allocating allotments. Merritt, of course, was the assistant commissioner of Indian Affairs under Cato Sells. Therefore the issue with Baum's ongoing allotment work was that he was employing Sells's policy, which Burke, as Sells's successor, needed to redress.[10]

In June 1921, *Wassaja* published Latimer's 1911 testimony before Congress, specifically the House Committee on Expenditures, Interior Department, in which Latimer pleaded the Yavapai case, informing committee members that the Camp McDowell reservation was arranged for them by "General Cooke [*sic*] . . . after they had proven their loyalty and bravery in fighting against the Apaches and finally capturing Geronimo, the famous Apache leader." Latimer berated the Indian Bureau's plans to relocate the Yavapai to Salt River for the sole purpose of commercially exploiting their land and water rights. Specifically, he made issue of the fact that the Yavapai were precluded from selecting their own attorney without Indian Bureau approval, which diminished their rights further: "Only through the philanthropy and expenditure of the personal money of Dr. Carlos Montezuma and the help of a Congressional Committee has this rape of the McDowell Indians been thus far prevented."[11]

The June 1921 issue also printed an undated letter from the "Assistant Commissioner" to SAI President Thomas Sloan, in which the assistant commissioner commented indirectly about the negative and unwanted influence that Montezuma had on the Indian Bureau's planned allotments to the Yavapai at Salt River. The assistant commissioner's letter was in response to a letter that Sloan had sent to him, "dated February 15, 1921," which indicated that the letter in hand was written by Merritt. Sloan was informed that the Yavapai's best interests were being considered, as evidenced by the Indian Bureau's consultation with irrigation engineer William Code, who determined that the Verde River was too turbulent to accommodate a dam, the building of which, aside from the extreme cost, would lead to flooding Yavapai land. Consequently, the water rights that were due to the Camp McDowell Indians would be better placed at Salt River.[12]

Lastly, another letter from Latimer to Burke, dated May 5, 1921, expressed growing concern over the lack of any response from Burke about the ongoing crisis at Fort McDowell. In addition to reiterating the Yavapai's grievance against the Indian Bureau, Secretary Fisher's admission of error and his proposed resolution, which was disrupted by Cato Sells, Latimer pointed out the role that the City of Phoenix played in how the Camp McDowell situation was perceived:

> I have heard it said: "What do three hundred (300) Indians amount to when twenty-five thousand (25,000) citizens in Phoenix, Arizona want this Verde River water to drink?" My answer is there is a wrong and a right way to get this water if its use is necessary, and I know the methods of the past twelve (12) years have been branded a "mistake" by an official of the Government [Secretary Fisher], and I know somewhere, somehow, some other official of the Government is going to see fair play and a deal given these Indians in spite of the opposition . . . of the Indian Bureau and the Public Utility Corporations of Arizona.[13]

On the front page of the July issue, *Wassaja* published a letter, dated May 30, 1921, from Latimer to Albert B. Fall, President Harding's secretary of the interior. Fall was misidentified as the "Commissioner of Indian Affairs." Latimer acknowledged clarification received from Fall regarding the reasons why the Indian Bureau had sought an executive order from former President Wilson. Interestingly, Latimer noted that the Department of the Interior "does not expect to remove these Indians from the Camp McDowell Reservation." Unfortunately, this did not mean that the Yavapai had won their case. In the remainder of Latimer's letter was a growing concern that the issue at Fort McDowell had not been resolved in the least. Why? Because of the nagging issue of President Wilson's executive order, which was signed after

Secretary Fisher's statement that the relocation plan was a mistake. Between Fisher's recommendation and Wilson's order, it appeared to Fall and Burke that Wilson's executive order was the final word. The implication was that it would take either another executive order, this time from Harding, or an act of Congress to overturn the directive to proceed with Yavapai relocation. On the assumption that Wilson's order nullified Fisher's recommendation, Secretary Fall was following Fisher's original pre-1911 opinion on the Camp McDowell issue. Thus, Latimer's objective was to disabuse Secretary Fall of his assumption, reiterating the importance of the 1911 congressional hearing that led to Fisher's redirection on the Fort McDowell case. The policy under Valentine's successor, Commissioner Sells, was to allot to the Yavapai grazing rights at Camp McDowell and water rights at Salt River, in addition to rejecting the request, based on Code's opinion, for an irrigation dam on the Verde River. Consequently, the Indian Bureau promoted its relocation plan as an economic opportunity—all the Yavapai had to do was relinquish their water rights to the Verde River, for which they would be compensated with an allotment and water rights at Salt River.

At one time, Secretary Fisher did support the aforementioned allotment plan. However, he changed his mind after learning from Montezuma at the 1911 congressional hearing about the consequences of the allotment plan. Specifically, as of 1911, Fort McDowell was suffering immense economic hardship. Following through with the splitting of grazing and water rights between two reservations would only spell the ruin of the Yavapai, not prosperity. With respect to Secretary Fall, Latimer tried to convince him to review all of the documentation, including the 1911 congressional hearing testimony, and come to the same conclusion as Fisher: "If you will not amend your decision as indicated in your said letter of April 30th, we shall again undertake the task of combating the determination of the Indian Bureau, and, as stated, if you will indicate a willingness and if you want, suggest how to prefer—we will try to cheerfully co-operate with your department to again establish the engineering or any other facts needed."[14]

In the remaining seven issues of *Wassaja*, the Fort McDowell crisis did not resurface in its pages again until the February and March 1922 issues. In two installments, the "Evils of Indian Bureau System" appeared, which consisted of substantial excerpts from the booklet that Latimer assembled, titled *The Rape of McDowell Reservation, Arizona, by the Indian Bureau.*[15] The booklet was an anthology containing Latimer's and Montezuma's letters, an excerpt from the 1911 Hearing before the House Committee on Expenditures, Interior Department, and Secretary Fisher's letter describing the plan to allot five-acre plots to Yavapai at Salt River a "mistake." Latimer wanted to provide the general public with a primer on the Yavapai case that was presented to President Harding, his secretary of the interior, and his commissioner of Indian Affairs. The February 1922 issue also contained a lengthy letter from Latimer and Montezuma to Harding, reminding him what Fisher said about a mistake, along with enumerating the consequences of the relocation policy on Yavapai lives.[16] When "Evils of Indian Bureau System" continued in the March issue, readers saw an elaborate condemnation of the Indian Bureau by "Congressman [M. Clyde] Kelly of Pennsylvania, who was for two years a member of the House Indian Affairs Committee."[17]

The last meaningful reference to Arizona in *Wassaja* appeared in an article dedicated to Carl Hayden. Titled "Hon. Carl Hayden of Arizona," the April 1922 piece was an opprobrium to Hayden's impact on the "Pimas," whose suffering began when "civilization infested Arizona in (1871)," leading to a severe water crisis on the Gila River Reservation. Hayden was accused of abandoning "his friends," whom he always remembered as a much-valued part of his life growing up in Arizona. Yet as of 1922: "They [the Pimas] roam as abject objects and scratch up what they can to exist, waiting for the fulfillment of the phantom promises of the 'Washington Father,' over which Carl Hayden made his oration."[18] Montezuma, of course, referred to the ongoing water crisis that Akimel O'odham faced, along with the Piipaash, on the Gila River Reservation. While Hayden would be credited with the Salt River Project and the Central Arizona Project, which secured the state of Arizona enough water to grow its population and economy, including the City of Tempe—once known as Hayden's Ferry—Hayden's work on behalf of Indian water rights was more ambivalent.[19] On the one hand, he could speak assertively for Pima water rights, complete with admiring their historic aptitude for agriculture.[20] On the other, he did not diverge from the aggrandizement he enjoyed from exploiting Akimel O'odham and Piipaash lands.[21] Tempe, after all, was home—it still is—to Oidbag Doag, which is a sacred site that generations of Arizona State University students regard alternately as A Mountain, Tempe Butte, and Hayden Butte.[22]

Interestingly, as *Wassaja* approached its final issue—the last appearing in May 1922—there was never any indication that Montezuma knew that he had won his battle with the Indian Bureau and that the Yavapai would be

spared the travails of relocation to Salt River. No final words. No reflection
on the struggle. No memoir about his career as an Indian rights activist. It
is likely that as the Salt River Project progressed—in addition to a number
of other reclamation projects that circumnavigated Indian reserved water
rights, such as the Central Arizona Project, the Florence-Casa Grande Diversion Dam, and the San Carlos Irrigation Project—and as the Yavapai remained on their Fort McDowell reservation, the need to relocate them simply became less important over time. In fact, government records referred to
"Camp McDowell" and "Mohave Apache" during the years 1920 to 1923 only
in terms of the data that was kept for the reservation system. For example,
in Burke's 1920 annual report as the commissioner of Indian Affairs, the
Mohave Apache turned up three times: in reference to Camp Verde School,
Salt River School, and Camp Verde Reservation, which was acknowledged as
consisting of "24, 971" acres and whose boundaries were established by "Executive order Sept. 15, 1903: act of Apr. 21, 1904, vol. 33, p. 211 (See Ann. Rept.
1905, p 98)."[23] Otherwise, the Yavapai land and water crisis was nowhere to be
seen. An important exception to the federal indifference that emerged after
Montezuma's death was the homage that Latimer paid to his friend, keeping
the Yavapai struggle alive, in a 1923 booklet titled *Our Indian Bureau System*.
Consisting of three chapters and an appendix, Latimer documented how
Indian tribes lost their freedom and independence as they were herded onto
reservations where they have been kept to this day. In a precursor to the Meriam Report of the later 1920s, Latimer enumerates in his second chapter a
narrative of explaining the Indian Bureau's purpose, its massive expenditures
on supposedly civilizing the Indian, and its egregious failure at achieving its
stated goals. In the concluding chapter and appendix, Latimer argued, as had
his longtime friend, Montezuma, that only "unrestricted citizenship" was the
solution to the so-called Indian Problem; which, in the appendix, was the
premise on which the "Committee of 100" was formed by Interior Secretary
Work. Latimer prefaced his book with a dedication to Montezuma:

> We know no worthier purpose than to dedicate this booklet to the memory
> of CARLOS MONTEZUMA, M.D.
>
>   His death occurred suddenly in Arizona a few months ago. The facts
> herein were compiled especially for the purpose of assisting him in his cease-
> less, unselfish and patriotic appeal to our citizens, to "ABOLISH THE IN-
> DIAN BUREAU, AND LET MY PEOPLE GO . . ."

The life of Dr Montezuma . . . portrays most glaringly the farce and in-
humanity of our present Indian Bureau System, the avowed existence of
which is solely "to educate and make citizens" of the Indian, but which in
reality exploits the Indian in order to foster an immense billion dollar political estate.[24]

A few years later, in a series of letters dated August 5, 1929, to March 26,
1930—several years after Montezuma's demise—Joseph W. Latimer addressed his concerns to commissioner of Indian Affairs Charles J. Rhodes,
after the threat to Yavapai land and water rights was once again raised. The
letters were presented unexpectedly in a 1930 congressional report titled
Survey of Conditions of the Indians in the United States, part 10, *Flathead
Reservation, Mont.*, which was created under the auspices of a subcommittee
of the Senate Committee of Indian Affairs. Latimer on this occasion did not
mention his comrade-in-arms.[25]

Two years after Montezuma sent his 1921 letter to Mike Burns, Harrison
and Williams recounted escorting their legendary relative to Skeleton Cave:

In 1923 we went with Carl (Carlos) Montezuma (also known by his Yavapai
name, Wassaja) to get the bones from the cave. In that cave, on the wall, it
looked like oil sprayed on. Down on the floor it looked like oil. There is that
'oil' all over. It is the blood. When the bullets hit the bodies, the blood got
scattered all around. Looks awful. We found many bones. Lots of little bones
also. When we bring the bones, Montezuma is standing there crying. And
we all start crying right there. We see that blood on the wall. It is too bad for
us. It is here that all our people died. For nothing. And when I got back to
Prescott and told my grandmother; my grandmother sure cried.[26]

If the date was accurately recalled, then Montezuma visited his slain ancestors' remains not long before he passed away on January 31. However, the
exact date matters less than the story itself, which reveals a side to Montezuma that was hidden behind his "fiery Apache" reputation as an Indian
rights advocate. Certainly, Montezuma's tears indicate a deep connection
with his family, tribe, and homeland, washing away his image as a staunch
assimilationist. At the very least, the story complicates Montezuma's legacy,
and obliges one to reread his speeches and editorials, less from the vantage
point of federal Indian policy and the SAI's pan-Indian struggle for citizen-

ship, and more from the point of view of his Yavapai community. From that vantage point, one can also see how Montezuma determined to aid his people's ancient enemy, the Salt River and Gila River Pima, or Akimel O'odham. What he saw was not an enemy, but more victims like the Yavapai of Indian Bureau injustice and abuse.

CHAPTER SEVEN

An Unexpected O'odham Hero

Montezuma's Legacy Beyond Fort McDowell

Whereas what preceded demonstrated how Montezuma, or Wassaja, maintained his kinship relations with the Yavapai community through his correspondence, his annual hunting trips, and his activism on behalf of Yavapai land and water rights, what follows is an account of how Montezuma became a prominent figure in the O'odham communities, as they anxiously fought off the consequences of reduced water rights, land allotment, and the potential population influx of hundreds of relocated Yavapai. With the O'odham-Yavapai alliance in mind, this chapter shows that Montezuma's work was central to the development of "self-determination" in American Indian politics. More to the point, while the O'odham and Yavapai communities were forbidden from organizing in common cause, due to the heavy-handed control that the Indian Bureau maintained over its "wards," through Montezuma an alliance emerged nonetheless, in which their collective fate depended on recognizing that the issues they confronted were created by a mutual nemesis, namely the Indian Bureau.

Montezuma's relationship with the Akimel O'odham began early in his life, when they played a prominent and dramatic role. In a 1913 issue of the *Quarterly Journal of the Society of American Indians*, Montezuma set a tone that drove his political agenda for the rest of his life. In "Light on the Indian Situation," Montezuma recounted his life story, including his legendary abduction by "Pima raiders," his childhood in Chicago, and his graduation from medical college. He also gave a brief account of his career as an Indian Service physician, in which he said of the Western Shoshone Agency:

There I saw in full what deterioration a reservation is for the Indians. I
watched these Indians, cut off from civilized life, trying to become like Yan-
kees with the aid of a few government employes. Because of my own experience I was now able to fully realize how their situation held them to their old
Indian life, and often wondered why the government held them so arbitrarily
to their tribal life, when better things were all around them.[1]

Based on his Indian Service experience, Montezuma launched a three-
pronged political crusade: (1) creating outrage about reservation conditions,
(2) calling for the abolition of the Indian Bureau, and (3) advocating for the
assimilation of Indians into mainstream American society. "Colonization,
segregation and reservation are the most damnable creations of men," Montezuma declared. "They are the home, the very hothouse of personal slavery—
and are no place for the free and the 'home of the brave.'"[2] If nothing else, the
preceding six chapters have detailed this agenda.

As one reads Montezuma, one should not oversimplify what he meant by
assimilation—it was less about becoming like the Whites and more about
acquiring the same rights as them, as protected under the U.S. Constitution.
We have acknowledged this before. Assimilation entailed enfranchising Indians under the Fourteenth Amendment, a legal status to which Indians have
a right and which should not be forbidden to them simply because they are
culturally or racially different from their White peers. Since the Whites did
not have to live with an Indian Bureau or the like dominating them from cra-
dle to grave, why must Indians endure this indignity? This question turned
up repeatedly in the eight volumes of *Wassaja*, with many instances of this
appearing in the foregoing chapters. As an example of the racial segregation
policy imposed through the reservation system, Montezuma argued in his
1922 editorial criticizing Arizona Congressman Carl Hayden, who spear-
headed the Salt River Project: "if the Pimas in the Salt River Valley had the
same chance in the battle of life as Carl Hayden, from his youth up, those
Pimas would have made as good a showing as the Congressman from Arizona. But the blockade from that same chance that made Carl Hayden what
he is, has been and is the Indian Bureau of the Interior Department of our
government."[3]

Benefiting from the advantages of a modern education only occurred for
Montezuma because he was reared in an urban environment, far from reservation life and the obstacles the Indian Bureau created to impede Indian

success. Furthermore, because of his non-reservation education, Montezuma developed a point of view on Yavapai affairs that was precluded for the Yavapai at Fort McDowell. Yet as Leon Speroff summarizes, "Beginning in 1901, Montezuma returned to Arizona in the early fall of nearly every year."[4] Consequently, he became acquainted with Yuma Frank, who led the Fort McDowell Yavapai Nation until succeeded by George Dickens in 1914, and with his cousins. Charles Dickens solicited Montezuma's help against the Indian Bureau and the Salt River Valley Water Users Association (forerunner to the Salt River Project), which wanted the Yavapai removed. Dickens broke the news to Montezuma in a letter dated March 29, 1910: "Lately I learned that our agent have heard from Washington that we are to move to the Pima Indian Reservation."[5] Montezuma did not hesitate to answer the call for help and accepted the power of attorney. "In these forty years' absence from my people I have not forgotten them. They have been in my heart day and night. For them my pen and tongue have not been idle."[6]

It was only a matter of time before Montezuma took interest in the situation on the Salt and Gila River Reservations, which faced their own land and water crisis. The evidence was clear: the Indian Bureau was fomenting a humanitarian disaster.

> The original grand, noble and ideal object of the Indian Bureau was to aid and protect the Indian and prepare him to emerge from his wigwam into civilization, and it has been a total failure.
>
> Within my period of years there have been ten or twelve commissioners of Indian affairs. Most of them are dead, and the machine still exists to be greased and tinkered with. It is a political machine, where one goes out and another comes in, taking turns greasing and adjusting the Indian machine.[7]

During the twelve years in which Montezuma contended with the Indian Bureau, three different commissioners served in office: Robert G. Valentine (1909–1913); Cato Sells (1913–1921); and Charles H. Burke (1921–1929). The work that the "Indian machine" did on its "wards" included seizing land, selling mineral rights, building fences, controlling the tribal economy, and forcibly removing them whenever the Indian Bureau deemed it in the Indian's "best interest." Forced removal did not end with the Cherokee "Trail of Tears," as the Yavapai learned. They were the latest victims, struggling to retain the rights promised them in Theodore Roosevelt's 1903 Executive

Order that established the Fort McDowell reservation, which proclaimed: "that so much of the land of the Camp McDowell abandoned military reservation . . . be . . . set aside and reserved for the use and occupancy of such Mohave-Apache Indians as are now living thereon or in the vicinity, and such other Indians as the Secretary of the Interior may hereafter deem necessary to place thereon."[8] While implying the possibility of "other Indians" being placed on their reservation, what the Yavapai did not anticipate was the proposal to remove them to the Salt River Reservation. The "Pimas" at Salt River, as expected, were just as alarmed by this development as the Yavapai.

As for the significance of the Yavapai crisis in Arizona history, the literature on this epoch has been sparse. In the introduction to the book in hand, a survey of works about Montezuma was conducted for the purpose of demonstrating how the author of "Let My People Go" went from being one of the most well-known Indian rights activists in the country to being nearly forgotten after his death, only to be resurrected in the works of Spicer, Hertzberg, and Iverson. In this chapter is a more focused survey covering the modest but immensely important references to Montezuma's activism on behalf of the Akimel O'odham, which spread to other O'odham communities across southern Arizona. Toward that end, a major part of this chapter consists of an analysis of the writings of two Akimel O'odham, George Webb (1892–?) and Anna Moore Shaw (1898–1975).

In *Cycles of Conquest*, Edward H. Spicer referred to the Gila River Pimas, or Akimel O'odham, who were in a crisis due to a severe water loss caused by up-river damming. Many O'odham opted to move from their homes along the Gila to what they hoped would be more fruitful stakes along the Salt River. Naturally, the Akimel O'odham along the Onk Akimel or Salt River were now fearful, as of the 1910s, that moving the Yavapai there would put them in the same predicament they had sought to escape from in the first place. Employing the 1887 General Allotment Act, the Indian Bureau pressured O'odham into accepting 10-acre allotments, which would supposedly be complete with water rights. However, unallotted land would be put on the open market.

In 1918 [Montezuma] began to devote his time to the problems of Indians and came frequently to the Pima [Akimel O'odham]. . . . He published a monthly magazine [*Wassaja*] and espoused the view that the Indian Bureau had no right to allot land, it being the property of the Indians to dispose of as they saw fit. Pimas, called "Montezumas," listened to him and opposed the allotment program.[9]

Thus, a movement was born. Spicer subsequently observed that in 1925 a Tohono O'odham opposition group, the "League of Papago Chiefs," formed for the purpose of holding out "for traditional ways and a minimum of interference in village affairs by the superintendent and his assistants." Support came not only from traditionalists but also from "those conservatives sometimes called 'Montezumas' who had listened with approval to Dr. Carlos Montezuma in his speeches at Sacaton [on the Gila River Reservation] denouncing the Bureau of Indian Affairs and advocating its elimination."[10] Montezuma voiced O'odham concerns and shaped their political thinking as a result. Although there was no reference to the Tohono O'odham, the Akimel O'odham appeared roughly a dozen times in *Wassaja*, as in the article about Carl Hayden cited above. In the March 1919 issue, Montezuma focused on Indian Bureau land theft in "The Indian Bureau: Sells Indian Lands and Spends Indian Money Without the Approval of the Indians": "The wrong method is being pursued in the Salt River Valley of Arizona, where Indian land is so valuable. From reliable information the Pima and Maricopa Indians were put in jail because they would not be allotted because they did not want to give up their land that they had been living on for many years, but force was used to move them."[11]

Unlike anyone else who had written about Montezuma, Spicer made a surprising claim about Montezuma's legacy in terms of "religious diversification": "Strictly speaking, it [Montezuma's influence] was not a religious movement in the sense of resting on supernatural belief. Yet it had religious repercussions and in some ways affected Pimas and Papagos as a religious movement." Spicer referred in particular to Montezuma's impassioned drive to abolish the Indian Bureau and protect Indian rights: "His meetings at Sacaton on the Pima Reservation gained him many adherents, who were deeply dissatisfied with reservation conditions; at the same time he incurred the disapproval of the Indian Bureau [which refused to allow him to formally represent either of the Pima reservations]. After several years of preaching he died of tuberculosis on the Salt River Reservation." Montezuma, of course, passed away on his homeland at Fort McDowell, where he was buried.

Spicer evoked a mythic narrative, influenced perhaps by Montezuma's grandiloquent writing style as well as the O'odham history that contextualized Spicer's discourse, in which their anti-Bureauism meant a stance for the O'odham Himdag, which was to say Akimel O'odham culture—not land allotment. One might say, moreover, that Spicer portrayed how the O'odham understood this remarkable Indian man, who seemed to come from out of nowhere to defend them against a beast, the Indian Bureau. Montezuma had become a part of O'odham oral tradition. True to the Montezumas' cult status, there were instances when Akimel O'odham risked prosecution just for being known acquaintances of the Yavapai physician.

> As this Monday evening, I am going to write to you and . . . tell you about what I have heard a short time ago. I went out to work on my dam about twelve o'clock and I was working hard. Somebody came to me and told me that somebody wanted me at the corner and I went over to see who was on the corner. It was Lewis Nelson. He said "I am going to take you down to jail," and I said, "Why?" He said: "Because you are Montezuma's friend; that Montezuma is nothing—just like sick cat." I said, "But he is my friend, how is it? Why are you going to put me in jail? I don't know what for. I never stole any money, now why go to jail?" I would like to hear from you soon. I have no time to write a long letter. It is time to go. This will be all for this time. So, I will say good-bye.[12]

Spicer affirmed that Montezuma's effect was "based chiefly on the dignity and worth of the Indian racial and cultural heritage" and that he preached that Indigenous values and beliefs were superior to those of white Americans; moreover, that Indians ought to turn to their own ways instead of mainstream society. Montezuma, furthermore, promoted the idea that "Indians should reassume the independence they had practiced before the Indian Bureau had taken them over, take up their land again in their own name, and demonstrate the fundamental greatness of the Indian way of life."[13] While Montezuma would have questioned Spicer's interpretation of his ideas, he did galvanize Indians across the reservation system to empower themselves and assert their rights. What may explain Spicer's unique perspective is how the O'odham remembered him, which was based more on what he did for their community than on his publications.[14]

One thing Spicer did not raise in his explanation of the "Montezumas" is the possibility that this was a result of the factionalism that erupted as a consequence of Indian Bureau policy. As related in chapter 4, James Rhoades of Lehi, Arizona, on the Salt River Reservation, wrote a letter (dated February 17, 1918) on behalf of Chief Sam Eldridge about the factions that developed between those who took allotments and those who refused. While Rhoades and Eldridge did not make any reference to Montezumas, they were clear about an increasingly divided community. In fact, *Wassaja* was one source of friction between the two sides: "Mr. Card Sell [Cato Sells] came and took the paper home. A few days after that we had trouble over it, because our enemy (allotted boys) say that you have written in this paper about the 'war.' The allotted boys took this matter to the Superintendent [Sharp], so they told us on that." What was even more distressing was the way in which the factionalism exacerbated the water crisis: "The other day we went to his [the superintendent's] office about our water. I told you about this before that the allotted boys get more water than we can with ours. He would not listen to us. He said himself that we can't go back to our 'old ways;' again, that we ought to go higher like the white man." Making things even worse was the tendency of the superintendent to persecute those he found disagreeable: "For anything we do or say we have to be chained up. Oh, my, it is awful!"[15]

Despite his prominent role as a founder of the Society of American Indians, Hazel W. Hertzberg scarcely mentioned Montezuma's activism in her 1971 book on the SAI. Obliquely, Hertzberg quoted Spicer, associating Montezuma with his Aztec namesake: "Montezumas . . . were older village headmen who came to identify Montezuma with both Jesus and a tribal deity and believed that 'Montezuma would one day return and restore better times and good moral behavior.'"[16] What Montezuma thought of this, if he heard about it at all, is not preserved in the historical record. Moreover, although Montezuma's ideas and opinions emboldened "older leaders among Yavapais on the Fort McDowell and San Carlos reservations and . . . Apaches at San Carlos," neither turned these ideas into a political organization like their O'odham counterparts. Consequently, "by 1950 Dr. Montezuma the man was but a vague memory to the Indians with whom he had come in contact."[17] The exception, of course, was how Montezuma was remembered among the Yavapai. Nonetheless, he had largely faded from O'odham memory. Perhaps because of Spicer's and Hertzberg's distinctions as historians, the embers of Montezuma's memory began to glow again, the fire not completely extinguished.

William R. Coffeen mentioned Montezuma's name exactly twice in his 1972 article "The Effects of the Central Arizona Project on the Fort McDowell

Indian Community." Only in the second instance did Coffeen refer to Montezuma's advocacy work on behalf of Fort McDowell: "It was primarily through
the efforts of one tribal member, Dr. Carlos Montezuma, who acted under
the power of attorney and authority of the tribe, that the Fort McDowell
Indians were never removed."[18] Not long after, Sue Abbey Chamberlain gave
a more substantial account of Montezuma's defense of Fort McDowell from
forced removal in her 1975 article "The Fort McDowell Indian Reservation:
Water Rights and Indian Removal, 1910–1930." While relatively short—a
mere seven pages, including endnotes—Chamberlain nonetheless articulated the political and legal developments in which Montezuma represented
the interests of his ancestral community. Sticking close to the facts contained
in archival documents, Chamberlain neither interpreted nor embellished her
historical discourse. Rather than demonstrate the significance of Montezuma's activism, let alone how this fit into his life-long animosity toward the Indian Bureau and his pursuit of Indian assimilation, Chamberlain maintained
her focus on Fort McDowell and its arduous struggle to protect its land and
water rights. Chamberlain, however, did acknowledge Montezuma's success
at frustrating the Indian Bureau's effort to remove the Yavapais to Salt River:

> Use of the publication Wassaja, combined with letters from Montezuma and
> [Joseph W.] Latimer, representing the [Fort] McDowell Indians, resulted in
> an investigation into the McDowell problems by Commissioner of Indian
> Affairs Charles Bourke [*sic*]. Although one BIA investigator, in an unsigned
> memorandum to Commissioner Bourke, blamed the McDowell problems
> solely on Montezuma's "mischievous intervention and agitation for his own
> personal gain," Commissioner Bourke decided that lands at McDowell that
> could be irrigated should remain as tribal lands.[19]

The 1970s ended with Montezuma being completely forgotten in Margot
Liberty's 1978 collection of essays, which she gathered from an American
Anthropological Association meeting and later published as *American Indian Intellectuals of the Nineteenth and Early Twentieth Centuries*.[20] While
there were certainly more American Indian intellectuals during this time
period than can possibly be covered in a single volume, Montezuma's absence nonetheless reflected his liminal status in American Indian historical research, particularly during the 1970s when, because of the Red Power
movement, there was much more interest in "traditional" Indian lives and

culture than in someone like Montezuma, who represented the "assimilated" world from which many in the American Indian community sought to free themselves.

The 1980s, on the other hand, witnessed the most significant development in the scholarly discourse on Montezuma's legacy with the 1982 publication of Iverson's biography. Although it was limited to a single chapter, Iverson provided the most detailed and expansive account to date of Montezuma's single-handed struggle against Indian Bureau imperialism. What ensued in Iverson's text was a historical discourse on this traumatic episode in Arizona Indigenous history, complete with more detailed references to the individual participants and an explanation of federal policy developments. In a major contribution to the scholarly record, Iverson portrayed Montezuma as a central figure in the fight for Yavapai and O'odham rights. A scholar of an earlier generation, such as Francis Paul Prucha, would have focused more on Joseph W. Latimer, a friend and attorney from Chicago, whom Montezuma relied on recurrently for legal advice, not to mention pro bono work for the two tribes.[21]

Still, Montezuma's status in modern American Indian history, Iverson's seminal work notwithstanding, remained marginal. In 1983, Sigrid Khera and Patricia S. Mariella only briefly acknowledged Montezuma in their article "Yavapai," which appeared in Volume 10 of the Smithsonian's monumental *Handbook of North American Indians*, in which he was again recognized as a leader in the Yavapai's struggle against removal.[22] Montezuma was then almost completely overlooked in *Indian Lives: Essays on Nineteenth- and Twentieth-Century Native American Leaders*, edited by L. G. Moses and Raymond Wilson, which appeared in 1985. Aside from the fact that Montezuma lived and worked within the editors' stipulated time frame—which was noted in the three scant references to his medical and activist career— there was the additional fact that one of the editors, Wilson, had written an important biography about one of Montezuma's closest allies in the SAI, Charles A. Eastman, who was curiously also omitted from the personages represented in *Indian Lives*.[23]

While there were occasional examples of Montezuma entering the scholarly discourse during the late 1980s and 1990s, including works by William Willard and Robert A. Warrior, none of them added more than meager recognition to Montezuma's prestige, either as an intellectual or as an activist. Certainly nothing was added to our understanding of his advocacy work for the Yavapais and O'odham and what this teaches about being an Indigenous activist-intellectual. Montezuma was overlooked once more in R. David Edmunds's *The New Warriors: Native American Leaders since 1900* in 2001.[24] Timothy Braatz, although he opened his 2003 book *Surviving Conquest: A History of the Yavapai Peoples* with an account of Montezuma's life narrative (going from his abduction from his ancestral home by Pima raiders to becoming a medical doctor and an Indian rights activist, complete with the founding of his seminal newsletter *Wassaja*), there was scarce mention of his struggle against the Indian Bureau on behalf of the Fort McDowell reservation. In fact, what little there was of Montezuma's activism in Braatz's discourse, in an otherwise masterfully written history of the Yavapai, exclusively relied on previously published works, namely Iverson and Chamberlain.[25] On the other hand, things looked substantially different in Leon Speroff's *Carlos Montezuma, M.D.: A Yavapai American Hero: The Life and Times of an American Indian, 1866–1923*, published the same year as Braatz's book.

Even more than Iverson, Speroff created a truly epic portrayal of Montezuma from birth to death, including reflections on his legacy. Of utmost importance in Speroff's historical portrait was Montezuma's renewed kinship connections, which explained why he did not hesitate to take up the Yavapai cause.[26] Looking back on what the Fort McDowell community and Montezuma accomplished, Speroff concluded this life-affirming chapter in Yavapai tribal history:

> It would have been relatively easy for the few Yavapai to become amalgamated into the Salt River Reservation and the nearby urban areas. Instead, a desire for their own land prevailed and made it possible to maintain an impressively high degree of tribal identity. The Fort McDowell Yavapai are proud of the role played by Montezuma from 1910 to 1922, and Montezuma would be proud today to see his band of the Yavapai on their own land, and doing well.[27]

Mike Burns, as may be recalled from previous chapters, referred to the Akimel O'odham in terms of their historic rivalry, which included O'odham scouts aiding the U.S. Army in its campaign to round up "Apaches." In Burns's letter to Montezuma dated July 16, 1913, he said of the Yavapai's historic enemy, in which he included the Maricopa or Piipaash: "you had ought not try to do much feelings in helping the Pima and Maricopa Indians. Just because them are the people who had made [you] fatherless and motherless. And they have slaughtered more of our people than any other people."[28] Curiously, there was evidence that Burns's disregard for the "Pima and Maricopa Indians" was more cautious than vengeful. On July 7, 1914, Burns said of Salt River Chief Juan Andrews: "I must say something to you Cousin: about the Pimas: We were invited to go down to Saltriver Agency: on the 4th of July: by Chief Juan Andreas [*sic*]: and with rest of his followers: to have a sociable time among the Pimas: So we all went down there: had a good dinner: and lots of watermellons and had a game of baseball: Our boys won the game by scoring 15 to 7 in favor of the McDowell Apache boys."

While Montezuma was probably pleased with the convivial image of Yavapai–O'odham relations that Burns shared in his letter, he was just as likely to wonder about Burns's change of heart: "When Inspector Good all [*sic*] was here: And was down at the Saltriver: but afew hours: Agent Cae [*sic*]: had gathered those had agreed to have 10 acres: and not let others known about."[29] Given that Burns sometimes worked as a translator, Montezuma must have been concerned that Otis B. Goodall and Charles Coe might lead his cousin into temptation. As for Montezuma's interest in Akimel O'odham affairs, he saw them as allies in common cause. On this point, Iverson quoted Montezuma as saying: "I am interested in the Pimas as much as I am in the McDowell Indians. . . . I want the Pimas and the Apaches always to be friends and brothers."[30]

Montezuma's generous opinion about the O'odham is all the more meaningful in light of the fact that he regularly told, which is to say relived, the story of his abduction by a Pima raiding party. In a handwritten account of this life-changing event, dated September 7, 1887, Montezuma recounted:

> I am a fullblooded Apache of Arizona. [I] was captured by the Pima tribe
> in 1871. They were friendly to the whites. I remained with them a few days.
> When I was carried from village to village and offered for sale. In one place
> they offered a horse for me, but my captors thought I was worth more. Towards evening we came to a village where I was sold for thirty dollars to Mr.
> Gentile[,] formerly a photographer of Chicago.[31]

In light of such an experience, one might have expected Montezuma to have been biased against the "Pima." Yet he wanted them to always be friends. From where did Montezuma's humanitarian spirit derive? Plausibly, this was the influence of Montezuma's Hippocratic oath, meaning that because

the O'odham were suffering the same affliction as the Yavapai, namely bureauism, they deserved care as much as the Yavapai. In this sense, Montezuma lived up to his principles and consistently treated Yavapai and O'odham
leaders and community members with unwavering respect.

On the other hand, Montezuma's animosity toward the Indian Bureau was
always obvious. It went without saying that there was no love lost between
Montezuma and his arch enemies at the Indian Office, be they local superintendents or Indian Affairs commissioners. Iverson observed that a critical
advantage Montezuma had over his nemeses in the Indian Bureau, which
inflamed their wrath all the more, was a better education and a sharper mind,
which earned him a nefarious reputation: "Montezuma gave voice and power
to the misgivings and unhappiness of Indian people. He made life more difficult. He was in the way."[32] As may be recalled from earlier in this discourse,
the mere mention of Montezuma's name to the superintendents charged
with supervising the Fort McDowell and Salt River Reservations, such as
Coe, was enough to infuriate them.

With respect to Montezuma's work in Arizona, Speroff did more than any
previous scholar on this topic, including Iverson. The reader is taken to Montezuma's 1901 return to Arizona, during which he learned that although part
of his tribe had been removed to the San Carlos Apache reservation, he was
in fact a member of the Yavapai community, which at the time alternated as
"Yavapai-Apache" and "Mohave-Apache."[33] Speroff recounted Montezuma's
emotional reunion with his extended family at Fort McDowell, including
people who remembered him and told him about the fate of his parents and
siblings, all of whom were now lost to him.[34] Nevertheless, with his Yavapai
identity reaffirmed, Montezuma found new life for a life-long ambition—to
abolish the Indian Bureau. Thus, in a point that is worth reiterating, when
Montezuma excoriated the SAI in his seminal 1915 speech "Let My People
Go," one can easily imagine that he had his family and community foremost
in mind. After belittling the SAI for doing little more than "the mere routine
of shaking hands, appointing committees, listening to papers, hearing discus-
sions, passing a few resolutions, electing officers, then reorganizing," Montezuma went on to express what he saw as the genuine urgency facing them:

> We are wards, we are not free! In a free country we are not free; our heritage
> is freedom, but we are not free. Wake up, Indians, all over America! We are
> hoodwinked, duped more and more every year; we are made to feel free

when we are not. We are chained hand and foot, we stand helpless, inno-
cently waiting for the fulfillment of promises, that will never be fulfilled, in
the overwhelming great ocean of civilization.[35]

Such proclamations as these are typically analyzed within the context of
Montezuma's assimilationist agenda as expressed in the *Wassaja* newsletter.
Yet in light of what has been documented about Montezuma's reconnection to the Yavapai community, including the lengthy and numerous letters
exchanged between Montezuma and his Fort McDowell family, it would
be misguided to conclude that Montezuma had simply sold his soul for a
middle-class life as a Chicago physician. More than anything else, Montezuma wanted the Yavapai, not to mention all other Indians, to enjoy the
freedom inherent to all, regardless of race or ethnicity. Indians, after all,
should not be oppressed into believing that their only option was to be impoverished and uneducated wards of the federal government.

At this point it is time to introduce the O'odham perspective on Montezuma's legacy. It is a point of view that complements the Yavapai narrative that
drove the previous chapters of this discourse, in which references to the Salt
and Gila River Reservations appeared in the context of the correspondence
that Montezuma received from Fort McDowell, such as Burns's account of
his interaction with Juan Andrews and the references to Arizona in *Wassaja*.
In the latter context, Montezuma emerged as a conduit through which information, opinions, and ideas regarding the Yavapai and O'odham communities circulated, which drew him into the middle of their mutual battle against
the Indian Bureau. Consequently, this confluence of protests against Cato
Sells, in particular, influenced what Spicer identified as the "Montezumas." In
turn, the Montezumas signified the respect that Montezuma earned among
the O'odham as a friend and as a defender of their rights. To the extent that
the Indian Bureau succeeded at creating division within the Salt and Gila
River communities ("allotted boys"), Montezuma provided the antiallotment
forces a much-needed layer of political protection. This became Montezuma's legacy among the O'odham, which was a perspective that informed
the work of George Webb and Anna Moore Shaw, who both wrote about
Montezuma years after it seemed he had been forgotten. Webb's *A Pima
Remembers* (1959) and Shaw's *A Pima Past* (1974) together documented the
most substantial testimony from the O'odham community about Montezuma's place of honor in O'odham history.

The contributions of Webb and Shaw to Montezuma scholarship have been largely overlooked and underappreciated. In fact, the nearly complete absence of Webb and Shaw's books from the scholarly discourse on Montezuma—including Iverson and Speroff—represents a common problem in American Indian historiography: the recurrent omission of American Indian writers from topics they have written about, frequently with firsthand knowledge. In Iverson and Speroff's work, Shaw was mentioned fleetingly, twice in Iverson's book and only once in Speroff's, whereas Webb was not mentioned at all in either one.[36] So what was missed and why does it matter?

When E. L. B. reviewed *A Pima Remembers* for the *New York Times*, the review characterized its 126 pages thusly: "The result is a book which seems to have grown right out of the Arizona earth—anecdotal, almost artless in its directness, but having the impact of reality."[37] In a chapter titled "The Old Ways," Webb recalled how the Apaches raided O'odham fields for the abundant food they offered, and during the raids it was common that some O'odham were killed defending their homes. Consequently, "the Pimas would follow the Apaches to their camp. In the fight the Pima would kill as many Apaches as they could, leaving the women and children."[38] It should be noted that both Yavapai and Apaches were regarded in O'odham language and thought as *o'ob*, or as enemies. This was not to say that the Pima were unaware they were confronting two different tribes. Nonetheless, the customs regarding battle, casualties, and captives were fundamentally similar, including the adoption of captives: "We have now among our tribe Pimas who have Apache ancestors, descendants of people in that period," among whom Webb counted himself. "But no Pima warrior was allowed to take any Apache woman or child home unless he was capable of giving them a decent home." This principle applied to all captives: "Among the Pimas, it was always a dishonor to kill a woman or child. Sometimes, rather than leave the women and children orphaned, the Pima warriors would bring home an Apache woman or child." It was in this context that Montezuma's abduction was recounted.

As Webb relayed O'odham oral tradition, a warrior brought home a boy they called "Hejel-wi'ikam . . . meaning 'Left Alone.'" However, instead of taking him to Florence (as others, including Montezuma, recounted), where Carlo Gentile "purchased" him, Webb claimed that Hejel-wi'ikam was given to "white people passing through the Pima village." Was this village near Florence? Webb did not specify the location. At first rejecting the Whites' request to take the little boy, they eventually agreed to terms. "This boy later became a noted man, the famous Doctor Montezuma, a great surgeon." As recounted by Montezuma in the speech about his life quoted above, he recalled being led from one village to the next, as his captors searched for someone to purchase him. This itinerary may have been conflated in Webb's account, in which Gentile and Florence were erased from memory, becoming simply "white people." Equally interesting, Webb said nothing about Montezuma's illustrious career as an Indian rights activist, let alone his fight against the Indian Bureau, which benefitted the Salt and Gila River Reservations. Did Webb know anything about these distinctions or about any O'odham calling themselves "Montezumas"? One can only imagine as Webb's brief portrayal ended with seeing Montezuma on his deathbed:

> Sometime ago [Webb did not specify] I happened to be at Fort McDowell and one of the boys told me that the Doctor was there and very sick. He asked me if I would like to see him. I said I would like to see him very much.
>
> He took me to an olas-ki made of willow poles and brushed cover with a canvas. There was a passage way about four feet high, three feet wide and about three yards long. To get in, I had to get down on my hands and knees. There, on the dirt floor, was spread an expensive blanket on which the Doctor lay. To one side was a suitcase full of expensive clothes. The room was full of people. My visit was brief as the Doctor was on his last stage of life.
>
> A few days later he died.

What is just as remarkable is how Webb segued into a story about an Akimel O'dham who dream-prophesied an Apache raid. In fact, as Webb recalled, the O'dham who foresaw this battle was nearly killed: "The spot where the Pimas and Apaches fought is now marked with good sized rocks, near the hills south of what is now the town of Maricopa," which today is immediately northeast of the Ak Chin Indian Community. The story concluded with an explanation of the purification ritual warriors underwent after killing an enemy, in which the medicine man sang "to drive the evil spirits away."[39] Webb thus understood that the Yavapai were considered o'ob and were categorically different from O'odham in that the former had once been enemies. But they were also friends because of Montezuma. Webb probably knew the way in which the Akimel O'odham Creation Story explained the origin of the warrior purification ritual he mentioned, a tale in which a boy avenges the killing of his father. Upon returning from his successful pursuit of his father's Apache killers, says the boy, "the news of victory which I brought caused my people to rejoice with singing and dancing. There was a magician's house [meaning a makai or medicine person], enveloped in white winds and white clouds, into which we went to perform our ceremonies."[40] Of course, Webb was not recounting having slain Montezuma. Yet Webb did travel into o'ob territory to witness the imminent demise of a great Yavapai leader. Webb may have felt that he needed to purify himself at the same time he admired this man. Certainly, the juxtaposition of these two anecdotes in Webb's narrative symbolizes how much things had changed between the O'odham and Apaches.

Before proceeding with an analysis of Shaw's writing about Montezuma, it is worth mentioning that a possible influence on Webb's discourse was the calendar sticks preserved at Casa Blanca, Gila Crossing, and Blackwater Village on the Gila River Pima-Maricopa Reservation. The Oos:hikbina, or Stick Cuts Upon, recorded the annals of the O'odham village that maintained its history. The two that remember Carlos Montezuma were kept at Gila Crossing, or Kuiwa, and Blackwater, or Shuckma hudag. In Gila Crossing, anthropologist Frank Russell recorded multiple calendar sticks in his 1908 Bureau of American Ethnology Report, titled *The Pima Indians*. For the years 1873–1874, the calendar stick keeper recorded:

> The Pimas went on a campaign against the Salt River Apaches [Yavapai] soon after a heavy rain. When they reached the Salt river it was too high to be safely forded, so they built a raft and tried to take their saddles and blankets across upon it. The raft sank and they lost all their effects. Some of the party who had not engaged in the raft enterprise found a safe ford and continued on their raid, in which they killed several of the enemy, and near Four Peaks captured an Apache lad.

Russell added in a footnote: "He [the Apache lad] afterwards became known as Doctor Montezuma, now a prosperous physician practising [*sic*] in the city of Chicago."[41] Then, as an unexpected product of the San Carlos Irrigation Project, archaeologist Odd S. Halseth, in collaboration with chief engineer C. H. Southworth, had the pleasure of documenting the calendar stick held by Juan Thomas, who also served as a Russell informant in *The Pima Indians*. Among the numerous events that Halseth and Southworth recorded, beginning in 1850–1851, was an entry for 1872–1873: "Apaches were slaughtered on top of a mountain known to the Indians as Black Butte, and Doctor Montezuma was captured. Two brothers were killed."[42] One will notice that the years do not match up exactly; however, they do overlap at 1873, when, if the estimate for Montezuma's birth is correct (1866), he was approximately seven years old.

When Kay M. Sands reviewed *A Pima Past* for *Studies in American Indian Literatures*, she expressed appreciation for the book as a rare example of an autobiography written by an American Indian woman.[43] W. David Laird, on the contrary, wanted another *Ishi*, finding Anna Moore Shaw's book to be "all too often . . . vague," lacking in "detail useful to the ethnologist, and . . . emotionally white-washed by an overlay of religious or ethnic platitudes."[44] Both reviewers, however, observed the significant influence that Montezuma had had on how Shaw perceived her life as an Indian during the Progressive Era. In 1974, Shaw included a section titled "My Indian Hall of Fame," in which she paid homage to five men and one woman she most admired. In addition to William Thomas Moore, Russell "Big Chief" Moore, Dr. Roe Blaine Lewis, and Mae Fern Perkins, a well-known "Apache," Carlos Montezuma, was most distinguished. Shaw fondly recalled hosting the revered Pan-Indian leader in her home, not long before he passed away. More than others, Montezuma met Shaw's criterion of "cultural adjustment," meaning "those whose lives have shed special light on the process of bridging the gap between two cultures and living together in brotherly love."[45] Clearly, Shaw turned a blind eye to the impact of federal Indian policy on Indigenous people trapped in the reservation system, not to mention the fact that the "bridge" between Indian and white only went one way.

Along with remembering Montezuma's brief stay in her home, Shaw retold his life story, which Montezuma famously told in countless speeches, such as the one referenced earlier. Indeed, Montezuma was his own best example that Indians could succeed in American society. Curiously, Shaw did not talk about Montezuma's work on behalf of the Yavapai and O'odham. As in Webb's book, those efforts were conspicuously missing from her recollections. Shaw instead emphasized what she and her family experienced firsthand. Thus *A Pima Past* was about an Akimel O'odham family making the arduous transition into modern American life when opportunities for Indians to succeed were few and far between. Yet the Shaw family story validated the adaptations that they pursued in a world not of their making, affirming by turns their decision to follow Montezuma's example. Ultimately, they prevailed over social obstacles, especially the racial prejudice in their midst, which was the same prejudice that Montezuma regularly maligned.

Shaw prefaced her account with an anecdote about her husband, Ross, who worked for the American Railway Express Company. After acknowledging Ross's work ethic and his conscientiousness, Shaw observed the special burden that her husband bore due to the fact that he was the only Indian employed: "The trunks he carried were as heavy as lead, but he was young and strong, and he never dropped one. His customers appreciated the assistance he gave them, and this helped ease the prejudice against Indians which was so prevalent in those early days." Nevertheless, Ross could not avoid racist attitudes altogether, attitudes that became evident when some customers did not want him attending to them. As Shaw confided: "Sometimes Ross would tell me stories of how he had encountered similar attitudes when he was defending his country in the war." This was something that Montezuma and his SAI peers repeatedly reminded their white audiences every chance they got. Fortunately, back in the Rosses' neighborhood things were much different. The people who knew them well easily accepted and liked their Pima neighbors.

Montezuma entered the Shaws' home by way of Anna's brother, Bill Moore, a musician living in Chicago who took in his nephew, Russell, who became a respected jazz trombonist and played with Louis Armstrong and Lionel Hampton, among others.[46] Bill got to know Carlos when Russell was boarding in Montezuma's home on Michigan Avenue. It was during this time when Montezuma contracted "diabetes, then an incurable disease." Shaw, of course, was mistaken on this point. Montezuma, as noted earlier, died from tuberculosis. At the same time, given that Montezuma was a medical doctor, he may have disclosed something about his condition to Anna, which may have explained his tuberculosis. Did Montezuma know that he was diabetic? According to Speroff, another learned physician:

> Tuberculosis was an occupational disease for health care workers. Montezuma could easily have been infected with tuberculosis either during his [medical] student days, his work on the Indian reservations or at the Carlisle Indian School, or even from his private patients. . . . Although the world learned that bacteria caused tuberculosis in 1882, it took decades to bring about the proper procedures that minimize infection.[47]

Once ill, his "Masonic brothers" urged Montezuma to return to Arizona for his health, "where the mild climate might prolong his life." Thus, Bill arranged for Montezuma to stay at his sister's Phoenix home, which created excitement: "We had both heard so much about him since the time when we were children on the reservation. Now we were going to meet him in our home!"

Shaw was unfortunately elusive about what she and Ross heard about Montezuma as children. Instead, she recalled her nervous arrangements for her distinguished guest, who, upon his arrival, quickly set her mind at ease, telling her how much she reminded him of her brother Bill. The rest of Shaw's account was relatively brief, a mere nine pages, focusing exclusively on the five days "Dr. Montezuma stayed in our home, waiting for his Apache relatives to take him to Fort McDowell." Was Charles Dickens among the expected? Montezuma constantly wondered when his relatives would come for him, as Shaw remembered. He was also anxious about seeing an "Apache medicine man," who "might be able to cure him." Shaw mentioned the medicine man matter-of-factly, noting: "Modern medicine had been able to do nothing for his illness." It should be underscored again that Shaw is the only one on record to claim that Montezuma ever relied on any traditional Indigenous healers. Equally significant is how Montezuma's ideas and opinions, as expressed in speeches like "Let My People Go," taught Shaw and her family how to live in a society that once nearly brought about her tribe's extinction. Striking a personal tone, Shaw admitted that her political awareness began to grow because of Montezuma's presence in her home:

> Sometimes, when he was feeling good, Dr. Montezuma would sit with me and talk about the subject uppermost in his mind—the struggle for freedom for the American Indian. For years he had been giving speeches which urged the Indian to tolerate the white man's prejudice no longer. Now I was hearing those stirring phrases right in the living room of my home!

While it may not seem remarkable today to exclaim such principles, we have to take into account that there was a time when saying such things was uncommon. For many Indians, Montezuma was the first fellow Indian they knew of who dared to accuse the Indian Bureau of racism. Although Shaw did not mention subscribing to *Wassaja*, she did give a lengthy quotation from "Let My People Go," which, she carefully explained, "Montezuma made before the Society of American Indians in Lawrence, Kansas, in 1915." In the passages Shaw quoted, Montezuma made his familiar case that Indians were not free, that they were burdened with prejudice, and that the way out of this crisis was for Indians to reclaim their freedom and assert their place in American society.

Emphatically, Montezuma implored his Indian audience to "make yourselves feel at home as one of the units in the big family of America." In an era defined by segregation, this was nothing short of astounding. Indeed, Shaw titled the chapter in which she told this story "A Unit in the Family of America." Shaw, moreover, did not hesitate to credit Montezuma for empowering her husband to handle instances of racial bias at work, in addition to providing them the courage to move into "an all-white, 'restricted' neighborhood." Once Montezuma finally departed for Fort McDowell, Shaw discovered that her guest had left her "five silver dollars," to which Ross responded: "The white man says we Indians are not a competitive race. Well, I guess they are right, and I am glad of it! The Indian would rather share with his fellow man than to horde [sic] money and worldly goods. We cannot take it with us when death calls." Shaw thought that her husband had been so impressed with Montezuma that "he was starting to sound like him!" Thus, the Montezuman tradition took root in another O'dham mind.

Not long after Mary Montezuma arrived in Arizona, she moved her renowned but ailing husband from the "Apache wickiup," in which she found him, "lying on the dirt floor," to "a little frame house nearby and cared for him" until his final moments. Carlos Montezuma, Wassaja, passed away on January 23, 1923. "The medicine men had been powerless to heal the diabetic man."[48] Shaw recounted in the most economical of terms the funeral services held for Montezuma, which she and Ross attended. She even recalled a deathbed wish that they could not fulfill, which was to bury his remains "on top of Superstition Peak," the place of his birth. Instead, Montezuma "was placed in the Fort McDowell cemetery, where a beautiful monument marks his grave."[49] In the aftermath of her husband's passing, "Mary" Montezuma stayed with the Shaws over winter, during which time she regaled her hosts with "her reminiscences of her famous husband." Shaw acknowledged that the biography appearing at the end of A Pima Past "has been based on these conversations with his widow after his death."[50] Shaw then delved further into an account of how Montezuma's words motivated them to move into a new home and neighborhood, where they enjoyed the company of Mexican and Black neighbors, whom they and their children befriended:

Throughout our lives this conviction [that minority people can climb the ladder of success by hard work] so eloquently preached by Dr. Carlos Montezuma, was proved out again and again. It was the philosophy we tried to instill in our children as they grew up in the white man's world, still encountering occasional examples of racial prejudice. At such times we would remind them of the words of the great Indian doctor: "To fight is to forget ourselves as Indians in the world. To think of one's self as different from the mass is unhealthy. Make good, deliver the goods, and convince the world by your character that the Indians are not as they have been misrepresented to be." Rod and Adeline [the Shaws' children], today completely at home in the big family of America, bear out the value of this teaching.[51]

At this point, we have clearly left Montezuma's legendary fight against the Indian Bureau far behind. Yet the story that Shaw told of her experience with Montezuma is a poignant example of an O'odham perspective not only on his life and work but also on his legacy and ongoing influence. Although it is true that there was no mention of the struggle for Yavapai land and water rights in *A Pima Past*, one can argue that this reflected two fundamental facts: first, by the time Montezuma entered the Shaw household, the Yavapai had won their battle against the Indian Bureau, allowing Montezuma to concentrate more on his failing health; second, the Yavapai story simply was not Shaw's story to tell, as it belonged to the people who lived this struggle. Shaw's history focused more on the change and transition occurring in the Salt and Gila River Pima community, such as their conversion to Christianity, taking wage-labor jobs, acquiring off-reservation homes, sending their children to school, and enlisting in the military.

Thus, in the spirit of the Progressive Era that Montezuma represented, Shaw's narrative may be read as a demonstration of how the author of "Let My People Go" and *Wassaja* advocated not just for Indian rights but also for valuing Indian unity. To forget oneself as "Indian in the world" meant, among other things, to overcome those things that kept Indigenous communities divided and at odds with one another, thereby preventing them from organizing to achieve common goals. This was a lesson not lost on the founders of the National Congress of American Indians, the National Indian Youth Council, and the American Indian Movement, to name a few. As observed multiple times throughout this narrative, the Indian Bureau did not hesitate to violate O'odham and Yavapai civil liberties, including their First

Amendment rights to gather together and petition the government. Insofar as Montezuma thought that thinking of oneself as "different" was tantamount to accepting segregation, then this was problematic for both Indian-White and intertribal relations alike. The Yavapai and Akimel O'odham did not want to share a reservation because of their historic rivalry; however, together they prevailed because Montezuma had the acumen to see that they shared a common interest against the Indian Bureau. For Shaw, Montezuma represented a new generation of Indian leader, one who recognized that the Indian struggle for rights was being waged in the battlefield of modern life, not against traditional rivals. Times had irreversibly changed. After the Akimel O'odham engaged in their last skirmish with the Apaches on the Bradshaw Mountains, it was their legendary leader Antonio Azul who had the foresight to see that the Pimas had entered a new epoch: "The white man had been pressuring Chief Antonio Azul to lay down his weapons and live peaceably with the Apache. The wise old chief could see that the old way of life was changing and agreed that it was time to stop the earth's rumbling and tremblings in war."[52]

Yet Shaw did not fail to recognize that the new era of Indian unity was forged in a past defined by old rivalries and bloody conflicts. "When I gaze at the majestic Four Peaks from my Salt River home," Shaw wrote, "the events of a long-ago saga parade before me."[53] Shaw imagined Montezuma's legendary abduction by Pima raiders as something markedly different from the one recounted by Webb. Even though Shaw's account was based on what she learned from Montezuma's widow, Shaw interpreted Montezuma's story from her own Akimel O'odham perspective, beginning with informing her readers that the "Pima raiders" were not "savages" preying upon their "enemies" but rather had sound reason for embarking on a campaign against the "Apaches." The O'odham village Shaw mentioned without naming was located in Mazatzal or Snaggle Teeth, which today is called "Four Peaks." Moreover, Shaw stated that the O'odham were after something more important than the White man's money.[54] In contrast to the apprehensive village that Montezuma portrayed in one of his autobiographical pieces, Shaw pictured, on one side, an idyllic scene in which a loving Apache mother puts her children to bed; and on the other side, Pima raiders who did not see the Apache village as idyllic:

> The Pima braves who saw the Apache wickiups, which had grown up like mushrooms beside the flowing creek, were not so merry. Their hearts were filled with the bitterness of revenge for the painful personal losses and crop

failures they had suffered due to Apache raids. As soon as they had found a moment free from their fields they had headed for these mountains, for they knew that the Apaches, just like the Pimas themselves, could not resist the temptation of mescal ripe for roasting. Surely this area would be the place to find a poorly protected party of Apache squaws and children out gathering the delicacy. Pima revenge would be quick and sure.[55]

Shaw then went against the grain of most popular non-Indian accounts of Indian revenge when she emphasized the conscientiousness with which captives were treated.[56] Echoing Webb, Shaw pointed out that Montezuma and his fellow-captives "need not have feared for their lives, for it was Pima custom to adopt women and children captives. They were never tortured but treated with all possible kindness." Yet, as Webb pointed out earlier, one could bring home captives only if they could be supported. "However, these were days of great poverty for the Indians." Under these circumstances captives could not be taken home. Therefore Montezuma, like so many others, was sold and the money used "to provide for [the captor's] own family."

After his purchase by "Charles Gentile" in Florence, Arizona, which the Akimel O'odham called S-auppagk (Many Cottonwood Trees)—which may well be the same village that Webb alluded to in his narrative—Shaw gave a sentimental account of Montezuma's transformative journey back East, where he became a formidable proponent of Indian rights. Leaving tribal rivalry and the reservation hardships behind, Shaw narrated a respectful portrayal of Montezuma's destiny of becoming a renowned Indian leader. However, rather than lionizing his accomplishments as a physician, working first for the Indian Bureau (which gave him his first exposure to reservation conditions), then for the Carlisle Indian School (where he met Richard H. Pratt, who influenced his political ideals), Shaw turned her attention to Montezuma's frequent visits to his Yavapai homeland, where he gave "his speeches and visit[ed] with his cousins, his mother's nephews, Charley and George Dickens of Fort McDowell. These trips must have awakened strong emotions in the doctor."

> Once he [Montezuma] told me how he used his first savings to return to Sacaton just to meet his Pima captor. He called for a meeting, but the Indian warriors eyed him suspiciously. No one wanted to admit the deed for fear Montezuma would seek revenge.

The doctor tried to convince the braves that he held no rancor. He only
wanted to thank his captor for doing him a good deed; without him he would
still be an uneducated person on the reservation.

In "The Indian Problem from an Indian's Standpoint," which was published
in an 1898 Report of the Commissioner of Education, Montezuma stated, "If
the choice of my life had been left to my mother and father or myself, I would
not be here. Ignorance and the very depths of barbarism would have been
my fate."[57] Shaw concluded her story by describing how an "old warrior tim-
idly . . . approached Montezuma. The doctor shook his hand, and the old man
smiled." Over time, the Pimas came to like and respect Montezuma a great
deal, regarding him as "kind and generous . . . with no bitterness in his heart
for anyone." Then, adding nuance to the earlier stories about Montezuma's
influence on the O'odham, Shaw claimed that her husband, Ross, remembered "a group of Salt River old men who called themselves 'Montezuma's
Friends,' so great was their respect for this educated Indian."[58]

Despite his being Yavapai, an "ohb," the source of the O'odham's respect
for Montezuma came from seeing another Indian show the kind of courage
in the face of adversity that he showed them. Citing his 1915 speech again,
Shaw summarized a story encountered before, namely the outrage Montezuma felt when advised not to return to Chicago, lest he face the blatant
racism that surely awaited him. Montezuma took this as a challenge. Having resigned his Carlisle appointment, Montezuma "returned to Chicago
[in 1896] to crusade for his cause and to set an example for his people." Of
course, as has been referenced repeatedly, including in Iverson and Speroff,
Montezuma succeeded.[59] Shaw then enumerated brief stories about Montezuma's generosity, especially toward the poor, who often could not pay
him for his medical services. After which, tactfully omitting his tumultuous
relationship with Gertrude Bonnin (better known as Zitkala-Sa),[60] Shaw
happily told how Montezuma met his wife-to-be and the happy home they
made together.

As Shaw emphasized, in a fleeting allusion to his activist work, "his
active social life did not keep Carlos Montezuma from crusading for his
people. . . . Freeing the American Indian from the bonds of prejudice was
always uppermost in his mind." Shaw illustrated Montezuma's unwavering commitment with a meeting held at Lehi, Arizona, where he spoke to

a group of Onk Akimel O'odham, or Salt River O'odham, "with Lancisco Hill as interpreter. 'Get rid of the yoke that weighs you from rising to a higher plane!' he invoked his brothers." Lehi, as may be recalled, is where the 1918 letter from Chief Sam Eldridge about problems with the "allotted boys" working in cahoots with the Indian Bureau originated. The risks that Montezuma took because of his activism were underscored. Because the Indian agent—likely a reference to Sharp—at Lehi did not approve of what Montezuma was telling the Indians under his charge, he ordered the Indian police to break up the meeting. "The officer threatened to arrest the listeners and throw them in jail; then he seized Dr. Montezuma and escorted him to the outskirts of the reservation." Montezuma reacted to this treatment with aplomb.[61]

Shaw's biographical sketch concluded with the dignified way in which Montezuma faced his imminent death, returning to his Yavapai homeland. "During the time he lay dying, many Indians came to see the revered surgeon who had been such an outstanding leader of his people," among whom, as noted, was the author of *A Pima Remembers*. Finally, in the spirit of brotherhood inspired by Montezuma's life and words, Shaw honored his memory by recognizing the lasting influence he left in the hearts and minds of those who knew him: "Carlos Montezuma spent most of his life in the white man's world, but his heart was always with his people. He came home to us in his dying days, and it was to us that he uttered his last inspiring words: 'Our hearts must throb with love, our souls must reach to God to guide us. In behalf of my people, with the spirit of Moses I ask, 'Let my people go!'"[62]

Sadly, we do not have Montezuma's final reflections on his life's work, or, since Shaw's encounter with Montezuma occurred during his last days, his impressions of the Shaws.[63] For O'odham and Yavapai alike, Montezuma's lasting legacy is seen not just in his storied opposition to the Indian Bureau but in something more essential to their existence as tribes. As observed above, both communities were distressed at the idea of the Yavapai being forcibly removed to the Salt River Reservation, due in part to the fact that many still remembered their rivalry as living history, preserved in their respective oral traditions. Consequently, when Montezuma prevented the Indian Bureau from carrying out the injustice of removing the Yavapai to Salt River, not only were two rival tribes spared the collective upheaval of sharing a reservation with scant resources, especially water, but more importantly they were allowed to keep a vital part of their worlds in balance—their connection to their homelands. While both nations went on to face other challenges to their sovereignty and well-being, they could do so from a place of power—this is the essence of tribal self-determination—where they could look around them, see the mountains named in their Creation Stories, and remember who they are.[64]

Conclusion

During the fall semester 2020, on October 20, to be precise, I partook in a roundtable organized for an annual meeting of the Society for United States Intellectual History, which, like so many events during the COVID-19 pandemic, was held online. The title of our gathering was "Centering Native Voices in Intellectual History." Joining me were Philip J. Deloria, author of *Playing Indian* and many other works; Kiara Vigil, author of *Indigenous Intellectuals: Sovereignty, Citizenship, and the American Imagination, 1880–1930*; Christine DeLucia, author of *Memory Lands: King Philip's War and the Place of Violence in the Northeast*; Linford D. Fisher, author of *The Indian Great Awakening: Religion and the Shaping of Native Cultures in Early America*; and Sandy Littletree (Diné), a librarian at the University of Washington specializing in Indigenous Systems of Knowledge. With the roundtable's theme in mind, ahead of the discussion we were each asked to think about how we center Native voices in our work. Given that my career has been defined by centering American Indian activist-intellectuals, from Charles Eastman to Vine Deloria Jr., it would appear that answering this request would be easy. And if all I did was point to my publications, then it would be quite simple indeed. However, the deliberate act of centering a person's or group's voice, such as the group to which a given person belongs, takes consideration for why certain voices are privileged over others. After all, generations of historians did not consider the "discovery," "exploration," and "conquest" of the continent from an Indigenous perspective. So, then, how did I answer the question set before the roundtable participants, and what does this have to do with Carlos Montezuma?

My answers were premised on the fact that everywhere you roam across North America, "You're on Indian Land," to use a popular sentiment that sprang from the days of the Alcatraz Island occupation. Consequently, there are Native voices all around you. Some are historical, like Chief Seattle and his famous speech. Others are contemporary. And by contemporary, I mean the here and now in which I am writing these words, as an Indigenous person living in a world replete with Indigenous peoples. Indigenous peoples have always spoken up about the events happening around them, which is a part of our collective intellectual history. Not all Indigenous intellectuals spoke English—or any other colonizer language—or published their writings or were recognized by settler-colonial society, but many were recognized, thereby becoming a unique part of Indigenous history. This is where persons like Montezuma fit in. What researching and writing books about Indigenous activist-intellectuals such as Eastman, Deloria, and now Montezuma has taught me is that they are more than the sum of their publications.

As Indigenous people, Indigenous intellectuals are first and foremost someone's relative. They are members of their people's kinship relations who, because of their work and legacy, became revered ancestors. Their legacy, it should be acknowledged, is often colored by the divisions that defined any given intellectual's life and community. For example, by no means do all Paiute regard Sarah Winnemucca as a respected figure, just as not all Apaches think fondly of Geronimo. Nevertheless, there are always people at home, wherever that may be, who remember these men and women, even if, as in Montezuma's case, they otherwise appear to have been forgotten by history. What were thoroughly and abundantly documented and analyzed in the foregoing chapters of this book were the meaningful relations that Montezuma maintained with his family and tribe across his career as an Indian rights thinker and activist. While Montezuma possessed a learned understanding of the issues confronting American Indians, which stemmed from their problematic place in the federal system, not to mention the Indian Bureau's gross mismanagement of the reservation system, Montezuma's informed opinion about Indian affairs included what he learned from Yavapai leaders, such as Yuma Frank and George Dickens. Montezuma also learned about Yavapai history from Mike Burns. Equally important were the countless anecdotes that Charles Dickens shared with him on a regular basis.

What is also important to remember, and this was quite true of Montezuma, is that Indigenous intellectuals' so-called White man's education did not place them beyond the effects of historical trauma. If one did not know any better, one might think that Montezuma was spared the consequences of the wars, diseases, and forced removals that other Yavapai endured in the years after he was taken away by Carlo Gentile for a privileged life in New York and Chicago, complete with becoming a medical doctor. Certainly, Montezuma was known for counting his blessings due to not having grown up in the reservation system. Yet acknowledging the charity that he received from others, beginning with Gentile, who took on the responsibility of caring for Montezuma as a young boy, did not mean that he was freed from shouldering the burden of his people's past. As noted above, Montezuma told and retold the story of his abduction numerous times, which signified a lasting effect from that earth-shattering experience. Moreover, as recounted by others, such as Iverson, Speroff, and Crandall, Montezuma did desperately seek out his family, wanting to learn what became of his parents, siblings, and extended family. In addition, there was the Yavapai history that exposed him to the horrors of the Skeleton Cave Massacre, history that Burns shared with Montezuma in both his correspondence and his book manuscript.

It is important to observe that Burns and Montezuma expressed their trauma differently. Crandall describes Burns as having been profoundly affected by the tragedies he experienced, and he expressed this through his writing in a way that was fundamentally different from Montezuma's. Crandall quotes Burns as saying in his much-mentioned book manuscript:

> I am . . . horrified to mention what happened to my people in that cave. It brings tears to my eyes to mention [it] because this is the place where my father with two children, my aunt with five children, my uncle, and my poor grandpa were all slaughtered . . . with over 225 others—men, women, and children . . . soldiers. . . . After all were killed, I was led near the cave and noticed dead men and women lying around in all shapes, and so horrid to look on. I was shown where my grandpa lay. . . . I stood at the west entrance of the cave and sat there crying to death. . . . No more hope; no more kinfolk in the world.[1]

Except for the anecdote that Harrison and Williams told about showing Montezuma Skeleton Cave, where he cried at the sight of the slaughter shortly before he passed away, there does not exist any example of Montezuma expressing himself as candidly as did Burns. Which is not to say that Montezuma did not experience trauma or that his trauma was in any way less than Burns's. It only suggests that Montezuma expressed his trauma in ways that were unique to his life and personality. With respect, then, to the American Indian intellectual history that began this conclusion, one might say that Burns's account of Yavapai historical trauma is comparable to the excruciating episodes recounted in Sarah Winnemucca's *Life Among the Piutes*, while Montezuma hid his trauma behind his fiery rhetoric against the Indian Bureau. In a sense, Montezuma did not bare his soul, but rather, like his fellow physician Charles Eastman, maintained a more stoic attitude. For comparison, one can read Eastman's account of the Wounded Knee Massacre in *From the Deep Woods to Civilization*.

In the end, every Indigenous intellectual, including ones who were taken from their land and family, like Montezuma, is a part of a people, a nation. Each is bound by kinship (Montezuma found relatives who never forgot about him); bound by language (Montezuma remembered his Yavapai name, Wassaja); bound by homeland (Montezuma knew he belonged to the Verde Valley); and bound by a sacred history (Montezuma knew about his Yavapai origins, the American invasion, and his abduction by Pima raiders). Despite their respective distinctions in American society as writers, speakers, or public servants, within their Indigenous nations they are each only one of a community of voices, in which each voice has a story to tell about enduring, surviving, resisting, and overcoming the occupation and exploitation of their ancestral homes. Sometimes, as was the case with Montezuma, one's community may ask them to be a first among equals. Toward this end, one may recall the instances when Montezuma was asked to represent the Yavapai before the Indian Bureau, Congress, and the American people. However, more than speaking truth to power, an Indigenous intellectual, or what was once called glibly an "educated Indian," also had to speak truth to their own people, as was exemplified in Montezuma's letter to Burns. As cultural mediators, especially during a time of crisis, persons like Montezuma must take on the risk and responsibility for when things go wrong. As recollected above, there were people at Fort McDowell who did not appreciate Montezuma's role in Yavapai affairs, and so they talked about him, while others allied themselves with the Indian Bureau superintendent. At the Salt River Reservation, there were "allotted boys" who did not like Montezuma's criticisms of the American war effort during World War I. Yet confronting acrimony, calumny, and adversity is what makes Indigenous men and women like Montezuma courageous. It is why their lives mattered to so many. It is also why we, their descendants, have so much to learn from them.

Notes

Introduction

1. According to Timothy Braatz, in *Surviving Conquest: A History of the Yavapai Peoples*, "The early Yavapais were essentially four peoples: Yavapés, Wipukepas, Tolkepayas, and Kwevkepayas" (Lincoln: University of Nebraska Press, 2003), 38. During the American Period, which began in the 1850s, the Yavapai were organized into three reservations.

2. Mike Harrison, John Williams, and Sigrid Khera, *Oral History of the Yavapai* (Tucson: University of Arizona Press, 2015), 72.

3. For more of the story about how the Montezuma archives were rescued from destruction, see note 32.

4. For more about the contemporary Fort McDowell Yavapai Nation, see https://www.fmyn.org/. For the Yavapai-Apache Nation, see https://yavapai-apache.org/. For the Yavapai-Prescott Indian Tribe, see https://www.ypit.com/about_ypit.htm. As for the Yavapai name origin in the historical record, see Sigrid Khera and Patricia S. Mariella, "Yavapai," *Handbook of North American Indians*, ed. William C. Sturtevant, vol. 10, *Southwest*, ed. Alfonso Ortiz (Washington, D.C.: Smithsonian, 1983), 38–54. It is pertinent here that Khera and Mariella state: "Since the Fort McDowell Reservation was established in 1903 it has been designated a 'Mohave-Apache Reservation' by the federal government. Only the reservation in Prescott, officially established in 1935, was designated a 'Yavapai Reservation'" (38). Also, in the section on synonymy, Khera and Mariella observe, "Since at least 1686 the Yavapai have often been referred to in Spanish and in English as Apaches [citation omitted]. This usage appears to be an extension of the term used for the Athapaskan-speaking Apacheans since 1598 and not based on the coincidentally similar Yavapai word ʔpačƏ 'people,' which some modern Yavapai give as the source" (53). Maurice Crandall enumerates military

establishments in nineteenth-century Central Arizona as a consequence of the push of settlements around Prescott: "When Anglo-Americans—both settlers and soldiers—came to Arizona in increasing numbers in the 1860s, they compounded the pressures on Arizona Indians. An 1863 gold discovery around Prescott, in the heart of northern Yavapai territory, led to an influx of settlers, followed by the United States Army, which quickly established Fort Whipple that same year. Meanwhile, settlers resumed crossing southern Arizona on their way to California. In the decade that followed, the U.S. Army established Camp Verde (1865), Camp Reno (1867), Camp McDowell (1865), Camp Grant (1866), Camp Date Creek (1867), and other installations in central Arizona. Yavapais were hemmed in on every side by Anglo settlements, military installations, and other Indian nations" ("Wassaja Comes Home: A Yavapai Perspective on Carlos Montezuma's Search for Identity," *Journal of Arizona History* 55, no. 1 [Spring 2014]): 4.

5. See note 8 below for full citation. Sigrid Khera is also listed as author and editor ahead of Butler. The book is organized into five parts and twenty-four chapters. The narrative is a synthesis of Khera's, Harrison's, and Williams's voices. More specifically, the first four parts consist of a relatively short overview of Yavapai ethnohistory, while part 5, the lion's share of the book, comprises Harrison and Williams's oral history. The book is "Dedicated to the bravery of the Yavapai." Indeed, my personally inscribed copy states: "History from the Indians' point of view. Carolina C. Butler."

6. Harrison, Williams, and Khera, *Oral History of the Yavapai*, 76.

7. For George Dickens's letter, Khera cited U.S. House of Representatives, Committee on Indian Affairs, Washington, D.C., 1911, Memorial and Papers from the Mohave-Apache Indians of McDowell Reservation, Arizona, in Relation to Their Removal from McDowell Reservation to the Salt River Reservation, Arizona, Butler Collection. For Charles Dickens, Leon Speroff, in *Carlos Montezuma, M.D.: A Yavapai American Hero: The Life and Times of an American Indian, 1866–1923* (Portland, Ore.: Arnica Publishing, 2003), 285–86, 497n31, cited J. W. Larner Jr., ed., *The Papers of Carlos Montezuma*, microfilm edition (Wilmington, Del.: Scholarly Resources, 1984), Reel 2, May 7, 1910.

8. Mike Harrison and John Williams, *Oral History of the Yavapai*, ed. Sigrid Khera and Carolina C. Butler (Gilbert, AZ: Acacia Publishing, 2012), 72, 76, 92, 106, 161, 316–17, 361, 363, 365. Noted on the book's back cover is the fact that when "Sigrid Khera died in 1984, the Yavapai requested that her remains be buried at their cemetery. We are unaware of any other anthropologist who has been so honored." As for Khera's original manuscript and audio tapes, the publisher stated, also on the back cover: "These materials are being donated to the Labriola National American Indian Data Center at Arizona State University." According to Alex Soto, the operations supervisor for the Labriola Center, Fletcher Library, ASU West Campus, in an email to the author: "Upon reviewing our collection, the [Sigrid Khera] manuscript and audio recordings are held

in our High Density Collection located on the Polytechnic campus" (email dated May 4, 2020). More specifically, the Khera collection is held within two separate, larger collections, specifically, the Kenneth Stewart Papers (http://azarchivesonline.org/xtf/view?docId=ead/asu/stewart.xml) and the Accession Records of The Labriola Center (http://azarchivesonline.org/xtf/view?docId=ead/asu/labriolacenter.xml) (both accessed May 4, 2020). In addition, a web address is posted after the index, inviting readers to "enjoy color photos of places within the Yavapai Indians' ancestral territory and see the beauty of the land where they lived and roamed": https://www.oralhistoryoftheyavapai.com/ (accessed May 1, 2020).

9. Edward H. Peplow Jr., "Seeds of Wounded Knee? Carlos Montezuma Collection, a Timely Acquisition, Boosts Stature of ASU's Hayden Library," *Arizona Statesman* 33, no. 12 (March 1974): 1, 3; Box 13, Folder 2, Carlos Montezuma Collection, 1887–1980, Labriola National American Indian Data Center, Arizona State University Library. Peplow's major distinction as a historian was the three-volume *History of Arizona* (New York: Lewis Historical Publishing, 1958).

10. Each of the four Montezuma archival collections is unique. The collection at Arizona State University, whose handwritten correspondence is the primary focus of the work in hand, is not the only archive to possess correspondence from Montezuma's close relations at Fort McDowell but nonetheless contains an abundance that far surpasses the other three collections. With respect to letters cited throughout this book, as pointed out in the acknowledgments, I transcribed all of the handwritten letters contained in the Montezuma Collection, which is curated by the Labriola National American Indian Data Center: https://lib.asu.edu/labriola (accessed August 16, 2021). As of this writing, the document containing the transcribed correspondence was being processed into the Collection.

11. For more on this phenomenon, see William Leap, *American Indian English* (Salt Lake City: University of Utah Press, 1993); Amelia V. Katanski, *Learning to Write "Indian": The Boarding School Experience and American Indian Literature* (Norman: University of Oklahoma Press, 2007).

12. The Salt River Valley Water Users Association—later known as the Salt River Project—is not mentioned in Peplow's article, but their role in the Indian Bureau's attempt at removing the Camp Verde Mohave Apache to the Salt River reservation is documented by Khera and Mariella, "Yavapai," 42–43.

13. Montezuma would be reappointed as representative of the Mohave Apache tribe on April 11, 1921. See letter dated April 11, 1921, "McDowell Reservation Arizona," Box 12, Folder 4, Montezuma Collection, ASU Library.

14. Joseph W. Latimer, ed., *The Rape of McDowell Reservation, Arizona, by the Indian Bureau* (Washington, D.C.: Hayworth Publishing House, 1921).

15. Biographical information about Latimer is sketchy, in particular the years prior to his 1910–1923 collaboration with Montezuma. Peter Iverson stated in *Carlos Montezuma and the Changing World of American Indians*: "Montezuma had

recently [prior to June 1911] retained an attorney, Joseph W. Latimer, to assist him. It marked the beginning of a lifelong association between the two" (Albuquerque: University of New Mexico Press, 1982), 89. John William Larner Jr. stated in his *Guide to the Scholarly Resources Microfilm Edition of the Papers of Carlos Montezuma, M.D.*: "Maria Montezuma [wife] and Joseph W. Latimer were among the most important people in Carlos Montezuma's life. Little is known about either of these persons." As for Latimer: "Joseph W. Latimer was born and raised in Galesburg, Illinois. Possibly he and Carlos Montezuma became acquainted during Montezuma's brief sojourn in Galesburg prior to his student days in Urbana. Chicago directories place Latimer as an attorney in that city from 1891 until 1915 when, no longer listed as a lawyer, he was shown as secretary of the Climax Container Corporation. By 1918 Latimer departed Chicago, practicing law in Cleveland, San Francisco, and New York. It is impossible to determine why Latimer quit his Chicago law practice. Latimer's use of such phrases as 'nightmare in Chicago' to describe his final days in that city suggests that he must have encountered some unpleasantness there" (Wilmington, Del.: Scholarly Resources, 1984), 9. Speroff scarcely mentions Latimer at all, providing no information that other sources, including Iverson's, did not already document. See Speroff, *Carlos Montezuma, M.D.*, 286, 296–97, 323.

16. Both Peter Iverson and Leon Speroff cover this chapter in Montezuma's life in their respective books. See Iverson, *Carlos Montezuma and the Changing World of American Indians*, 63–146; and, Speroff, *Carlos Montezuma, M.D.*, 277–331.

17. Peplow, "Seeds of Wounded Knee," 3. Interestingly, on June 5, 1973, the Fort McDowell Mohave Apache Tribal Council passed a resolution (Ft McD 182–73) for the purpose of authorizing "Glenn Solomon, Counselor, University of Oklahoma and author of a book on Dr. Montezuma to be announced later this year, to proceed in trying to recover papers and artifacts of Dr. Montezuma and return to the Tribe." See Box 12, Folder 1B, Montezuma Collection, ASU Library. Solomon never published his book on Montezuma. However, he did produce a master's thesis, titled "The Odyssey of Carlos Montezuma" (University of Oklahoma, 1973). Additionally, Solomon wrote an article that appeared in the now defunct, but historically important, *Wassaja* journal, titled "Fort McDowell Indians Face Loss of Land," *Wassaja: "Let My People Know"* 1, no. 4, (1973): 1–10.

18. Iverson, *Carlos Montezuma and the Changing World of American Indians*, xi. Spicer recounts Montezuma's legacy as being based on his affirmation that "Indians should cleave to their traditions in religion and moral behavior and not look to the Whites for guidance." Moreover, Montezuma's influence survived his 1923 death some twenty-five years. In the end, "no organized movement came into existence. It was apparent that [Montezuma's] influence had been very diffuse, but it had been powerful here and there," including among the "Pimas, Papagos, Yavapais, and Western Apaches." See Edward H. Spicer, *Cycles*

of Conquest: The Impact of Spain, Mexico, and the United States on the Indians of the Southwest, 1533–1960 (Tucson: University of Arizona Press, 1962), 350–51.

19. The legislative event that instigated the Yavapai fight against Orme Dam occurred when Congressman Wayne N. Aspinall (D-CO) introduced HR 3300 on January 23, 1967. The purpose of the bill was "to authorize the construction, operation, and maintenance of the Colorado River Basin project, and for other purposes." HR 3300 was then reported to the House on April 24, 1968. See 90 HR 3300 (1967–1968). On May 16, 1968, HR 3300 was raised as a topic of discussion by Congressman Aspinall, labeled as the "Colorado River Basin Project." Of particular interest were remarks made by Representative John Jacob Rhodes (R-AZ) regarding easements. Referring to the text of the proposed bill: "Mr. Chairman, under section 302(a), the Secretary of the Interior is authorized to acquire either fee title to, or easements over, lands within the Fort McDowell land Salt River Reservations for the Orme Dam and Reservoir. The purpose of my amendment is to make clear, as I understand the committee intended that the two Indian communities involved may not be prevented from developing and operating recreation facilities within their reservations—particularly on lands to which the United States has acquired only flowage easements—by arbitrary action of some future Secretary of the Interior." For the complete discussion, see Congressional Record, May 16, 1968, 90th Cong., 2nd Sess. (1968), 13566–13589.

20. Jennings C. Wise, *The Red Man in the New World Drama*, revised and edited with an introduction by Vine Deloria Jr. (New York: Macmillan, 1971), 359. Deloria is credited with the above quotation because the revised edition included five new chapters that Deloria added to cover the years 1934–1970, which Wise's original 1931 book did not cover.

21. Robert Allen Warrior, *Tribal Secrets: Recovering American Indian Intellectual Traditions* (Minneapolis: University of Minnesota Press, 1995), 6.

22. Iverson mentions Montezuma's work on behalf of the Pima, or Akimel O'odham, in *Carlos Montezuma and the Changing World of American Indians*, 79, 126, 128, 132, 137–38. Speroff also recounts Montezuma-Pima relations in *Carlos Montezuma, M.D.*, 298–304. For a dedicated discourse about what Montezuma did for the Pima-Maricopa, see David Martínez, "Carlos Montezuma's Fight Against 'Bureauism': An Unexpected Pima Hero," *Studies in American Indian Literatures* 25, no. 2 (Summer 2013): 311–30.

23. Hazel W. Hertzberg, *The Search for an American Indian Identity: Modern Pan-Indian Movements* (Syracuse: Syracuse University Press, 1971), 137, 140.

24. Hertzberg, 44.

25. Hertzberg, 193.

26. Hertzberg, 197. Iverson took Hertzberg's contribution into consideration when he observed: "In the 1970s prospects improved immeasurably for a proper biography of Carlos Montezuma. In 1972 [*sic*], Hazel Hertzberg published her pioneering study of early twentieth century pan-Indianism, *The Search for an*

American Indian Identity. Hertzberg's book gave attention to Montezuma, particularly in terms of his role with the Society of American Indians. While sometimes presenting an unflattering picture of Montezuma, she acknowledged his influence on the national level. During the decade, in addition, two collections of Montezuma's papers were acquired and made available to researchers. These collections, at the State Historical Society of Wisconsin, and the Arizona State University Library [Hayden], made possible a far more comprehensive portrayal. When consulted with other useful collections, such as the Arthur C. Parker papers at the New York State Museum, the Richard H. Pratt papers at Yale University, and the additional Montezuma file at the University of Arizona, the biography became an exciting possibility" (*Carlos Montezuma and the Changing World of American Indians*, xii-xiii). To Iverson's list of Montezuma-related resources, it is worth adding the Carlos Montezuma Papers, 1888–1936, held at the Newberry Library, Chicago, Illinois. The Newberry notes the provenance for the collection as "received in 1984 by David Miller and Frederick Hoxie of the Newberry Library's D'Arcy McNickle Center for American Indian History. Papers were found in a trunk after the death of Montezuma's wife and eventually were brought to the Newberry Library." As for the content of the Newberry collection, the library states: "Correspondence, writings, miscellaneous documents and memorabilia, clippings and photographs relating to Carlos Montezuma. Mainly incoming correspondence, much of which is from educator and activist Richard H. Pratt. Other correspondents range from relatives and other Indians including Indian author Simon Pokagon and other individuals concerned with Indian affairs, to Chicago patients, social contacts and admirers. The few outgoing letters and drafts of letters concern both Montezuma's medical practice and his activist views. Among his writings are drafts of an article on the Carlisle School on what he calls 'the Indian question,' manuscript copies of several speeches on that subject, a pamphlet, 'Let My People Go,' and a group of miscellaneous notes for articles or speeches. The miscellaneous material includes a manuscript transcript 'Account of the capture of Maria Ruiz's mother, July 3, 1889,' ads, brochures, bills and receipts, clippings and a periodical of 1921 'The Sagamore,' and other bits of memorabilia presumably retained by Montezuma. There are a few photographs and photoduplications, only one of which is of Carlos Montezuma." See the Newberry Library, "Inventory of the Carlos Montezuma Papers, 1888–1936, Bulk 1888–1922," https://mms.new berry.org/xml/xml_files/montezuma.xml (accessed June 3, 2020).

27. Iverson's work is a standard biography, consisting of eight chapters following Montezuma's life story from his origins in 1860s Arizona Territory, from which he was abducted by "Pima scouts" working for the U.S. Army, to his career as a physician and Indian rights activist, ending back in Arizona, where he died among his Mohave Apache family. In a sense, Iverson bases his narrative on the heroic tale that Montezuma retold before countless audiences and in print about his success as an "educated Indian."

28. Iverson, *Carlos Montezuma and the Changing World of American Indians*, xiii.
29. Speroff's substantial biography exceeds Iverson's earlier work in its scope, attempting to be about not only Montezuma but also American Indian history. In its eighteen chapters, Speroff goes over the same highlights as did Iverson, but with substantially more detail about all of the topics covered, including a bevy of images. When a copy was sent to me at the University of Minnesota, where I taught in the Department of American Indian Studies, the publisher's intent was to promote this book as an Introduction to American Indian Studies, hence the numerous digressions into areas of American Indian law and policy, culture, and politics. As for Iverson's work, it was cited in the 1984 book *Native Americans in the Twentieth Century* by James S. Olson and Raymond Wilson (Urbana-Champagne: University of Illinois Press), and in L. G. Moses and Raymond Wilson's edited volume *Indian Lives: Essays on Nineteenth- and Twentieth-Century Native American Leaders* (Albuquerque: University of New Mexico Press, 1985). With respect to Raymond Wilson, it is worth noting that earlier in 1983 he published *Ohiyesa: Charles Eastman, Santee Sioux* (Urbana-Champagne: University of Illinois Press). For a selected bibliography, see David Martínez, ed., *The American Indian Intellectual Tradition: An Anthology of Writings from 1772 to 1972* (Ithaca, N.Y.: Cornell University Press, 2011), 379.
30. For more about Speroff's distinguished medical career, see "2008 DeLee Humanitarian Award Goes to Leon Speroff, MD, of Oregon Health Sciences University," U Chicago Medicine, February 22, 2008: https://www.uchicagomedicine.org/forefront/news/2008-delee-humanitarian-award-goes-to-leon-speroff-md-of-oregon-health-sciences-university (accessed June 8, 2020).
31. Speroff resumes his account of Summit in the back pages of his book, in which he summarizes the four microfilm collections that he used to research Montezuma's life story. Regarding the entry for *Supplement to the Papers of Carlos Montezuma*, ed. John William Larner Jr., Speroff wrote: "Leon Summit was writing a story about the Great Chicago Fire and kept encountering Montezuma's name in old newspaper articles. Intrigued, Summit pursued Montezuma's history and discovered that the story ended with the trash man in 1956. Summit told me that he learned, with the help of the Chicago Historical Society, that at least a portion of the collection had been saved by the trash man and stored in an old barn that was about to be demolished for a construction project. Summit purchased what was in the barn for $3,000 and rescued the collection within an hour of the barn's destruction. Leon Summit acquired his Montezuma collection in late 1966. The *Chicago Tribune*, November 30, 1966, and the *Tucson Daily Citizen*, January 5, 1967, reported that his holdings were expanded by items given freely by people from all parts of the country, and that Summit intended to donate the documents to the University of Arizona after completing a biography. Photocopies of the Summit collection were made in 1980 by Jack Larner and Roger Bruns in Summit's basement using a rented copier. These copies were indexed with The Papers of Carlos Montezuma, Microfilm Edition,

but the copies were held until 2001 when they were put on microfilm at the
National Archives" (*Carlos Montezuma, M.D.*, 527).

32. Speroff, *Carlos Montezuma, M.D.*, v, 526–27. Was the Summit collection
merely a set of copies of the Wisconsin and Larner papers? It remains unclear.
As for the Wisconsin-held collection, titled The Papers of Carlos Montezuma,
1892–1937, Speroff notes: "This part of the Montezuma collection was held by
Marie Montezuma Moore until her death in 1956. It subsequently appeared at
an auction house near Huntsville, Alabama. According to the *Huntsville Times*,
September 15, 1966, an old trunk containing Indian papers and artifacts was
purchased by Richard Dahlman of Franklin, Wisconsin, who sold it in 1971
to his friends, John and Carol Fryer, owners of the Memorabilia Antique Co.
of Denver," who then sold it during a 1972 national auction "to the University
of Wisconsin and the Wisconsin History Foundation, which donated the collection to the institute that became the Wisconsin Historical Society" (526).
Speroff's reference to the Carlos Montezuma Collection held at ASU's Hayden
Library comes up in passing in his account of the Papers edited by John William
Larner Jr. In this instance, the origin of the collection once again begins with
Montezuma's widow, Marie, who "reported to Will C. Barnes that Montezuma's
papers were packed and placed in storage after his death." Barnes intended to
write a biography but, like Summit after him, never completed that project.
Instead, Barnes gave notes to Oren Arnold, who went on to write *Savage Son*.
"In January 1935, the Arizona Historical Society appealed to Mrs. Moore to
donate the papers or to provide for a donation in her will. She did neither. The
papers that Will Barnes borrowed ended up at the Arizona Historical Society
in the Will C. Barnes Collection. After Marie Montezuma Moore died in 1956,
her house was raided by looters. Three trunks containing the disrupted collection were put at the street curb, perhaps by neighbors, to be taken by the
trash man. From there the story is foggy. The University of Arizona received its
Montezuma collection in 1967 as a gift from James G. Lotter of Chicago. The
Arizona State University Hayden Library collection was purchased in 1973 from
Frank D. Novak, Sr., of Calument Park, Illinois. Newspaper stories report that
Novak found the collection in an old trunk that he purchased in 1962, but didn't
open for many years" (526–27). For more on the Barnes papers, see William
Croft Barnes, Papers, 1878–1945, Manuscript Collections Finding Aids, Ari-
zona Historical Society Library and Archives: https://arizonahistoricalsociety
.org/wp-content/uploads/2019/02/library_Barnes-William-Croft.pdf (accessed
June 11, 2020).

33. Warrior's book was largely about Osage novelist and essayist John Joseph
Mathews, who was regarded as exemplary of the American Indian intellectual
generation of "free agents," who were defined by a historical era (1925–1960) in
which writers and thinkers were not motivated by an ongoing political movement such as those occurring during the Progressive Era (1890–1916) and the
Red Power Movement (1960–1973). Montezuma appears briefly as an example

of the Progressive Era, which Warrior claimed was characterized by "assimilationism" and "apocalypticism," meaning the drive for U.S. citizenship rights and the end of pre-reservation life.

34. Oren Arnold distinguished himself as a writer of western novels in the tradition of Zane Grey and Alan Lemay. In the case of Arnold's novelization of Montezuma's much-told life story, he dramatizes Wassaja's story as the son of "Co-cu-ye-vah" and as a member of the "N'de." While Arnold misidentifies Montezuma as Apache, which was commonplace, he nevertheless refers his readers to the actual people who were significant in Montezuma's real life story, including Carlo Gentile. In fact, the middle of the novel is illustrated with a gallery of images, namely an artist's rendition of Wassaja as a boy (bow and arrow in hand), a sample of Montezuma's handwriting, a photograph of Wassaja and his two sisters (taken by Gentile), Gentile himself in a self-portrait, along with a photograph described as "Typical Apache Woman" taken at "San Carlos About 1920," reproductions of *Wassaja: Freedom's Signal* for the Indian masthead, a 1915 photograph of Montezuma in profile, and an "Apache Wickiup" described as being like the one in which "Carlos Montezuma Died January 31, 1923." Clearly, Arnold wanted to emphasize the authenticity of his novel's story. In spite of all the work that Arnold put into his novel, Iverson referred to *Savage Son* as an ultimately minor work: "Arnold's novel, as it must be labeled, centered almost entirely on Montezuma's early life and gave little attention to his career. It hardly represented an advance in scholarship, and as the title suggests, left something to be desired as a portrait of Indian life" (*Carlos Montezuma and the Changing World of American Indians*, xii).

35. Adele R. Arnold's novelization of Montezuma's life is not only much shorter than her husband Oren's book but also deliberately targeted toward adolescent readers, which is reflective of Arnold's career as an elementary school teacher in Phoenix. Otherwise, *Red Son Rising* covered the usual highlights of Montezuma's life and career, from captive to doctor to Indian rights legend (Minneapolis: Dillon Press, 1974).

36. William S. Burroughs, *The Place of Dead Roads: A Novel* (New York: Holt, Rinehart and Winston, 1983), 85–88. The reference to Montezuma's infamous abduction by the Akimel O'odham appears subtly when reference is made to "thirteen Pima Indians," a photographer named "Tom," and "a look of sheer panic" on an Indian boy's face.

37. Kevin Bruyneel, *The Third Space of Sovereignty: The Postcolonial Politics of U.S.-Indigenous Relations* (Minneapolis: University of Minnesota Press, 2007), 102–9. Montezuma was noted for his radical solution of abolishing the Indian Bureau as a means for according American Indians all of the rights and privileges of U.S. citizenship. Parker was a gradualist who proposed a tiered system of promoting Indians from wardship to citizenship, in which the Indian Bureau would be charged with facilitating the process. Eastman, in turn, who identified as an "Indian" and an "American," argued for an understanding of citizenship

that accommodated maintaining one's Indigenous culture. Lastly, Zitkala-Sa argued for citizenship based on the assertion that they had more than sufficiently proven their loyalty to the United States, making an implicit reference to the numerous treaties between tribes and the United States.

38. Similar to Adele Arnold's juvenile reader, Gina Capaldi's illustrated children's book is meant to bring Montezuma's story to young people—in this case, ages 8–12. It is worth noting that among Capaldi's other publications is a similar book on Zitkala-Sa, Gertrude Bonnin, titled *Red Bird Sings: The Story of Zitkala-Sa, Native American Author, Musician, and Activist*, which she edited but was written by Querida Lee Pearce. See *A Boy Named Beckoning: The True Story of Dr. Carlos Montezuma, Native American Hero* (Minneapolis: Carolrhoda Books, 2008).

39. For resources, see "Carlos Montezuma Guide to Collections," American Indian Studies, Arizona State University Library: https://libguides.asu.edu/c.php?g=263762&p=1765040 (accessed June 8, 2020).

40. This article was prepared in honor of the centennial of the Society of American Indians' first meeting during October 1911 in Columbus, Ohio. The focus is on the work that Montezuma did on behalf of the Salt and Gila River reservations, which were under threat from the Indian Bureau's plan to forcibly relocate the Mohave Apache to the Salt River Reservation, which likely would have worsened an already serious water crisis. A major feature of this paper was how Pima, or Akimel O'odham, writers George Webb and Anna Moore Shaw remembered Montezuma. In fact, Shaw recounted hosting Montezuma in her home near the end of this life. For more on the Society of American Indians Centennial Symposium, see "SAI Centennial Symposium Archive," American Indian Studies, Ohio State University: https://americanindianstudies.osu.edu/symposium (accessed May 31, 2020).

41. Newmark's article was also prepared for the SAI Centennial Symposium. She examined the print-run for Montezuma's self-published newsletter *Wassaja* for the way in which it reflected his love-hate relationship with the Society of American Indians, which Montezuma regarded as too Indian Bureau–friendly, and Arthur C. Parker, the longtime editor of *The Quarterly Journal of the Society of American Indians*, who advocated a gradualist approach to reforming federal Indian policy, as opposed to Montezuma's call for the immediate abolition of the Indian Bureau.

42. Crandall's paper asserts itself as the first work focusing on Montezuma's life and legacy from a Yavapai perspective. Toward that end, Crandall states: "As a people, we Yavapais regard Carlos Montezuma as a favorite son, and so I decided to quickly skim over the Carlos Montezuma Papers at the Newberry [Library in Chicago, IL]. Not to do so would be to miss out on a rare opportunity to study primary documents of my people's history" (1). What Crandall commits to is reading some of the correspondence between Montezuma and his Yavapai kinfolk, most importantly Mike Burns. As Crandall acknowledged in his intro-

ductory paragraph, he limited his analysis of the correspondence to the items held at the Newberry, which came out to thirteen references in the endnotes. Crandall's objective, with respect to his Yavapai point of view, is to highlight the ways in which people like Burns and Charles and George Dickens accepted Montezuma as one of their relatives from the beginning of his reappearance in their lives. In fact, despite the limited Montezuma sources available at the Newberry, Crandall argues convincingly not only that the Yavapai had remembered their long-lost cousin but also that the desire to reconnect with his family and tribe was always a driving force in Montezuma's life.

43. Cristina Stanciu, "'Americanism for Indians': Carlos Montezuma's 'Immigrant Problem,' *Wassaja*, and the Limits of Native Activism," *Studies in American Indian Literatures* 33, nos. 1–2 (Spring–Summer 2021): 126–58.

44. Thomas Constantine Maroukis, *We Are Not a Vanishing People: The Society of American Indians, 1911–1923* (Tucson: University of Arizona Press, 2021).

45. These items document the political agenda that Montezuma would maintain throughout his career as an Indian rights activist. See Box 1, Folders 1–2, Montezuma Collection, ASU Library.

46. The letters from Charles Dickens are contained throughout the Collection and document both a political interest in Fort McDowell tribal affairs and the more mundane interests shared between cousins. As for the letter to Interior Secretary Ballinger, Montezuma is responding to a letter from the Department of the Interior (not in the Collection) regarding "the removal of the Camp McDowell Indians to the Salt River Reservation." In his response, Montezuma stated: "After a thorough investigation of the question in Arizona by myself, consulting with the leaders of the tribe and the tribe themselves, and further consultation with eminent men in full position to pass judgment on such a question, I thoroughly disagree with your department that it is to the best interests of these Camp McDowell Indians to move, and I positively know it is not their wish to move." For more, see Carlos Montezuma to Hon. R. A. Ballinger, January 20, 1911, Box 3, Folder 3, Montezuma Collection, ASU Library.

47. HR 6294 was entered into the Congressional Record on April 20, 1911. See CR-1911–0420. See also Memorial and Papers from the Mohave-Apache Indians of McDowell Reservation, Arizona, in Relation to Their Removal from McDowell Reservation to the Salt River Reservation, Arizona, Committee on Indian Affairs, House, 62nd Cong., 1st Sess. (1911); and Allotment Bill for McDowell Reservation, Box 3, Folder 3, Montezuma Collection, ASU Library.

48. See Mike Burns to Dr. Carlos Montezuma, January 22, 1915, Box 4, Folder 1, Montezuma Collection, ASU Library. In part, Burns stated to Montezuma: "We are undersigne [*sic*] oldest residence [*sic*] here on McDowell reservation, and ask your aid: as we are the members of the Mojaves [*sic*] Apaches.—Very respectfully: 1 Geo Dickens (chief head)."

49. Both Peter Iverson and Leon Speroff wrote about Montezuma's futile effort at acquiring tribal membership, be it at San Carlos or Fort McDowell. See Iver-

son, *Carlos Montezuma and the Changing World of American Indians*, 147–73. Within chapter 7, "The Circle Closes," there is a section titled "Application for Enrollment." See also Speroff, *Carlos Montezuma, M.D.*, 258–76. Within chapter 11, "Rediscovering the Yavapai: They're All Related to Me," there is a section titled "Montezuma's Effort to Enroll in a Tribe."

50. Crandall inferred from the letters that Mike Burns wrote to Montezuma with the expectation that Montezuma would relearn his Yavapai language. In the Carlos Montezuma Collection held at ASU's Hayden Library, there are no references in Burns's letters to teaching Montezuma Yavapai, be it via correspondence or during Montezuma's annual hunting trips. For Crandall's claim, see "Wassaja Comes Home," 18.

51. Carlos Montezuma, "Superintendent Sharp and Dr. Montezuma," *Wassaja* 5, no. 7 (October 1920): 2.

52. Harrison, Williams, and Khera, *Oral History of the Yavapai*, 363.

53. Bruyneel, *The Third Space of Sovereignty*, 105.

54. Kiara Vigil, *Indigenous Intellectuals: Sovereignty, Citizenship, and the American Imagination, 1880–1930* (New York: Cambridge University Press, 2015), 104.

55. Crandall, "Wassaja Comes Home," 17.

Chapter 1

1. Peter Iverson, *Carlos Montezuma and the Changing World of American Indians* (Albuquerque: University of New Mexico Press, 1982), 14, 25.

2. Manuel Ruiz to Dr. Carlos Montezuma, May 1, 1901, Box 3, Folder 1, Carlos Montezuma Collection, 1887–1980, Labriola National American Indian Data Center, Arizona State University Library.

3. "Juan Ruiz Student Information Card," Carlisle Indian School Digital Resource Center, http://carlisleindian.dickinson.edu/student_files/juan-ruiz-student-information-card (accessed June 10, 2020).

4. "Manuel Ruiz Student Information Card," Carlisle Indian School Digital Resource Center, http://carlisleindian.dickinson.edu/student_files/manuel-ruiz-student-information-card (accessed June 10, 2020).

5. According to the Arizona Memory Project, they have on record a possible descendant of the Ruiz family. See "Oral History with Manuel Ruiz, January 14, 2011," Arizona Memory Project, https://azmemory.azlibrary.gov/digital/collection/asacapture/id/244/ (accessed June 11, 2020).

6. Crandall argues: "As early as 1888, Wassaja asked individuals to help him find more information about his family. He was specifically concerned with the fate of his sisters and parents. We only have the return correspondence from individuals to whom he turned for help, but their letters are very telling." See Maurice Crandall, "Wassaja Comes Home: A Yavapai Perspective on Carlos Montezuma's Search for Identity," *Journal of Arizona History* 55, no. 1 (Spring 2014): 12.

7. Grace Thumbo is listed as a student at Carlisle Indian School. Thumbo was seventeen years old when she enrolled on September 23, 1899, and was identified

as a "full blood" and a "Mohave." She left Carlisle on September 23, 1904. See "Grace Thumbo Student Information Card," Carlisle Indian School Digital Resource Center, http://carlisleindian.dickinson.edu/student_files/grace-thumbo -student-information-card (accessed July 28, 2020).

8.　Charles Dickens to Dr. Carlos Montezuma, November 2, 1901, Box 3, Folder 1, Montezuma Collection, ASU Library.

9.　Charles Dickens to Dr. Carlos Montezuma, December 7, 1908, Box 3, Folder 2, Montezuma Collection, ASU Library.

10.　Mike Burns to Dr. Carlos Montezuma, August 6, 1903, Box 3, Folder 2, Montezuma Collection, ASU Library.

11.　Crandall, "Wassaja Comes Home," 22.

12.　Iverson, *Carlos Montezuma and the Changing World of American Indians*, 41–42.

13.　Charles Dickens to Dr. Carlos Montezuma, February 9, 1911, Box 3, Folder 3, Montezuma Collection, ASU Library.

14.　Yuma Frank to Dr. Carlos Montezuma, March 3, 1911, Box 3, Folder 3, Montezuma Collection, ASU Library.

15.　Charles Cook to Dr. Carlos Montezuma, June 10, 1911, Box 3, Folder 3, Montezuma Collection, ASU Library. It is worth pointing out that Cook's letter included an account of him having seen Montezuma not long after his capture: "I have very often thought of you since I first met you, I believe it was in 1841 [1871?], a prisoner with the Pimas & with a prospect of being sold for a pony to Mexicans and taken to that country a slave." On the topic of slavery among the Akimel O'odham, Frank Russell provided a brief note in *The Pima Indians*: "The slaves taken by the Pimas were chiefly from the ranks of the Apaches or their allies. Though war was waged for many years against the Yumas it was not of a character to enable them to capture many Yuma children. When captured, Apache children were not killed; they were soon forwarded to Tucson, Altar, or Guaymas and sold to the Spaniards or Mexicans. These captives were well treated, but their origin was never forgotten and the fear and suspicion of the tribe found expression at times in the decrees of the medicine-men that certain misfortunes were caused by the presence of the aliens" (Tucson: University of Arizona Press, 1975), 197.

16.　For more about the struggle to protect Indian water rights, see Daniel McCool, *Native Waters: Contemporary Indian Water Settlements and the Second Treaty Era* (Tucson: University of Arizona Press, 2006).

17.　Sigrid Khera and Patricia S. Mariella, "Yavapai," *Handbook of North American Indians*, ed. William C. Sturtevant, vol. 10, *Southwest*, ed. Alfonso Ortiz (Washington, D.C.: Smithsonian, 1983), 42.

18.　David H. DeJong, *Stealing the Gila: The Pima Agricultural Economy and Water Deprivation, 1848–1921* (Tucson: University of Arizona Press, 2009), 112–13.

19.　Hazel W. Hertzberg, *The Search for an American Indian Identity: Modern Pan-Indian Movements* (Syracuse: Syracuse University Press, 1971), 44.

20. Hertzberg, 45.

21. Crandall, "Wassaja Comes Home," 10–11.

22. David R. Berman, *George Hunt: Arizona's Crusading Seven-Term Governor* (Tucson: University of Arizona Press, 2015).

23. For more, see "Hayden, Carl Trumbull (1877–1972)," Biographical Directory of the United States Congress, https://bioguide.congress.gov/search/bio/H000385 (accessed March 27, 2021).

24. Jack L. August Jr., "Water, Politics, and the Arizona Dream: Carl Hayden and the Modern Origins of the Central Arizona Project, 1922–1963," *Journal of Arizona History* 40, no. 4 (1999): 391–414.

25. Leon Speroff, *Carlos Montezuma, M.D.: A Yavapai American Hero: The Life and Times of an American Indian, 1866–1923* (Portland, Ore.: Arnica Publishing, 2003), 277.

26. Speroff, 284. *Hurley v. Abbott* was newsworthy, taking up two full pages of the *Arizona Republican,* which reported on the court's opinion on Wednesday, March 2, 1910, 7–8.

27. Speroff, *Carlos Montezuma, M.D.,* 285.

28. Temple may be the same person noted as the friend of Gila County Sheriff John Thompson, accused of murdering a bartender in Globe, Arizona, in 1911. See Clare V. McKanna Jr., *Homicide, Race, and Justice in the American West, 1880–1920* (Tucson: University of Arizona Press, 1997), 34.

29. Charles Dickens to Dr. Carlos Montezuma, January 3, 1912, Box 3, Folder 4, Montezuma Collection, ASU Library.

30. Charles Dickens to Dr. Carlos Montezuma, January 28, 1912, Box 3, Folder 4, Montezuma Collection, ASU Library.

31. Charles Dickens to Dr. Carlos Montezuma, February 10, 1912, Box 3, Folder 4, Montezuma Collection, ASU Library.

32. Charles Dickens to Dr. Carlos Montezuma, February 10, 1912.

33. Likely a reference to the U.S. Bureau of Reclamation, which oversaw what became the Salt River Project. See "A History of Canals in Arizona," SRP, https://www.srpnet.com/water/canals/history.aspx (accessed December 10, 2020); see also Ninth Annual Report of the Reclamation Service (U.S. Government Printing Office, 1911), 57–70.

34. Charles Dickens to Dr. Carlos Montezuma, January 28, 1912, Box 3, Folder 4, Montezuma Collection, ASU Library. The reference to the "Arizona Canal Reclamation Service" was likely in regard to the Salt River Project, which impacted both the Verde and Salt Rivers. For an extensive report on the project, see F. H. Newell, Ninth Annual Report of the Reclamation Service, 1909–1910, House Committee on Irrigation and Arid Lands, 61st Cong., 3rd Sess. (1910).

35. Charles Dickens to Dr. Carlos Montezuma, April 1, 1912, Box 3, Folder 4, Montezuma Collection, ASU Library.

36. Dickens was likely referring to Secretary of the Interior Walter Lowrie Fisher, who served 1911–1913 under President William Howard Taft. See "Past Secre-

taries," U.S. Department of the Interior, https://www.doi.gov/whoweare/past
-secretaries#fisher (accessed August 6, 2020).

37. Samuel H. Adams served as first assistant secretary of Interior under Fisher.
See "Samuel Adams, 68, Attorney, Is Dead; Chicagoan First Assistant Secretary
of the Interior in Taft Administration," *New York Times*, May 21, 1935, https://
www.nytimes.com/1935/05/21/archives/samuel-adams-68-attorney-is-dead
-chicagoan-first-assistant.html (accessed August 6, 2020).

38. Charles Dickens to Dr. Carlos Montezuma, August 28, 1912, Box 3, Folder 4,
Montezuma Collection, ASU Library.

39. Harry Temple was at one time employed at the San Carlos Agency as an "Industrial teacher." See Annual Report of the Commissioner of Indian Affairs, for
the Year 1888, United States Office of Indian Affairs (Washington, D.C.: GPO,
[1888]), 404.

40. Charles Dickens to Dr. Carlos Montezuma, August 28, 1912.

41. Iverson, *Carlos Montezuma and the Changing World of American Indians*,
89–90.

42. "Indians Hold Reservation of M'Dowell," *Arizona Republican*, August 24, 1912, 1.

43. "Indians Hold Reservation of M'Dowell," 10.

44. Grace Pelcher to Dr. Carlos Montezuma, January 5, 1912, Box 3, Folder 4, Montezuma Collection, ASU Library.

45. Burns is actually referring to the Skeleton Cave Massacre, one of the most infamous events in Yavapai history. See Timothy Braatz, *Surviving Conquest: A
History of the Yavapai Peoples* (Lincoln: University of Nebraska Press, 2003),
2–3, 6, 13, 16, 17, 19, 85, 138–39. Harrison and Williams also recount this; see
Mike Harrison, John Williams, and Sigrid Khera, *Oral History of the Yavapai*
(Tucson: University of Arizona Press, 2015), 28, 73–74, 76, 82, in which they
explain why Burns was so reviled by many Yavapai.

46. Mike Burns to Dr. Carlos Montezuma, January 7, 1913, Box 3, Folder 5, Montezuma Collection, ASU Library.

47. Mike Burns to Dr. Carlos Montezuma, March 28, 1913, Box 3, Folder 5, Montezuma Collection, ASU Library.

48. For more about the history behind what became Fort McDowell, see "Period
History," Fort Verde State Historic Park, https://azstateparks.com/fort-verde
/about-the-fort/period-history (accessed June 18, 2020).

49. Mike Burns to Dr. Carlos Montezuma, May 28, 1913, Box 3, Folder 5, Montezuma Collection, ASU Library.

50. Crandall, "Wassaja Comes Home," 5.

51. The Camp Grant Massacre occurred on April 30, 1871, along the San Pedro
River, Arizona. In this instance, the U.S. Army violently assaulted Western
Apache northeast of Tucson. For more, see Dan L. Thrapp, *The Conquest of
Apacheria* (Norman: University of Oklahoma Press, 1975) and Patricia Nelson
Limerick and Karl Jacoby, *Shadows at Dawn: An Apache Massacre and the
Violence of History* (New York: Penguin, 2009).

52. Mike Burns to Dr. Carlos Montezuma, June 29, 1913, Box 3, Folder 5, Montezuma Collection, ASU Library.
53. Braatz, *Surviving Conquest*, 3.
54. Mike Burns to Dr. Carlos Montezuma, July 16, 1913, Box 3, Folder 5, Montezuma Collection, ASU Library. Burns tells a similar story in his letter to Montezuma of June 29, 1913.
55. Khera and Mariella, "Yavapai," 41.
56. Crandall, "Wassaja Comes Home," 2.
57. DeJong, *Stealing the Gila*, 179.
58. Charles Dickens to Dr. Carlos Montezuma, June 28, 1913, Box 3, Folder 5, Montezuma Collection, ASU Library. The reference to the "Reclamation Service" was likely the same Salt River Project noted above. See Newell, Ninth Annual Report of the Reclamation Service.
59. Charles Dickens to Dr. Carlos Montezuma, July 11, 1913, Box 3, Folder 5, Montezuma Collection, ASU Library. Speroff identified Morgan specifically as "George N. Morgan, a classmate [of Montezuma's] at the University of Illinois and now an attorney in Chicago"; while Gibson was noted as "Charles B. Gibson, a physician from Chicago." Gibson's wife, however, was not identified. For more on the 1913 hunting trip, see Speroff, *Carlos Montezuma, M.D.*, 266–67.
60. Charles Dickens to Dr. Carlos Montezuma, July 28, 1913, Box 3, Folder 5, Montezuma Collection, ASU Library.
61. Cato Sells, Annual Report of Commissioner of Indian Affairs (Washington, D.C.: Government Printing Office, 1913): 45.
62. George Dickens to Dr. Carlos Montezuma, February 7, 1913, Box 3, Folder 5, Montezuma Collection, ASU Library.
63. Speroff, *Carlos Montezuma, M.D.*, 267–68.
64. Iverson, *Carlos Montezuma and the Changing World of American Indians*, 44–45, 75.
65. Yuma Frank to Dr. Carlos Montezuma, August 9–13, 1913, Box 3, Folder 5, Montezuma Collection, ASU Library. Harrison and Williams recount Yuma Frank's tenure as the Fort McDowell Yavapai headman in *Oral History of the Yavapai*, 146–57.
66. Letter to Dr. Carlos Montezuma, August 24, 1913, Box 3, Folder 5, Montezuma Collection, ASU Library.
67. Charles Dickens to Dr. Carlos Montezuma, September 5, 1913, Box 3, Folder 5, Montezuma Collection, ASU Library.
68. Charles Dickens to Dr. Carlos Montezuma, December 16, 1913, Box 3, Folder 5, Montezuma Collection, ASU Library.
69. Cristina Stanciu does an excellent job at analyzing the "immigrant trope" in Montezuma's writings on Indian rights. More to the point, Stanciu argues that the analogy to the immigrant experience enabled Montezuma to make Indian rights, especially the necessity of citizenship, accessible to his American reader

by making a comparison with something more familiar. Stanciu attributes this affiliation with immigrants to Montezuma's guardian, Carlo Gentile, an Italian immigrant, and his wife, Marie, a Romanian immigrant. See Stanciu, "'Americanism for Indians': Carlos Montezuma's 'Immigrant Problem,' *Wassaja*, and the Limits of Native Activism," *Studies in American Indian Literatures* 33, nos. 1–2 (Spring-Summer 2021): 129–36.

70. Iverson, *Carlos Montezuma and the Changing World of American Indians*, 100–101.

71. "Gem Valley of Them All," *Arizona Republican*, August 10, 1913, 10.

Chapter 2

1. Mike Burns to Dr. Carlos Montezuma, March 19, 1914, Box 3, Folder 6, Carlos Montezuma Collection, 1887–1980, Labriola National American Indian Data Center, Arizona State University Library. The letter contains a postscript on a separate sheet, titled "Part 2," in which Burns largely reiterates concerns about Francisco Hill but begins with a reference to a planned new church construction: "Other Indians come: and says that there is a church is going to be built on the reservation: and with out [*sic*] their consent: And pulling Juan on them." No further details are given about the planned new church.

2. Peter Iverson, *Carlos Montezuma and the Changing World of American Indians* (Albuquerque: University of New Mexico Press, 1982), 132–33.

3. Mike Burns to Dr. Carlos Montezuma, July 7, 1914, Box 3, Folder 6, Montezuma Collection, ASU Library.

4. Mike Burns to Dr. Carlos Montezuma, July 22, 1914, Box 3, Folder 6, Montezuma Collection, ASU Library.

5. Mike Burns to Dr. Carlos Montezuma, August 7, 1914, Box 3, Folder 6, Montezuma Collection, ASU Library.

6. Iverson, *Carlos Montezuma and the Changing World of American Indians*, 141.

7. Mike Burns to Dr. Carlos Montezuma, September 12, 1914, Box 3, Folder 6, Montezuma Collection, ASU Library.

8. This may actually be referring to Hans B. Klingenberger, who was listed as a teacher at the Camp McDowell Day School. See Camp Notes, *Native American*, April 1, 1916, 130.

9. Mike Burns to Dr. Carlos Montezuma, December 25, 1914, Box 3, Folder 6, Montezuma Collection, ASU Library.

10. Mike Nelson was remembered both as a medicine man and as Fort McDowell's first Indian policeman. See Mike Harrison, John Williams, and Sigrid Khera, *Oral History of the Yavapai* (Tucson: University of Arizona Press, 2015), 30, 155. Nelson is mentioned multiple times throughout this volume.

11. George Dickens to Dr. Carlos Montezuma, April 30, 1914, Box 3, Folder 6, Montezuma Collection, ASU Library.

12. Charles Dickens to Dr. Carlos Montezuma, July 3, 1914, Box 3, Folder 6, Montezuma Collection, ASU Library.

13.   Richard Dickens to Dr. Carlos Montezuma, July 13, 1914, Box 3, Folder 6, Montezuma Collection, ASU Library.

14.   Yuma Frank to Dr. Carlos Montezuma, November 30, 1914, Box 3, Folder 6, Montezuma Collection, ASU Library.

15.   Harrison, Williams, and Khera, *Oral History of the Yavapai*, 359–61. Burns, as one may infer from his portrayal here, had a life that paralleled and diverged from Montezuma's in interesting ways. Burns's effort at publishing his Yavapai history did not bear fruit until 1998 when Elaine Waterstrat and Mount McDowell Press released a single volume titled *Hoomothya's Long Journey, 1865–1897: The True Story of a Yavapai Indian*, which was published again in 2012 when Gregory McNamee edited Burns's manuscript into another single volume titled *The Only One Living to Tell: The Autobiography of a Yavapai Indian*, which the University of Arizona Press published. Iverson, however, only mentions Burns a handful of times, one of these in regard to a 1915 visit to the Fort McDowell reservation, at the behest of Montezuma, by Fayette McKenzie, a sociologist remembered for the critical role he played in organizing the Society of American Indians. According to Iverson: "McKenzie had a good word for almost everyone, including [Superintendent] Coe and the farmer [Shafer]; he complained only about Mike Burns, who had missed a meeting because, according to McKenzie, he had concluded the professor had no power" (*Carlos Montezuma and the Changing World of American Indians*, 142). Leon Speroff, in *Carlos Montezuma, M.D.: A Yavapai American Hero: The Life and Times of an American Indian, 1866–1923* (Portland, Ore.: Arnica Publishing, 2003), also mentions Burns a handful of times, and these instances shed light on Burns's place in Yavapai society. In a section of Chapter 1 recounting Montezuma's capture by Akimel O'odham scouts titled "Corbusier: An Army Doctor," Speroff notes: "Mike Burns (Hoo-moo-thy-ah, Little Wet Nose) was named after Captain James Burns, who captured him about two weeks before the Skeleton Cave Massacre. Burns was about the same age as Wassaja [Montezuma], maybe five years older. All of Burns' relatives were killed in the Battle of the Caves, or the Skeleton Cave Massacre. In 1869, several hundred Indians (Tonto [Apache] and Yavapai) came to Camp McDowell to make peace and treaty. Burns and his family were with this group" (9–10). With respect to William H. Corbusier, Speroff notes: "Corbusier knew Michael Burns, Wassaja's cousin, very well. Burns learned English as a frequent guest in the Corbusier home in the Verde Valley (Burns was later to attend the Carlisle Indian School)." Corbusier later attempted to assist Burns in getting his manuscript published, then titled *The Indian Side of the Question*, but to no avail (9). Burns's name appears periodically in the literature about the Yavapai, as in Dan L. Thrapp's *The Conquest of Apacheria* (Norman: University of Oklahoma Press, 1967), 112, 126; Timothy Braatz's *Surviving Conquest: A History of the Yavapai Peoples* (Lincoln: University of Nebraska Press, 2003), 1–11, 16, 20, 51, 88, 204, 207; and Daniel J. Herman's *Rim Country Exodus: A Story of Con-*

quest, Renewal, and Race in the Making (Tucson: University of Arizona Press, 2012), 80, 81, 102, 150, 159–60, 218, 260, 263, 296–97, 306, 311. Burns's life story was also told in a master's thesis by Louise Alflen submitted at Arizona State University (2011) titled "Yavapai Indians Circle Their Wagons: Indians to Arizona: 'It's a Good Day to Declare War,'" in which there is a subsection of section 2, "Case Studies of Yavapai Warrior Leaders," titled "Hoomothya: The Mike Burns Story" (35–44). For more of Alflen's work, see ASU Digital Repository, Arizona State University Library, https://repository.asu.edu/attach ments/93373/content//tmp/package-CmMAJk/Alflen_asu_0010N_11303.pdf (accessed June 24, 2020).

16. Maurice Crandall, "Wassaja Comes Home: A Yavapai Perspective on Carlos Montezuma's Search for Identity," *Journal of Arizona History* 55, no. 1 (Spring 2014): 8. Crandall cites a passage from what was for many years Burns's unpublished manuscript, in which he expressed his horror at the carnage. See Mike Burns, *All of My People Were Killed: The Memoir of Mike Burns (Hoomothya), a Captive Indian* (Prescott, Ariz.: Sharlot Hall Museum, 2010), 27–28.

17. Crandall, "Wassaja Comes Home," 9.

18. Joint letter to Dr. Carlos Montezuma, January 22, 1915, Box 4, Folder 1, Montezuma Collection, ASU Library.

19. For more on Horseshoe Ranch, see "History of Horseshoe Ranch," Cornerstone Environmental, https://www.cornerstone-environmental.com/publications/item /a-brief-history-of-horseshoe-ranch (accessed December 11, 2020).

20. George Dickens to Dr. Carlos Montezuma, January 11, 1915, Box 4, Folder 1, Montezuma Collection, ASU Library.

21. Letter to Dr Carlos Montezuma, McDowell, Arizona, July 10, 1915, *Carlos Montezuma Collection, 1887–1980*, Arizona State University Libraries, Labriola National American Indian Data Center, Box 4, Folder 1. This farmer may have been William W. Moore (d. 1929): "The area surrounding the Rio Verde community, northeast of Scottsdale, was settled by small farmers in the 1880s, who grew hay and alfalfa to provide for the nearby Fort McDowell US Army camp (1865–1890) (now the Fort McDowell Yavapai Nation). In the late 1890s, William W. Moore acquired several of the small farm plots on the Verde River, combining them into what became the Box Bar Ranch. After his death in 1929, Moore's sons, Glenn and Lin Moore, operated the Box Bar as a partnership, under the name 'Moore Bros Cattle Co.,' with grazing leases both east and west of the Verde River. Lin Moore also ran the X2 Ranch, 12 miles (19 km) to the west, where he and his wife, Ada Lucille, had homesteaded in the 1920s. William Moore's father, Ranse B. Moore, had emigrated to Arizona from California in 1883 and ranched for many years on the Reno Ranch, just west of the community of Punkin Center, Arizona. The 'Asher Hills' were named for Frank Asher, who had been Glenn Moore's brother-in-law and William Moore's partner for a time. The granddaughter of Asher's wife Ella, Jacque Mercer, was selected as Miss Arizona and then Miss America in 1949." See "Rio Verde, AZ," MapQuest,

https://www.mapquest.com/us/arizona/business-rio-verde/rio-verde-az-2820 31090 (accessed October 12, 2020).

22. George Dickens to Dr. Carlos Montezuma, July 10, 1915, Box 4, Folder 1, Montezuma Collection, ASU Library.

23. George Dickens to Dr. Carlos Montezuma, August 28, 1915, Box 4, Folder 1, Montezuma Collection, ASU Library.

24. Harrison, Williams, and Khera, *Oral History of the Yavapai*, 157, 281.

25. Harrison, Williams, and Khera, 340, 359–60.

26. See An Act to Provide for the Allotment of Lands in Severalty to Indians on the Various Reservations, and to Extend the Protection of the Laws of the United States and the Territories over the Indians, and for Other Purposes, 24 Stat 388 (1887).

27. Grace Stewart to Dr. Carlos Montezuma, April 22, 1915, Box 4, Folder 1, Montezuma Collection, ASU Library.

28. Cato Sells, Annual Report of the Commissioner of Indian Affairs, 1915, 22, 25.

29. Cato Sells, Annual Report of the Commissioner of Indian Affairs, 1916, 43, 48.

30. Charles Vollan, "Yellowtail, Robert (1887/1889–1988)," in *Great Plains Indians*, ed. David J. Wishart (Lincoln: University of Nebraska Press, 2016), 224.

31. Frederick E. Hoxie, *Parading Through History: The Making of the Crow Nation in America, 1805–1935* (New York: Cambridge University Press, 1995), 259. In the same volume, Hoxie describes Kappler as "a Washington attorney who had served for a time as clerk to the Senate Indian Affairs Committee and who had begun to represent tribes' complaints against the [federal] government" (255). Kappler also compiled the legendary multivolume resource *Indian Affairs: Laws and Treaties* (1904–71); see "Kapplers," Digital Collections, Oklahoma State Library, https://dc.library.okstate.edu/digital/collection/kapplers (accessed December 14, 2020).

32. Hoxie, *Parading Through History*, 259n64.

33. Robert Yellowtail to Dr. Carlos Montezuma, November 20, 1915, Box 4, Folder 1, Montezuma Collection, ASU Library.

34. Vollan, "Yellowtail, Robert," 224.

35. Iverson, *Carlos Montezuma and the Changing World of American Indians*, 40.

36. Charles Dickens to Dr. Carlos Montezuma, July 10, 1915, Box 4, Folder 1, Montezuma Collection, ASU Library.

37. Charles Dickens to Dr. Carlos Montezuma, December 14, 1915, Box 4, Folder 1, Montezuma Collection, ASU Library. "Em Witter" was likely the "E. E. Witter" that Iverson identifies as the person described as being from "Des Moines" in an *Arizona Republican* story about Montezuma's visit to Phoenix (*Carlos Montezuma and the Changing World of American Indians*, 45).

38. Dwight Campbell to Dr. Carlos Montezuma, June 23, 1915, Box 4, Folder 1, Montezuma Collection, ASU Library. In a 1917 issue of the Phoenix Indian School publication *The Native American*, Dwight Campbell's name appeared in the Around the Campus section: "Dwight Campbell, a Mojave-Apache from McDowell, was a visitor at the school hospital during the week. Dwight is a

returned student of the Santa Fe and Fort Yuma schools." See Around the Campus, *Native American*, January 26, 1917, 19.

39. Harrison, Williams, and Khera, *Oral History of the Yavapai*, 156, 158.

40. Dwight Campbell to Dr. Carlos Montezuma, September 4, 1915, Box 4, Folder 1, Montezuma Collection, ASU Library.

41. Dwight Campbell to Dr. Carlos Montezuma, September 11, 1915, Box 4, Folder 1, Montezuma Collection, ASU Library.

42. Sigrid Khera and Patricia S. Mariella, "Yavapai," *Handbook of North American Indians*, ed. William C. Sturtevant, vol. 10, *Southwest*, ed. Alfonso Ortiz (Washington, D.C.: Smithsonian, 1983), 43. For a historical timeline of the Salt River Project, which claims to go back to the time of the Huhugam, see "Timeline," A History of Service, SRP, https://www.srpnet.com/about/history/timeline.aspx (accessed October 9, 2020).

43. Carlos Montezuma, "Let My People Go," in *The American Indian Intellectual Tradition: An Anthology of Writings from 1772 to 1972*, ed. David Martínez (Ithaca, N.Y.: Cornell University Press, 2011), 207–8.

44. Thomas C. Maroukis, *We Are Not a Vanishing People: The Society of American Indians, 1911–1923* (Tucson: University of Arizona Press, 2021), 111.

45. Maroukis, 110.

46. Maroukis, 119–20.

47. Thurma Dickens to Dr. Carlos Montezuma, November 27, 1915, Box 4, Folder 1, Montezuma Collection, ASU Library.

48. A 1917 issue of the Phoenix Indian School's newspaper, *The Native American*, aside from misidentifying Thurma Dickens as a boy, reported that she had been a patient in the school hospital: "Mr. and Mrs. George Dickens, of the McDowell Reservation, were visitors at the school hospital recently, they were here to see their son, Thurma Dickens, who is a patient." See Around the Campus, *Native American*, January 26, 1917, 19.

49. For more on the Phoenix Indian School, see Robert A. Trennert, *Phoenix Indian School: Forced Assimilation in Arizona, 1891–1935* (Norman: University of Oklahoma Press, 1988); see also Owen Lindauer, "Archaeology of the Phoenix Indian School," *Archaeology*, March 27, 1998, https://archive.archaeology.org /online/features/phoenix/ (accessed October 9, 2020).

50. For more, see Robert A. Trennert, "Educating Indian Girls at Nonreservation Boarding Schools, 1878–1920," *Western Historical Quarterly* 13, no. 3 (July 1982): 271–90.

Chapter 3

1. Peter Iverson, *Carlos Montezuma and the Changing World of American Indians* (Albuquerque: University of New Mexico Press, 1982), 183.

2. Julianne Newmark, "A Prescription for Freedom: Carlos Montezuma, *Wassaja*, and the Society of American Indians," *American Indian Quarterly* 37, no. 3 (Summer 2013): 145.

3.   As of this writing I was unsuccessful at locating any information on Howard
      Hughes. However, he may have been a descendant of Samuel Hughes, one of
      the so-called pioneers who settled the Arizona Territory. See Thomas Edwin
      Farish, *History of Arizona*, vol. 2 (San Francisco: Filmer Brothers Electrotype,
      1915), 210–11.

4.   Timothy Braatz, *Surviving Conquest: A History of the Yavapai Peoples* (Lin-
      coln: University of Nebraska Press, 2003), 153. On this point, Braatz cites Mike
      Burns's unpublished manuscript held at Arizona State University's Hayden Li-
      brary, adding: "According to Burns, Motha's papers passed to Marshall Pete,
      who was later shot by Tonto Lewis. The papers were in Pete's clothing, and no
      one thought to remove them before his body was placed in his uwa [traditional
      Yavapai home] and burned" (263n24).

5.   The Yavapai communities did utilize the Indian Land Claims Commission to
      acquire monetary compensation for some of their lost lands. See The Yavapai
      and the Groups and 1 Bands Thereof, ex. Rel. Calloway Bonnaha, Harry Jones,
      Fred Beauty and Warren Gazzam; The Yavapai Apache Indian Community;
      The Fort McDowell Mohave Apache Community v. United States, 20 Ind Cl
      Comm 361 (1969), "Indian Claims Commission Decisions," Edmon Low Library,
      Oklahoma State University.

6.   Braatz, *Surviving Conquest*, 171. For more, see George Crook, *General George
      Crook: His Autobiography*, ed. Martin F. Schmitt (Norman: University of Okla-
      homa Press, 1986), 173–86.

7.   George Dickens to Dr. Carlos Montezuma, January 18, 1916, Box 4, Folder 2,
      Carlos Montezuma Collection, 1887–1980, Labriola National American Indian
      Data Center, Arizona State University Library. Ellipses indicate where the letter
      was torn.

8.   George Dickens to Dr. Carlos Montezuma, February 22, 1916, Box 4, Folder 2,
      Montezuma Collection, ASU Library.

9.   Secretary of the Interior, "Appropriation of Support of Indian Schools, Etc.,
      Fiscal Year 1916," House Committee on Indian Affairs. 64th Cong., 2nd Sess.
      (1916), 2.

10.   For more about George W. P. Hunt, see "Gov. George Wylie Hunt," National
      Governors Association, https://www.nga.org/governor/george-wylie-hunt/ (ac-
      cessed October 13, 2020).

11.   George Dickens to Dr. Carlos Montezuma, March 28, 1916, Box 4, Folder 2,
      Montezuma Collection, ASU Library.

12.   Harrison and Williams recount a story in which Gilbert Davis agreed to help
      move the Yavapai "out of the Fort McDowell reservation," but the story is dated
      1920. See Mike Harrison, John Williams, and Sigrid Khera, *Oral History of the
      Yavapai* (Tucson: University of Arizona Press, 2015), 160–61. Did Harrison and
      Williams add to the 1916 narrative on the Davises that Chief Dickens shared
      with Montezuma or did Harrison and Williams misremember when their story
      took place?

13. George Dickens to Dr. Carlos Montezuma, September 18, 1916, Box 4, Folder 2, Montezuma Collection, ASU Library. Parts of the letter are either illegible or damaged from decay.

14. Mike Burns to Dr Carlos Montezuma, May 12, 1916, Box 4, Folder 2, Montezuma Collection, ASU Library.

15. For more about Fort Mohave, see Alfred Louis Kroeber and Clifton B. Kroeber, *A Mohave War Reminiscence, 1854–1880* (New York: Dover, 1994). See also Kenneth M. Stewart, "Mohave," *Handbook of North American Indians*, ed. William C. Sturtevant, vol. 10, *Southwest*, ed. Alfonso Ortiz (Washington, D.C.: Smithsonian Institution, 1983), 55–70.

16. During this era of environmental crisis across large swathes of Arizona, it was typical of Indians to rely on cutting and selling mesquite wood when they could not grow anything due to the lack of irrigation water or the low availability of wage labor. David H. DeJong documented this survival industry among the Akimel O'odham in *Stealing the Gila: The Pima Agricultural Economy and Water Deprivation, 1848–1921* (Tucson: University of Arizona Press, 2009), 104–7.

17. Mike Burns to Dr. Carlos Montezuma, May 12, 1916, Box 4, Folder 2, Montezuma Collection, ASU Library. In a comparable episode, Luther Standing Bear recounts working a fence around the Pine Ridge Reservation in *My People the Sioux* (Lincoln: University of Nebraska Press, 1975), 242.

18. Mike Burns to Dr. Carlos Montezuma, August 11, 1916, Box 4, Folder 2, Montezuma Collection, ASU Library.

19. Carlos Montezuma, "Let My People Go," in *The American Indian Intellectual Tradition: An Anthology of Writings from 1772 to 1972*, ed. David Martínez (Ithaca, N.Y.: Cornell University Press, 2011), 208.

20. Montezuma, "Let My People Go," 207.

21. Mike Burns to Dr. Carlos Montezuma, November 6, 1916, Box 4, Folder 2, Montezuma Collection, ASU Library.

22. Charles Dickens to Dr. Carlos Montezuma, January 6, 1916, Box 4, Folder 2, Montezuma Collection, ASU Library.

23. Harrison, Williams, and Khera, *Oral History of the Yavapai*, 158.

24. Likely referring to Marvin B. Clark, who was listed as the Camp McDowell teacher in a 1911 Department of the Interior report, which noted the average attendance of 80 and Clark's annual salary of $720. See Walter L. Fisher, Secretary of the Interior, "Expenditures for Indian School Buildings, 1911," Committee on Expenditures in the Interior Department, House, 6324 H.R. Doc. 196 (1911), 6.

25. Charles Dickens to Dr. Carlos Montezuma, January 25, 1916, Box 4, Folder 2, Montezuma Collection, ASU Library.

26. Possibly a reference to George H. Morgan, who was a second lieutenant under the command of Al Sieber, Chief of Scouts for the U.S. Army. See Dan L. Thrapp, *Al Sieber, Chief of Scouts* (Norman: University of Oklahoma Press, 2012), Kindle. Morgan's name appears in chapter 15, "The Battle of Big Dry Wash."

27. Charles Dickens to Dr. Carlos Montezuma, January 30, 1916, Box 4, Folder 2, Montezuma Collection, ASU Library.

28. Charles Dickens to Dr. Carlos Montezuma, June 9, 1916, Box 4, Folder 2, Montezuma Collection, ASU Library.

29. Charles Dickens to Dr. Carlos Montezuma, July 21, 1916, Box 4, Folder 2, Montezuma Collection, ASU Library.

30. Thurma Dickens to Dr. Carlos Montezuma, March 27, 1916, Box 4, Folder 2, Montezuma Collection, ASU Library.

31. Thurma Dickens to Dr. Carlos Montezuma, August 2, 1916, Box 4, Folder 2, Montezuma Collection, ASU Library.

32. In the pages of *Wassaja*, William Leading Cloud is credited with the first use of the term "bureauism," which appeared in a letter dated April 20, 1916, and was published in vol. 1, no. 2 (May 1916): 4. For more on what *Wassaja* meant to its readers and subscribers, as evidenced in the letters published in *Wassaja*, see Rochelle Raineri Zuck, "'Yours in the Cause': Readers, Correspondents, and the Editorial Politics of Carlos Montezuma's *Wassaja*," *American Periodicals* 22, no. 1 (2012): 72–93.

33. Elias Boudinot, "An Address to the Whites," in *The American Indian Intellectual Tradition*, ed. Martínez, 41.

34. An infamous example of this was *The Indian and His Problem* by Francis E. Leupp (New York: Charles Scribner's Sons, 1910). Leupp served as commissioner of Indian Affairs 1904–1909 under President Theodore Roosevelt.

35. Vine Deloria Jr., *Custer Died for Your Sins: An Indian Manifesto* (1969; Norman: University of Oklahoma Press, 1988), 12.

36. Deloria, 12–13.

37. Deloria, 14.

38. Carlos Montezuma, "The Repression of the Indian," *Wassaja* 1, no. 2 (May 1916): 1, 2.

39. Carlos Montezuma, "Error Dominates the Indian Bureau and Indian Bureau Dominates Indians," *Wassaja* 1, no. 3 (June 1916): 2. With respect to saving American taxpayer dollars and Indian lives, George Copway made a comparable argument in his "Address Before Both Houses of the Legislature of South Carolina" (1848), in which he advocated for a northern Indian Territory where tribes from the Northern Great Plains could relocate for the purpose of developing a common government and economy that would save money and lives. See *The American Indian Intellectual Tradition*, ed. Martínez, 79–84.

40. Carlos Montezuma, "More Scare-Crows to Keep the Indian Dependent," *Wassaja* 1, no. 3 (June 1916): 4. Vine Deloria Jr. raises the issue of federal Indian myths in *Custer Died for Your Sins*, presenting these: "paternalism exists in the governmental area, assistance is always available in the private sector, and the tribes dwell in primitive splendor. All three myths are false" (13).

41. Montezuma, "The Church and the Indian," *Wassaja* 1, no. 4 (July 1916): 2. For Deloria's critique of federal Indian policy and the Christian tradition, see *Custer*

Died for Your Sins, 101–24, and *God Is Red: A Native View on Religion* (1973; Golden, Colo.: Fulcrum Publishing, 1992), 61–148.

42. Montezuma, "The Church and the Indian," 3.

43. Carlos Montezuma, "Indians and Indians," *Wassaja* 1, no. 6 (September 1916): 2.

44. Montezuma, "Indians and Indians," 3.

Chapter 4

1. In addition to Montezuma's much-cited speech "Let My People Go," see Arthur C. Parker, "The Legal Status of the American Indian" (1914); Charles A. Eastman, "The Indian as a Citizen" (1915); and Zitkala-Sa, "Americanize the First American," in *The American Indian Intellectual Tradition: An Anthology of Writings from 1772 to 1972*, ed. David Martínez (Ithaca, N.Y.: Cornell University Press, 2011), 198–202, 213–21, 222–24.

2. Letter to Dr. Carlos Montezuma, sent from Santan, Arizona, January 11, 1917, Box 4, Folder 3, Carlos Montezuma Collection, 1887–1980, Labriola National American Indian Data Center, Arizona State University Library. The letter is incomplete and does not contain a signature from the author. The place of origin suggests that the letter writer is from the Gila River Indian Community, District 4.

3. For more about the struggle for Pima water rights in Gila River Indian Community history, including references to the village of Santan, see David H. DeJong, *Stealing the Gila: The Pima Agricultural Economy and Water Deprivation, 1848–1921* (Tucson: University of Arizona Press, 2009).

4. Carlos Montezuma, "Fear Rules the Indians," *Wassaja* 1, no. 11 (February 1917): 2.

5. DeJong, *Stealing the Gila*, 117, 127, 129. For further analysis of the allotment policy implemented at the Gila River Indian Community, see Jennifer Bess, *Where the Red-Winged Blackbirds Sing: The Akimel O'odham and Cycles of Agricultural Transformation in the Phoenix Basin* (Boulder: University Press of Colorado, 2021), 123–49.

6. "Gibby" may have been a reference to George H. Gebby, who was assigned as the Presbyterian missionary for the "Mojave-Apache Indians." See Arthur Swazey et al., *The Interior* (n.p.: Western Presbyterian Publishing Company, 1913), 126.

7. The quoted amount was calculated using US Inflation Calculator: https://www.usinflationcalculator.com/ (accessed May 17, 2022).

8. For a historical analysis of the Phoenix Indian School, see Robert A. Trennert, *The Phoenix Indian School: Forced Assimilation in Arizona, 1891–1935* (Norman: University of Oklahoma Press, 1988).

9. George Dickens to Dr. Carlos Montezuma, May 14, 1917, Box 4, Folder 3, Montezuma Collection, ASU Library.

10. According to Vigil, "The Tomahawk Publishing Company was run by the Minnesota Chippewa from 1918 until 1926. The Tomahawk published articles about Indian citizenship, the administration of Indian affairs, and, in particular, spe-

cific issues related to Chippewa natural resources." See Kiara Vigil, *Indigenous Intellectuals: Sovereignty, Citizenship, and the American Imagination, 1880–1930* (New York: Cambridge University Press, 2015), 134.

11. Carlos Montezuma, "This Is Law," *Wassaja* 2, no. 8 (November 1917): 1.

12. For more see "U.S. Entry into World War I, 1917," Office of the Historian, United States Department of State, https://history.state.gov/milestones/1914-1920/wwi (accessed January 10, 2021).

13. Carlos Montezuma, "Drafting Indians and Justice," *Wassaja* 2, no. 7 (October 1917): 3. Stanciu observes, "Montezuma's writings in *Wassaja* . . . showed his readers the incongruence between the assimilation of foreigners and the perpetual relegation of Native people to a complicated political status of wards of the federal government." See Cristina Stanciu, "'Americanism for Indians': Carlos Montezuma's 'Immigrant Problem,' *Wassaja*, and the Limits of Native Activism," *Studies in American Indian Literatures* 33, nos. 1–2 (Spring–Summer 2021): 140.

14. See An Act to Provide for the Allotment of Lands in Severalty to Indians on the Various Reservations, and to Extend the Protection of the Laws of the United States and the Territories over the Indians, and for Other Purposes, 24 Stat. 388 (1887), section 6. The 1906 Burke Act amended section 6 of the 1887 Act and gave the Indian commissioner discretionary power to judge individual applicants for land patents to be either "competent" or "incompetent" to manage their own affairs. See An Act to Amend Section Six of an Act Approved February Eighth, Eighteen Hundred and Eighty-seven, Entitled "An Act to Provide for the Allotment of Lands in Severalty to Indians on the Various Reservations, and to Extend the Protection of the Laws of the United States and the Territories over the Indians, and for Other Purposes," 34 Stat. 182 (1906). The bill was introduced into the House of Representatives on February 21, 1906, by Congressman Charles H. Burke (R-S.Dak.) and was heard by the Committee on Indian Affairs.

15. The most significant example of this is the multiple treaties that the United States signed with Cherokee Nation, which were cited in *Cherokee Nation v. Georgia* (1831).

16. Montezuma, "Drafting Indians and Justice," 3.

17. See Treaty of Fort Laramie with the Crow, 15 Stat. 649 (1868).

18. Montezuma, "Drafting Indians and Justice," 4.

19. Joseph W. Latimer to Dr. Carlos Montezuma, September 23, 1918, Box 4, Folder 4, Montezuma Collection, ASU Library.

20. Julianne Newmark, "A Prescription for Freedom: Carlos Montezuma, *Wassaja*, and the Society of American Indians," *American Indian Quarterly* 37, no. 3 (Summer 2013): 140.

21. Carlos Montezuma, "Wassaja's Plea to the Indians," *Wassaja* 2, no. 10 (January 1918): 1.

22. Carlos Montezuma, "Carter's Bill," *Wassaja* 2, no. 11 (February 1918): 1. See also 65 HR 9253, 65th Cong., 2nd Sess. (1918).

23. Correspondence, *Wassaja* 2, no. 12 (March 1918): 2–4.

24. The distinction that Montezuma appears to be making to Thackery was between receiving payment for services rendered ("mercenary") and serving pro bono ("philanthropic"). Since Montezuma was never once afforded remuneration for his advocacy efforts on behalf of either the "Mohave Apaches" or the "Pimas," Montezuma made a valid argument, which Thackery clearly did not appreciate.

25. Carlos Montezuma, "The Indian Bureau Is Autocracy," *Wassaja* 3, no. 6 (September 1918): 1–2.

26. "Consideration," Legal Information Institute, Cornell Law School, https://www.law.cornell.edu/wex/consideration (accessed February 13, 2021).

27. Oscar Hiram Lipps, *Laws and Regulations Relating to Indians and Their Lands*, (n.p.: Lewiston, 1913), 52.

28. The developer in question was the Salt River Valley Water Users Association, founded in 1903, which became the Salt River Project (SRP). See "Salt River Project," American Folklife Center, Library of Congress, http://memory.loc.gov/diglib/legacies/loc.afc.afc-legacies.200002705/ (accessed December 17, 2021).

29. Montezuma, "The Indian Bureau Is Autocracy," 1–2.

30. For more, see "'The N*gger' in the Woodpile," Prints and Photographs Online Catalog, Library of Congress, https://www.loc.gov/pictures/item/2003674571/ (accessed March 21, 2021).

31. Carlos Montezuma, "Carlisle Misunderstood," *Wassaja* 3, no. 7 (October 1918): 3–4.

32. Carlos Montezuma, "Carlisle U.S. Indian School," *Wassaja* 3, no. 8 (November 1918): 3–4.

33. Carlos Montezuma, "The Duty of Every Indian Soldier Who Entered the War," *Wassaja* 3, no. 11 (February 1919): 1–2.

34. Carlos Montezuma, "In Regard to Attorneys for Indians," *Wassaja* 3, no. 11 (February 1919): 3.

35. Select Committee on Indian Affairs, To Provide for Allotment of Lands of Crow Indians in Montana, 66th Cong., 1st Sess. (1919).

36. See M. Kaye Tatro, "Curtis Act (1898)," in *The Encyclopedia of Oklahoma History and Culture*, Oklahoma Historical Society, https://www.okhistory.org/publications/enc/entry.php?entry=CU006 (accessed March 7, 2021).

37. Montezuma, "In Regard to Attorneys for Indians," 3.

38. Carlos Montezuma, "The Indian Bureau Sells Lands and Spends Indian Money Without the Approval of the Indians," *Wassaja* 3, no. 12 (March 1919): 3.

39. Carlos Montezuma, "Is It Legal?," *Wassaja* 4, no. 3 (June 1919): 1.

40. Carlos Montezuma, "Bleeding the Indians More," *Wassaja* 4, no. 4 (July 1919): 1.

41. Carlos Montezuma, "Gold Against the Indians' Rights and Justice," *Wassaja* 4, no. 5 (August 1919): 1. For more about the authority invested in the Secretary of the Interior, as of June 30, 1919, see Leases of Unallotted Mineral Lands Withdrawn from Entry Under Mining Laws, 25 U.S.C. §309.

42. An Act Granting Citizenship to Certain Indians, 66 HR 5007 (1919).
43. For more about the 1919 annual meeting of the Society of American Indians, see Hazel W. Hertzberg, *The Search for an American Indian Identity: Modern Pan-Indian Movements* (Syracuse: Syracuse University Press, 1971), 184–94. See also David Martínez, *Dakota Philosopher: Charles Eastman and American Indian Thought* (St. Paul: Minnesota Historical Society, 2009), 83–121.
44. Martínez, *Dakota Philosopher*, 111. With respect to the controversial issue of peyote and the Native American Church, see Hertzberg, *Search for an American Indian Identity*, 239–84, and Thomas C. Maroukis, *The Peyote Road: Religious Freedom and the Native American Church* (Norman: University of Oklahoma Press, 2010), 103–29.
45. Peter Iverson, *Carlos Montezuma and the Changing World of American Indians* (Albuquerque: University of New Mexico Press, 1982), 93–94.
46. Iverson, 149.
47. Carlos Montezuma, "Society of American Indians' Conference," *Wassaja* 4, no. 8 (November 1919): 4.
48. DeJong, *Stealing the Gila*, 168. As for the Lockwood Decree, this was the result of a case brought before the Superior Court of Arizona, *Lobb v. Avenente* (1916), in which 35,000 acres in the Florence area was prioritized for Pima water rights. See DeJong, 154, 222n52.
49. Little has been written about the impact of the Spanish Influenza on the Yavapai, other than a brief reference to its effect on the overall population. See Sigrid Khera and Patricia S. Mariella, "Yavapai," *Handbook of North American Indians*, ed. William C. Sturtevant, vol. 10, *Southwest*, ed. Alfonso Ortiz (Washington, D.C.: Smithsonian, 1983), 45. See also Committee on Indian Affairs, House, *Indians of the U.S.*, vol. 1: *Hearings*, 66th Cong., 1st Sess. (1919).
50. Jose Rice, a former student at Phoenix Indian School, was once noted as having visited a hospital around Memorial Day: "Jose Rice and his mother from McDowell were visitors at the hospital during the week to see Lupe Rice who has been sick with rheumatic fever. Jose was a school boy here seven years ago." See John B. Brown, *Native American*, June 15, 1915, 273.
51. Although the wife's name is unrecorded in the historical record, George Norton was likely the superintendent of the Mohawk Canal Project, who was a trusted friend of the Yavapai community, in particular those at Fort McDowell. See Timothy Braatz, *Surviving Conquest: A History of the Yavapai Peoples* (Lincoln: University of Nebraska Press, 2003), 201, 219.
52. Possibly a reference to Ovea Johnson, who is remembered as playing a role in the selection of Yuma Frank as Yavapai chief, in addition to being a signatory of a letter of petition to Indian Commissioner Cato Sells. See Mike Harrison, John Williams, and Sigrid Khera, *Oral History of the Yavapai* (Tucson: University of Arizona Press, 2015), 146, and Iverson, *Carlos Montezuma and the Changing World of American Indians*, 85.

53. In a 1929 House Committee on Indian Affairs report, Dogka was listed as a "private policeman" in the service of the Fort McDowell reservation. See *Survey of Conditions of the Indians in the United States: Hearings Before a Subcommittee of the Committee on Indian Affairs* (U.S. Government Printing Office, 1929), 8229. Dogka was also noted as one of the organizers of an annual Fourth of July celebration at Fort McDowell: "The Mohave-Apache Indians of Camp McDowell are planning for a big Fourth of July celebration on their reservation and are anxious to have the Indians from outside places with them at this time. Football and baseball games, horse races, foot races for boys, girls, and men, tug-o-war, and other sports are scheduled to take place. The arrangements are in charge of a committee of four composed of Charles Dickens, Dock Dogka, Thomas Surrama and James Star." See *Native American*, June 29, 1912, 389. As for Dogka's wife, her name is not recorded anywhere, at least not conclusively. Mabel Dogka was quoted as remembering how difficult it was for the Yavapai to sustain themselves economically during the late nineteenth century. See Braatz, *Surviving Conquest*, 214.

54. Charles Dickens to Dr. Carlos Montezuma, January 1, 1919, Box 4, Folder 5, Montezuma Collection, ASU Library.

55. According to the April 29, 1916, issue of the *Native American*: "Thomas Little Bison, Sioux, has been transferred as farmer from Fort Bidwell, California, to Salt River, Arizona, being assigned to the Lehi district" (165). Then, in the November 25, 1916, issue, it stated under Hospital Notes that "Mrs. Bison and two children are spending the week at the hospital. Mr. Bison, farmer at Lehi, is looking after the Lehi exhibit at the State Fair" (364). As for Little Bison's reputation, Iverson noted in his book on Indian cowboys that Indian agent and ranchman C. W. Crouse "not only clashed with the commissioner of Indian Affairs but also battled local government stockman Thomas Little Bison, who seemed to cause problems wherever he went, and others." See Peter Iverson, *When Indians Became Cowboys: Native Peoples and Cattle Ranching in the American West* (Norman: University of Oklahoma Press, 1994), 102–4.

56. Mike Burns to Dr. Carlos Montezuma, February 1, 1919, Box 4, Folder 5, Montezuma Collection, ASU Library.

57. No author, "Three Countries to Get Rich In," *Adventure*, 1921, 188. Did Little Bison misrepresent himself to the unnamed author of this article, calling himself an "Indian agent," as opposed to a "stockman"? Prior to the article cited here, Little Bison was the topic of a January 16, 1919, article in the *Bisbee Daily Review* bearing the headline "Indian Boosting Southern Project." The report noted that Little Bison had stopped in Phoenix, Arizona, before proceeding to Honduras, where "fortunes await those of small capital and large initiative." Little Bison was looking to interest people in investing in Honduran "rubber, beef and sugar" imports, which included supposedly inexpensive "fertile land" (4). See

Arizona Memory Project, https://azmemory.azlibrary.gov/digital/collection /sn84024827/id/52013/ (accessed November 20, 2020).

58. Thurma Dickens to Dr. Carlos Montezuma, February 19, 1919, Box 4, Folder 5, Montezuma Collection, ASU Library.

59. Dwight Campbell to Dr. Carlos Montezuma, February 20, 1919, Box 4, Folder 3, Montezuma Collection, ASU Library.

60. See Donald W. Meyers, "It Happened Here: Native American Advocate, Actor Nipo Strongheart Born in White Swan," *Yakima Herald-Republic*, February 25, 2019, https://www.yakimaherald.com/news/local/it-happened-here-native -american-advocate-actor-nipo-strongheart-born-in-white-swan/article_4658 b610-37c3-11e9-b585-db75711b7292.html (accessed July 5, 2020).

61. Brother Ben to Dr. Carlos Montezuma, February 21, 1919, Box 5, Folder 1, Montezuma Collection, ASU Library.

62. Charles Dickens to Dr. Carlos Montezuma, February 23, 1919, Box 4, Folder 5, Montezuma Collection, ASU Library.

63. Charles Dickens to Dr. Carlos Montezuma, February 26, 1919, Box 4, Folder 5, Montezuma Collection, ASU Library.

64. Mike Burns to Dr. Carlos Montezuma, March 11, 1919, Box 4, Folder 5, Montezuma Collection, ASU Library.

65. What became known as the "Osage Oil Murders" sparked a Congressional investigation, an Indian Rights Association report, and a variety of novels dramatizing events. See Oil Lands in Osage Reservation: Hearings on S. Com. Res. 4 (1916); Gertrude Bonnin, Charles H. Fabens, and Matthew K. Sniffen, "Oklahoma's Poor Rich Indians: An Orgy of Graft and Exploitation of the Five Civilized Tribes, Legalized Robbery" (n.p.: Office of the Indian Rights Association, 1924); John Joseph Mathews, *Sundown* (Norman: University of Oklahoma Press, 1988); Linda Hogan, *Mean Spirit* (New York: Ivy Books, 1990); Charles H. Red Corn, *A Pipe for February: A Novel* (Norman: University of Oklahoma Press, 2002).

66. Mike Burns to Dr. Carlos Montezuma, March 11, 1919, Box 4, Folder 5, Montezuma Collection, ASU Library.

67. Mike Burns to Dr. Carlos Montezuma, April 17, 1919, Box 4, Folder 5, Montezuma Collection, ASU Library.

68. Burns to Montezuma, April 17, 1919.

69. Joshua Russell to Dr. Carlos Montezuma, June 3, 1919, Box 4, Folder 5, Montezuma Collection, ASU Library.

70. Bess, *Where the Red-Winged Blackbirds Sing*, 135–38.

71. See *Indians of the United States: Hearings Before the Committee on Indian Affairs, House of Representatives, Sixty-sixth Congress, First Session, on the Condition of Various Tribes of Indians. Act of June 30, 1919* (U.S. Government Printing Office, 1920), 862–74.

72. George Dickens to Dr. Carlos Montezuma, September 8, 1919, Box 4, Folder 5, Montezuma Collection, ASU Library. In the upper left-hand corner is written a note: "Sept 15th 1919 Sent copy to E.B. Meritt [*sic*] Assist Com."

73. This is likely the Lowell Mason listed as one of two "informants" on a 1921 document at the Smithsonian Institution labeled "Revised Yavapai Vocabularies": https://sova.si.edu/record/NAA.MS2249BC?s=0&n=10&t=C&q=Yavapai&i=0 (accessed November 20, 2020).

74. George Dickens to Dr. Carlos Montezuma, December 7, 1919, Box 4, Folder 5, Montezuma Collection, ASU Library. Written in pen next to "Good Bye" is "Dec 21st 1919."

75. George Dickens to Dr. Carlos Montezuma, December 28, 1919, Box 4, Folder 5, Montezuma Collection, ASU Library.

76. Charles Dickens to Dr. Carlos Montezuma, May 2, 1919, Box 4, Folder 5, Montezuma Collection, ASU Library.

77. Charles Dickens to Dr. Carlos Montezuma, May 25, 1919, Box 4, Folder 5, Montezuma Collection, ASU Library. "June 21st 1919" is written vertically and perpendicularly to the May 25 date. It is unclear what this means, if anything.

78. Charles Dickens to Dr. Carlos Montezuma, July 10, 1919, Box 4, Folder 5, Montezuma Collection, ASU Library.

79. According to the *Martindale-Hubbell Law Directory*, P. H. Hayes was listed as a partner of the Hayes, Stanford, Walton, Allee & Williams firm of Phoenix, Arizona, which specialized in irrigation and mining cases. Hayes was admitted into the Arizona Bar in 1907 with a degree from the National Normal University (now closed) in Lebanon, Ohio. See *The Martindale-Hubbell Law Directory* (New York: Martindale-Hubbell Law Directory, 1932), 20.

80. Charles Dickens to Dr. Carlos Montezuma, August 4, 1919, Box 4, Folder 5, Montezuma Collection, ASU Library.

81. The issue of Indian federal ward status, precluding them from the privileges of state citizenship, would be a major concern for Indians exercising their right to vote once the 1924 Indian Citizenship Act was passed. See Laughlin McDonald, *American Indians and the Fight for Equal Voting Rights* (Norman: University of Oklahoma Press, 2010).

82. Carlos Montezuma, "State Game Laws," *Wassaja* 2, no. 9 (December 1917): 2.

83. Charles Dickens to Dr. Carlos Montezuma, August 26, 1919, Box 4, Folder 5, Montezuma Collection, ASU Library.

84. Charles Dickens to Dr. Carlos Montezuma, September 20, 1919, Box 4, Folder 5, Montezuma Collection, ASU Library.

85. For more on the role of cotton in the Arizona economy, see Thomas E. Sheridan, *Arizona: A History* (Tucson: University of Arizona Press, 2012), 211–33, and Bess, *Where the Red-Winged Blackbirds Sing*. For an account of the pre-WWII urban Indian experience in Phoenix, Arizona, see Anna Moore Shaw, *A Pima Past* (Tucson: University of Arizona Press, 1974).

86. Charles Dickens to Dr. Carlos Montezuma, December 2, 1919, Box 4, Folder 5, Montezuma Collection, ASU Library. About three lines above the signature, "Dec 6th 1919" is written over script.

87. Khera and Mariella, "Yavapai," 43.

88.   Charles Dickens to Dr. Carlos Montezuma, December 15, 1919, Box 4, Folder 5, Montezuma Collection, ASU Library. Written in pen just below the return city and date is "Dec 19th 1919."

89.   Iverson, *Carlos Montezuma and the Changing World of American Indians*, 32.

90.   "President Woodrow Wilson's Fourteen Points," Avalon Project, Lillian Goldman Law Library, Yale Law School, https://avalon.law.yale.edu/20th_century /wilson14.asp (accessed July 31, 2021).

91.   Maurice Crandall, *These People Have Always Been a Republic: Indigenous Electorates in the U.S.-Mexico Borderlands, 1598–1912* (Chapel Hill: University of North Carolina Press, 2019), 8. It is worth noting that Crandall makes only a handful of fleeting references to Montezuma and the Yavapai in this volume. See pages 1, 215, 278, 281, 283, 289, 337n1, 337n188, 338n11.

Chapter 5

1.   Hazel W. Hertzberg, *The Search for an American Indian Identity: Modern Pan-Indian Movements* (Syracuse: Syracuse University Press, 1971), 179–209.

2.   Citizenship Act, 66 PL 75; 41 Stat. 350, Chap. 95; 66 Enacted HR 5007 (November 6, 1919).

3.   There have been numerous studies on alcoholism, Prohibition, public policy, and the law, too many to summarize here. With respect to the relation between Prohibition and American Indians, however, see William E. Unrau, *White Man's Wicked Water: The Alcohol Trade and Prohibition in Indian Country, 1802–1892* (Lawrence: University Press of Kansas, 1996), and Thomas J. Lappas, *In League Against King Alcohol: Native American Women and the Woman's Christian Temperance Union, 1874–1933* (Norman: University of Oklahoma Press, 2020). Also of interest are Lisa McGirr, *The War on Alcohol: Prohibition and the Rise of the American State* (New York: Norton, 2015), and Sean Beienberg, *Prohibition, the Constitution, and States' Rights* (Chicago: University of Chicago Press, 2019).

4.   Ben Buffalo to Dr. Carlos Montezuma, February 19, 1920, Box 5, Folder 1, Carlos Montezuma Collection, 1887–1980, Labriola National American Indian Data Center, Arizona State University Library.

5.   Wanda Shirt to Dr. Carlos Montezuma, March 20, 1920, Box 5, Folder 1, Montezuma Collection, ASU Library.

6.   Wanda Short, "On, Straight On to Freedom," *Wassaja* 4, no. 10 (January 1920): 4.

7.   Carlos Montezuma, "Leasing 30,000,000 Acres of Indian Mining Land," *Wassaja* 4, no. 10 (January 1920): 3–4.

8.   Joe Easchief was likely also known as "Jose Easchief," who was one of dozens of persons listed in a petition dated June 25, 1911 that was sent to the "United States Government to allow them to hold the whole amount of land on which they live, and which has been set aside for their home, and while it is their wish to be perfectly fair and just to the Government, they strongly protest against having any of the land from the resources of which they must earn their living taken from them." This petition was written by Larisco Hill. See "Memorial in

Re-Investigation of Pima Indians, Arizona," Native American Water Rights, http://water.library.arizona.edu/body.1_div.36.html (accessed March 8, 2021).

9. Joe Easchief to Dr. Carlos Montezuma, June 15, 1920, Box 5, Folder 1, Montezuma Collection, ASU Library.

10. John Hunter to Dr. Carlos Montezuma, June 29, 1920, Box 5, Folder 1, Montezuma Collection, ASU Library. Written in ink immediately below the postscript is "July 8th 1920." If the "Mr. Pierce" mentioned in this letter was Charles F. Pierce, he was the superintendent of Indian Schools under Indian Commissioner Cato Sells.

11. Nellie H. David was listed as a "housekeeper" in a 1911 issue of the *Native American*, the newspaper for the Phoenix Indian School, which meant that David was also a student. See *Native American*, "Changes in Indian Service Employees for the Months of Nov., Dec., 1910," March 25, 1911, 168. David was also listed as "Nellie H. Davis" in a 1920 House Committee on Indian Affairs investigation into the field service, in which "Davis" served for "6 mos." as "Housekeeping assistant" at the San Carlos Agency. See Committee on Indian Affairs, House, *Indians of the U.S.*, vol 3: *Investigation of the Field Service*, 66th Cong., 2nd Sess. (1920), 976.

12. In the same House Committee on Indian Affairs document that noted "Davis" as a "Housekeeping assistant," Merritt was incorrectly acknowledged as "Commissioner of Indian Affairs." Merritt served as assistant commissioner of Indian Affairs under Cato Sells. See *Indians of the U.S.*, 3:885.

13. The name of the physician listed in the same *Investigation of the Field Service* was "Dr. E. C. Williams," who served at San Carlos for two years (*Indians of the U.S.*, 3:977). The name "Ferrel" or "Ferrell" was nowhere to be found in this or any other government document listing San Carlos Agency employees.

14. For more about the history of wagon roads in Arizona, see "Good Roads Everywhere: A History of Road Building in Arizona," Arizona Department of Transportation, March 2004, https://azdot.gov/sites/default/files/2019/07/cultural_good_roads_everywhere.pdf (accessed November 25, 2020); see also "Arizona Transportation History," Arizona Department of Transportation, December 2011, http://www.ansac.az.gov/UserFiles/PDF/02032016/C040-EngelmanBergerCities%20Supplement/Arizona%20Transportation%20History%20Final%20Report%20660%20December%202011%20(00650539xB0704).PDF (accessed November 25, 2020).

15. Hazzarner does not exist anywhere in the historical record. It could be a phonetic spelling for another name, such as Hasner or Hefner. Other than the reference to San Carlos, David did not indicate clearly if this person was Indian or non-Indian, or if he was in the employ of the San Carlos Agency.

16. Nellie H. David to Dr. Carlos Montezuma, July 5, 1920, Box 5, Folder 1, Montezuma Collection, ASU Library.

17. Parker is listed as a member of the Chicago Historical Society. See their *Charter, Constitution, By-laws, Membership List, Annual Report* ([Chicago?]: The Society, 1913), 117. Parker is also credited as the recipient of numerous letters in re-

sponse to his interest in "individual remembrances of the Battle of Sharpsburg in Maryland, more commonly known as Antietam." See "Series 15: R.D. Parker, Civilian, 1896–1901—31 Letters," American Civil War Documents, Manuscripts, Letters and Diaries and Grand Army of the Republic Collections, Chicago Public Library, https://www.chipublib.org/fa-american-civil-war-documents-manu scripts-letters-and-diaries-and-grand-army-of-the-republic-collection/#P1S15 (accessed November 25, 2020).

18. Meyers is likely the "Leta V. Meyers Smart (Omaha)" in *Changing Is Not Vanishing: A Collection of American Indian Poetry to 1930*, ed. Robert Dale Parker (Philadelphia: University of Pennsylvania Press, 2011), 305–10.

19. Wheeler is mentioned only once in the Montezuma Collection archives and nowhere in the scholarly sources.

20. According to the Masonic Lodge, the acronym stands for "Ancient Free and Accepted Masons." See "AF and AM vs F and AM States," Masonic Lodge of Education, https://www.masonic-lodge-of-education.com/af-and-am-vs-f-and -am-states.html (accessed November 25, 2020).

21. R. D. Parker to Dr. Carlos Montezuma, July 14, 1920, Box 5, Folder 1, Montezuma Collection, ASU Library.

22. George Dickens to Dr. Carlos Montezuma, January 18, 1920, Box 5, Folder 1, Montezuma Collection, ASU Library.

23. George Dickens to Dr. Carlos Montezuma, July 14, 1920, Box 5, Folder 1, Montezuma Collection, ASU Library. Written on the back of the one-page letter are nine lines of shorthand.

24. George Dickens to Dr. Carlos Montezuma, September 14, 1920, Box 5, Folder 1, Montezuma Collection, ASU Library. Written in ink right below the signature is "sept. 19th 1920."

25. Carlos Montezuma, "Superintendent Sharp and Dr. Montezuma," *Wassaja* 5, no. 7 (October 1920): 1–3.

26. Charles Dickens to Dr. Carlos Montezuma, January 6, 1920, Box 5, Folder 1, Montezuma Collection, ASU Library.

27. Charles Dickens to Dr. Carlos Montezuma, January 16, 1920, Box 5, Folder 1, Montezuma Collection, ASU Library. Written in pen immediately below the signature is "Jan. 19th 1920."

28. Charles Dickens to Dr. Carlos Montezuma, February 17, 1920, Box 5, Folder 1, Montezuma Collection, ASU Library. Written in pen immediately below the cited date is "March 21st 1920."

29. Charles Dickens to Dr. Carlos Montezuma, August 30, 1920, Box 5, Folder 1, Montezuma Collection, ASU Library.

30. Montezuma, "Superintendent Sharp and Dr. Montezuma," 1.

31. Charles Dickens to Dr. Carlos Montezuma, September 13, 1920, Box 5, Folder 1, Montezuma Collection, ASU Library. Written in ink at the very top of the first page is "Sept. 19th 1920."

32. Burns was referring to Thomas Edwin Farish, the author of *History of Arizona*, vol. 2 (San Francisco: Filmer Brothers Electrotype, 1915).

33. Mike Burns to Dr. Carlos Montezuma, February 19, 1920, Box 5, Folder 1, Montezuma Collection, ASU Library.

34. For Burns's manuscript, see Mike Burns (Hoomothya) Papers, SHM MS-8, 1881–2010, Sharlot Hall Museum Library and Archives, Prescott, Arizona, http://www.azarchivesonline.org/xtf/view?docId=ead/sharlot/Burns_Mike_Hoomothya_Papers_SHM_MS-8.xml&doc.view=print;chunk.id=0 (accessed August 1, 2021); for published editions, see Mike Burns, *The Journey of a Yavapai Indian: A 19th Century Odyssey* (Princeton, N.J.: Elizabeth House, 2002), and *The Only One Living to Tell: The Autobiography of a Yavapai Indian* (Tucson: University of Arizona Press, 2012).

Chapter 6

1. John Baum is referenced as an allotting agent in *Indian Water Rights of the Five Central Tribes of Arizona: Hearings Before the Committee on Interior and Insular Affairs, United States Senate, Ninety-fourth Congress, First Session . . . October 23 and 24, 1975* (U.S. Government Printing Office, 1976), 56, 365.

2. Carlos Montezuma, "Horse Meat as Food for Man," *Wassaja* 6, no. 1 (April 1921): 3.

3. Nellie Davis [David] to Dr. Carlos Montezuma, February 12, 1921, Box 5, Folder 1, Carlos Montezuma Collection, 1887–1980, Labriola National American Indian Data Center, Arizona State University Library. Stamped over the original date is "FEB 21 1921." The anthropologist in question was Frances Densmore. According to the Smithsonian Institution, "In April, 1920, Miss Densmore visited the 'Mohave' Apaches living at Camp MacDowell [*sic*] near Phoenix, Ariz., with a view to recording songs among them next season, taking the Apache as the representatives of the Athapascan stock." See *Annual Report of the Board of Regents of the Smithsonian Institution 1920* (U.S. Government Printing Office, 1922), 66. Noteworthy in this context is Natalie Curtis, who wrote about the "Mohave Apache" in *The Indians' Book: An Offering by the American Indians of Indian Lore, Musical and Narrative, to Form a Record of the Songs and Legends of Their Race* (New York: Harper and Brothers, 1907). Curtis also published a 1919 article titled "The Winning of an Indian Reservation: How Theodore Roosevelt and Frank Mead Restored the Mohave-Apaches to Their Own" (*Outlook*, June 25, 1919, 327–30).

4. The Kent Decree refers to *Hurley v. Abbott*, Arizona Territorial Court, Cause No. 4564 (March 1, 1910); see Salt River Pima-Maricopa Indian Community Water Rights Settlement Agreement (February 12, 1988), Pub. L. 100–512, Oct. 20, 1988, 102 Stat. 2549., ¶ 7.0.

5. Dr. Carlos Montezuma to Mike Burns, March 24, 1921, Box 5, Folder 1, Montezuma Collection, ASU Library.

6. Carlos Montezuma, "Indian Has No Rights Whatsoever," *Wassaja* 5, no. 12 (March 1921): 1–2. Merritt was referring to An Act Relating to Rights of Way Through Certain Parks, Reservations, and Other Public Lands, 31 Stat. 790 (1901). The reference to Indian reservations is fleeting, appearing exactly once in the provision that reads, regarding permit approvals: "That such permits shall be allowed within or through any of said parks or any forest, military, Indian, or other reservation only upon approval of the chief office of the Department under whose supervision such park or reservation falls and upon a finding by him that the same is not incompatible with the public interest."

7. See An Act to Amend Section Six of an Act Approved February Eighth, Eighteen Hundred and Eighty-seven, Entitled "An Act to Provide for the Allotment of Lands in Severalty to Indians on the Various Reservations, and to Extend the Protection of the Laws of the United States and the Territories over the Indians, and for Other Purposes," (PL 59–149; 34 Stat. 182, 1906). Provided in this amendment is the statement "That the Secretary of the Interior may, in his discretion, and he is hereby authorized, whenever he shall be satisfied that any Indian allottee is competent and capable of managing his or her affairs at any time to cause to be issued to such allottee a patent in fee simple."

8. Carlos Montezuma, "The Commissioner of Indian Affairs," *Wassaja* 6, no. 1 (April 1921): 4.

9. Joseph W. Latimer, "Exposure and Injustices on McDowell Agency, Arizona," *Wassaja* 6, no. 2 (May 1921): 1–3.

10. Latimer, 3–4.

11. Joseph W. Latimer, "Brief History of Camp McDowell Indian Reservation," *Wassaja* 6, no. 3 (June 1921): 1–2.

12. Letter from Assistant Commissioner [Merritt] to Thomas L. Sloan, *Wassaja* 6, no. 3 (June 1921): 2–3.

13. Letter from Joseph W. Latimer to Albert H. Burke, *Wassaja* 6, no. 3 (June 1921): 3–4.

14. Letter from Joseph W. Latimer to Albert B. Fall, *Wassaja* 6, no. 4 (July 1921): 1–2.

15. Joseph W. Latimer, ed., *The Rape of McDowell Reservation, Arizona, by the Indian Bureau* (Washington, D.C.: Hayworth Publishing House, 1921), Box 13, Folder 4, Montezuma Collection, ASU Library.

16. Joseph W. Latimer, et al., "Evils of Indian Bureau System," *Wassaja* 8, no. 2 (February 1922): 3–4.

17. Joseph W. Latimer, et al., "Evils of Indian Bureau System," *Wassaja* 8, no. 3 (March 1922): 1–2. The description of Kelly comes from the previous issue, page 4.

18. Carlos Montezuma, "Hon. Carl Hayden of Arizona," *Wassaja* 8, no. 4 (April 1922): 1–2.

19. See Jack L. August Jr., "Carl Hayden: Born a Politician," *Journal of Arizona History* 26, no. 2 (Summer 1985): 117–44.

20. Diversion Dam on the Gila River at a Site Above Florence, Ariz.: Hearing Before the Committee on Indian Affairs, United States Senate, 64th Cong., 2nd Sess. (1917). See Carl Hayden's comments.

21. See David H. DeJong, "An Equal Chance? The Pima Indians and the 1916 Florence-Casa Grande Irrigation Project," *Journal of Arizona History* 45, no. 1 (Spring 2004): 63–102.

22. For a comprehensive survey of the site, see the Moore/Swick Partnership, "Hayden Butte Preserve: Management Plan," City of Tempe, Ariz., May 2017.

23. Charles H. Burke, Annual Report of the Commissioner of Indian Affairs, 1920, 85.

24. Joseph W. Latimer, *Our Indian Bureau System: A Summary and a Remedy in Three Chapters* (New York: 1923), 7.

25. Senate Subcommittee on S. Res. 79, Committee on Indian Affairs, Senate, *Survey of Conditions of the Indians in the United States*, part 10, *Flathead Reservation, Mont.* (U.S. Government Printing Office, 1930), 3519–26.

26. Mike Harrison, John Williams, and Sigrid Khera, *Oral History of the Yavapai* (Tucson: University of Arizona Press, 2015), 106.

Chapter 7

1. Carlos Montezuma, "Light on the Indian Situation," *Quarterly Journal of the Society of American Indians* 1, no. 1 (April 15, 1913): 51.

2. Montezuma, 53.

3. Carlos Montezuma, "Hon. Carl Hayden of Arizona," *Wassaja* 8, no. 4 (April 1922): 2.

4. Leon Speroff, *Carlos Montezuma, M.D.: A Yavapai American Hero: The Life and Times of an American Indian, 1866–1923* (Portland, Ore.: Arnica Publishing, 2003), 258.

5. Speroff, 285. Speroff cites for Dickens's letter, Larner, J.W., Jr. The Papers of Carlos Montezuma, Microfilm Edition, *Scholarly Resources, Inc., Wilmington, Delaware*, 1984, Reel 2.

6. Carlos Montezuma, "The Indian Problem from an Indian's Standpoint," in United States Commissioner of Education, *Annual Reports of the Department of the Interior for the Fiscal Year Ended June 30, 1897: Report of the Commissioner of Education*, vol. 2 (Washington, D.C.: Government Printing Office, 1898), 1521.

7. Carlos Montezuma, "Let My People Go," in *The American Indian Intellectual Tradition: An Anthology of Writings from 1772 to 1972*, ed. David Martínez (Ithaca, N.Y.: Cornell University Press, 2011), 203–12.

8. President Theodore Roosevelt, Executive Order, September 15, 1903; see American Presidency Project, https://www.presidency.ucsb.edu/node/206264 (accessed May 1, 2022).

9. Edward H. Spicer, *Cycles of Conquest: The Impact of Spain, Mexico, and the United States on the Indians of the Southwest, 1533–1960* (Tucson: University of Arizona Press, 1962), 150.

10. Spicer, *Cycles of Conquest*, 141.

11. Carlos Montezuma, "The Indian Bureau," *Wassaja* 3, no. 12 (March 1919): 3.

12. Anonymous, letter, *Wassaja* 4, no. 11 (February 1920): 2. Lewis D. Nelson was from Casa Blanca, Gila River Indian Community, and he regularly represented the Pima on behalf of their land and water rights.

13. Spicer, *Cycles of Conquest*, 530–31.

14. See Hazel W. Hertzberg, *The Search for an American Indian Identity: Modern Pan-Indian Movements* (Syracuse: Syracuse University Press, 1971), 44–45, 197.

15. Letter to Montezuma, *Wassaja* 2, no. 12 (March 1918): 2.

16. Hertzberg, *Search for an American Indian Identity*, 45. Hertzberg is referencing Spicer's work, in which the "tribal deity" was I'itoi, an O'odham cultural hero.

17. Spicer, *Cycles of Conquest*, 531.

18. William R. Coffeen, "The Effects of the Central Arizona Project on the Fort McDowell Indian Community," *Ethnohistory* 19, no. 4 (Autumn 1972): 352. The first instance in which Coffeen mentioned Montezuma is while quoting an observation on a missionary's successful work at turning the Yavapai into "good farmers" (351).

19. Sue Abbey Chamberlain, "The Fort McDowell Indian Reservation: Water Rights and Indian Removal, 1910–1930," *Journal of the West* 14, no. 4 (October 1975): 32.

20. To read more about some of Montezuma's peers, see Margot Liberty, ed., *American Indian Intellectuals of the Nineteenth and Early Twentieth Centuries* (1978; Norman: University of Oklahoma Press, 2002).

21. See, for example, Francis Paul Prucha, *American Indian Policy in Crisis: Christian Reformers and the Indian, 1865–1900* (Norman: University of Oklahoma Press, 2014).

22. Sigrid Khera and Patricia S. Mariella, "Yavapai," *Handbook of North American Indians*, ed. William C. Sturtevant, vol. 10, *Southwest*, ed. Alfonso Ortiz (Washington, D.C.: Smithsonian Institution, 1983), 42. Similar to other sources mentioning Montezuma's advocacy work for Fort McDowell, Khera and Mariella's article also includes a brief summary of his life and career. They make a point of noting that Montezuma "was a full-blood Yavapai" (42).

23. For the brief references to Montezuma, see L. G. Moses and Raymond Wilson, eds., *Indian Lives: Essays on Nineteenth- and Twentieth-Century Native American Leaders* (Albuquerque: University of New Mexico Press, 1985), 62, 154, 170. See also Raymond Wilson, *Ohiyesa: Charles Eastman, Santee Sioux* (Urbana-Champaign: University of Illinois Press, 1983), 152–56, 160–62, 170–71, 189.

24. For chapters relevant to Montezuma's era, see R. David Edmunds, ed., *The New Warriors: Native American Leaders Since 1900* (Lincoln: University of Nebraska Press, 2001).

25. Timothy Braatz, *Surviving Conquest: A History of the Yavapai Peoples* (Lincoln: University of Nebraska Press, 2003), 223–24.

26. Speroff, *Carlos Montezuma, M.D.*, 258–331.

27. Speroff, 331.

28. Mike Burns to Dr. Carlos Montezuma, July 16, 1913, Box 3, Folder 5, Carlos Montezuma Collection, 1887–1980, Labriola National American Indian Data

Center, Arizona State University Library. Burns made a similar statement in a letter to Montezuma dated June 29, 1913.

29. Mike Burns to Dr. Carlos Montezuma, July 7, 1914, Box 3, Folder 6, Montezuma Collection, ASU Library.

30. Peter Iverson, *Carlos Montezuma and the Changing World of American Indians* (Albuquerque: University of New Mexico Press, 1982), 121.

31. Montezuma's notes for an autobiographical speech, Box 6, Folder 21, Montezuma Collection, ASU Library.

32. Iverson, *Carlos Montezuma and the Changing World of American Indians*, 121, 130.

33. For a Yavapai synonymy, see Khera and Mariella, "Yavapai," 53.

34. Speroff, *Carlos Montezuma, M.D.*, 258–331. Speroff visited the Fort McDowell Yavapai Reservation for his research and interviewed some of Montezuma's descendants and other community members. Thus one can claim that in his emphasis on Montezuma's renewed kinship ties, Speroff, like Spicer, exposed his research findings to the way the Indigenous community remembered Montezuma, as opposed to relying only on the archival record.

35. Carlos Montezuma, "Let My People Go," in *The American Indian Intellectual Tradition: An Anthology of Writings from 1772 to 1972*, ed. David Martínez (Ithaca, N.Y.: Cornell University Press, 2011), 203, 204.

36. See Iverson, *Carlos Montezuma and the Changing World of American Indians*, 5, 175; and Speroff, *Carlos Montezuma, M.D.*, 441.

37. E. L. B., "Things Past," review of *A Pima Remembers* by George Webb, *New York Times*, October 11, 1959, 36.

38. George Webb, *A Pima Remembers* (Tucson: University of Arizona Press, 1959), 30.

39. Webb, 30–33.

40. Frank Russell, *The Pima Indians* (Washington, D.C.: Government Printing Office, 1908), 356.

41. Russell, 55.

42. C. H. Southworth, "A Pima Calendar Stick," *Arizona Historical Review* 4 (1931–1932): 48.

43. Kay M. Sands, review of *A Pima Past* by Anna Moore Shaw, *Studies in American Indian Literatures* 5, no. 1 (Winter 1981): 3.

44. W. David Laird, review of *A Pima Past* by Anna Moore Shaw, *Arizona and the West* 17, no. 2 (Summer 1975): 178.

45. Anna Moore Shaw, *A Pima Past* (Tucson: University of Arizona Press, 1974), 237.

46. For more about Russell "Big Chief" Moore, see David Martínez, "Living Large During the Jazz Age: 'Big Chief' Russell Moore, Pima Memories, and the Changing Roles of American Indians in the 20th Century," *Journal of Arizona History* 55, no. 2 (Summer 2014): 127–44.

47. Speroff, *Carlos Montezuma, M.D.*, 437.

48. Shaw, *A Pima Past*, 162–63.

49. Shaw, *A Pima Past*, 163.

50. Shaw, *A Pima Past* 163.

51. Shaw, *A Pima Past*, 166.

52. Shaw, 63. For more on Antonio Azul, see Charles H. Cook and Isaac T. Whittmore, *Among the Pima, or The Mission to the Pima and Maricopa Indians* (Albany, N.Y.: Ladies' Union Mission School Association, 1893). See also Robert A. Trennert, "John H. Stout and the Grant Peace Policy Among the Pimas," *Journal of the Southwest* 28, no. 1 (Spring 1986): 45–68. By David H. DeJong, see "Forced to Abandon Their Farms: Water Deprivation and Starvation among the Gila River Pima, 1892–1904," *American Indian Culture and Research Journal* 28, no. 3 (2004): 29–56; "'Good Samaritans of the Desert': The Pima-Maricopa Villages as Described in California Emigrant Journals, 1846–1852," *Journal of the Southwest* 47, no. 3 (Autumn 2005): 457–96; and "'Left High and Dry': Federal Land Policies and Pima Agriculture, 1860–1910," *American Indian Culture and Research Journal* 33, no. 1 (2009): 23–45.

53. Shaw, *A Pima Past*, 238.

54. For Montezuma's own account of his well-known abduction by Pima raiders, see Carlos Montezuma, *The Indian of Yesterday: The Early Life of Dr. Carlos Montezuma Written by Himself* (Chicago: National Christian Women's Temperance Union, 1888), no pagination.

55. Shaw, *A Pima Past*, 238–39.

56. Shaw, 239. For more on how Pimas treated captives and a note on Montezuma's capture recorded on a history stick, see Frank Russell, *The Pima Indians*, re-edition, ed. Bernard L. Fontana (Tucson: University of Arizona Press, 1975), 55, 197.

57. Montezuma, "Indian Problem from an Indian's Standpoint," 1521. An editorial note states that this article first appeared as "an address delivered before the Fortnightly Club, of Chicago."

58. Shaw, *A Pima Past*, 239, 243–44.

59. See Iverson, *Carlos Montezuma and the Changing World of American Indians*, 31–45, and Speroff, *Carlos Montezuma, M.D.*, 175–205.

60. Speroff spent a considerable amount of time recounting Montezuma's relationship with Zitkala-Sa, as fellow progressive and as the object of his affection. See *Carlos Montezuma, M.D.*, 206–46.

61. Shaw, *A Pima Past*, 246. See also Iverson, *Carlos Montezuma and the Changing World of American Indians*, 164–65.

62. Shaw, *A Pima Past*, 247–48.

63. See Martínez, ed., *American Indian Intellectual Tradition*, 203–12.

64. See Thomas E. Sheridan, "The Other Arizona," *Journal of the Southwest* 36, no. 3 (Autumn 1994): 255–86.

Conclusion

1. Mike Burns, quoted in Maurice Crandall, "Wassaja Comes Home: A Yavapai Perspective on Carlos Montezuma's Search for Identity," *Journal of Arizona History* 55, no. 1 (Spring 2014): 8.

Works Cited

Archive Collections

Accession Records of the Labriola National American Indian Data Center. Arizona State University Library. http://azarchivesonline.org/xtf/view?docId=ead/asu/labriolacenter.xml.

Arizona Historical Digital Newspapers. Arizona Memory Project. https://azmemory.azlibrary.gov/digital/custom/newspapers.

Arizona State University Library Digital Repository. https://repository.asu.edu/.

Barnes, William Croft. Papers, 1878–1945. Manuscript Collections Finding Aids. Arizona Historical Society Library and Archives. https://arizonahistoricalsociety.org/wp-content/uploads/2019/02/library_Barnes-William-Croft.pdf.

Carlos Montezuma Collection, 1887–1980. Labriola National American Indian Data Center. Arizona State University Library.

Carlos Montezuma Guide to Collections. American Indian Studies, Arizona State University Library. https://libguides.asu.edu/c.php?g=263762&p=1765040.

Carlos Montezuma's Wassaja Newsletter. https://repository.asu.edu/collections/195.

Carlos Montezuma's Wassaja Newsletter: Access, Engagement, and Collaboration. Digital Repository, Arizona State University Library. https://repository.asu.edu/items/44713.

"Inventory of the Carlos Montezuma Papers, 1888–1936, Bulk 1888–1922." Newberry Library, Chicago, Illinois. https://mms.newberry.org/xml/xml_files/montezuma.xml.

"Kapplers." Oklahoma State Library, Oklahoma State University. https://dc.library.okstate.edu/digital/collection/kapplers.

Kenneth Stewart Papers, 1946–1981. Arizona State University Library. http://azarchivesonline.org/xtf/view?docId=ead/asu/stewart.xml.

Larner, J. W. Jr., ed. *Guide to the Scholarly Resources Microfilm Edition of the Papers of Carlos Montezuma, M.D.* Wilmington, Del.: Scholarly Resources, 1984. https://swcenter.fortlewis.edu/finding_aids/inventory/MontezMflmGuide.pdf.

Larner, J. W. Jr., ed. *The Papers of Carlos Montezuma.* Microfilm edition. Wilmington, Del.: Scholarly Resources, 1984.

Mike Burns (Hoomothya) Papers, SHM MS-8, 1881–2010 (Bulk Dates 1923–2010). Sharlot Hall Museum Library and Archives, Prescott, Arizona. http://www.az archivesonline.org/xtf/view?docId=ead/sharlot/Burns_Mike_Hoomothya_Papers _SHM_MS-8.xml&doc.view=print;chunk.id=0.

Wassaja: A Carlos Montezuma Project http://wassaja.lib.asu.edu/.

The Yavapai and the Groups and 1 Bands Thereof, ex rel Calloway Bonnaha, Harry Jones, Fred Beauty and Warren Gazzam; The Yavapai Apache Indian Community; The Fort McDowell Mohave Apache Community v. United States, 20 Ind Cl Comm 361 (1969). "Indian Claims Commission Decisions," Edmon Low Library, Oklahoma State University.

Books

Arnold, Adele R. *Red Son Rising.* Minneapolis: Dillon Press, 1974.

Arnold, Oren. *Savage Son.* Albuquerque: University of New Mexico Press, 1951.

Berman, David R. *George Hunt: Arizona's Crusading Seven-Term Governor.* Tucson: University of Arizona Press, 2015.

Bess, Jennifer. *Where the Red-Winged Blackbirds Sing: The Akimel O'odham and Cycles of Agricultural Transformation in the Phoenix Basin.* Boulder: University Press of Colorado, 2021.

Bonnin, Gertrude, Charles H. Fabens, and Matthew K. Sniffen. "Oklahoma's Poor Rich Indians: An Orgy of Graft and Exploitation of the Five Civilized Tribes, Legalized Robbery." N.p.: Office of the Indian Rights Association, 1924.

Braatz, Timothy. *Surviving Conquest: A History of the Yavapai Peoples.* Lincoln: University of Nebraska Press, 2003.

Bruyneel, Kevin. *The Third Space of Sovereignty: The Postcolonial Politics of U.S.-Indigenous Relations.* Minneapolis: University of Minnesota Press, 2007.

Burns, Mike. *All of My People Were Killed: The Memoir of Mike Burns (Hoomothya), a Captive Indian.* Prescott, Ariz.: Sharlot Hall Museum, 2010.

Burns, Mike. *The Journey of a Yavapai Indian: A 19th Century Odyssey.* Princeton, N.J.: Elizabeth House, 2002.

Burns, Mike. *The Only One Living to Tell: The Autobiography of a Yavapai Indian.* Tucson: University of Arizona Press, 2012.

Burroughs, William S. *The Place of Dead Roads: A Novel.* New York: Holt, Rinehart and Winston, 1983.

Capaldi, Gina. *A Boy Named Beckoning: The True Story of Dr. Carlos Montezuma, Native American Hero.* Minneapolis: Carolrhoda Books, 2008.

Chicago Historical Society, *Charter, Constitution, By-laws, Membership List, Annual Report.* [Chicago?]: The Society, 1913.

Cook, Charles H., and Isaac T. Whittmore. *Among the Pima, or The Mission to the Pima and Maricopa Indians*. Albany, N.Y.: Ladies' Union Mission School Association, 1893.

Crandall, Maurice. *These People Have Always Been a Republic: Indigenous Electorates in the U.S.-Mexico Borderlands, 1598–1912*. Chapel Hill: University of North Carolina Press, 2019.

Crook, George. *General George Crook: His Autobiography*. Edited and annotated by Martin F. Schmitt. Norman: University of Oklahoma Press, 1986.

Curtis, Natalie, *The Indians' Book: An Offering by the American Indians of Indian Lore, Musical and Narrative, to Form a Record of the Songs and Legends of Their Race*. New York: Harper and Brothers, 1907.

DeJong, David H. *Stealing the Gila: The Pima Agricultural Economy and Water Deprivation, 1848–1921*. Tucson: University of Arizona Press, 2009.

Deloria, Vine Jr. *Custer Died for Your Sins: An Indian Manifesto*. 1969. Norman: University of Oklahoma Press, 1988.

Deloria, Vine Jr. *God Is Red: A Native View on Religion*. 1973. Golden, Colo.: Fulcrum Publishing, 1992.

Edmunds, R. David, ed. *The New Warriors: Native American Leaders Since 1900*. Lincoln: University of Nebraska Press, 2001.

Farish, Thomas Edwin. *History of Arizona*. Vol. 2. San Francisco: Filmer Brothers Electrotype, 1915.

Herman, Daniel J. *Rim Country Exodus: A Story of Conquest, Renewal, and Race in the Making*. Tucson: University of Arizona Press, 2012.

Hertzberg, Hazel W. *The Search for an American Indian Identity: Modern Pan-Indian Movements*. Syracuse: Syracuse University Press, 1971.

Hogan, Linda. *Mean Spirit*. New York: Ivy Books, 1990.

Hoxie, Frederick E. *Parading Through History: The Making of the Crow Nation in America, 1805–1935*. New York: Cambridge University Press, 1995.

Iverson, Peter. *Carlos Montezuma and the Changing World of American Indians*. Albuquerque: University of New Mexico Press, 1982.

Iverson, Peter. *When Indians Became Cowboys: Native Peoples and Cattle Ranching in the American West*. Norman: University of Oklahoma Press, 1994.

Kroeber, Alfred Louis, and Clifton B. Kroeber. *A Mohave War Reminiscence, 1854–1880*. New York: Dover, 1994.

Latimer, Joseph W. *Our Indian Bureau System: A Summary and a Remedy in Three Chapters*. New York: 1923.

Latimer, Joseph W., ed. *The Rape of McDowell Reservation, Arizona, by the Indian Bureau*. Washington, D.C.: Hayworth Publishing House, 1921.

Leupp, Francis E. *The Indian and His Problem*. New York: Charles Scribner's Sons, 1910.

Liberty, Margot, ed. *American Indian Intellectuals of the Nineteenth and Early Twentieth Centuries*. 1978; Norman: University of Oklahoma Press, 2002.

Limerick, Patricia Nelson, and Karl Jacoby. *Shadows at Dawn: An Apache Massacre and the Violence of History*. New York: Penguin, 2009.

Lipps, Oscar Hiram. *Laws and Regulations Relating to Indians and Their Lands*. N.p.: Lewiston, 1913.

Maroukis, Thomas Constantine. *We Are Not a Vanishing People: The Society of American Indians, 1911–1923*. Tucson: University of Arizona Press, 2021.

The Martindale-Hubbell Law Directory. New York: Martindale-Hubbell Law Directory, 1932.

Martínez, David. *Dakota Philosopher: Charles Eastman and American Indian Thought*. St. Paul: Minnesota Historical Society, 2009.

Martínez, David, ed. *The American Indian Intellectual Tradition: An Anthology of Writings from 1772 to 1972*. Ithaca, N.Y.: Cornell University Press, 2011.

Mathews, John Joseph. *Sundown*. Norman: University of Oklahoma Press, 1988.

McDonald, Laughlin. *American Indians and the Fight for Equal Voting Rights*. Norman: University of Oklahoma Press, 2010.

McKanna, Clare V. Jr. *Homicide, Race, and Justice in the American West, 1880–1920*. Tucson: University of Arizona Press, 1997.

Montezuma, Carlos. *The Indian of Yesterday: The Early Life of Dr Carlos Montezuma Written by Himself*. Chicago: National Christian Women's Temperance Union, 1888.

Moses, L. G., and Raymond Wilson, eds. *Indian Lives: Essays on Nineteenth- and Twentieth-Century Native American Leaders*. Albuquerque: University of New Mexico Press, 1985.

Olson, James S., and Raymond Wilson, eds. *Native Americans in the Twentieth Century*. Urbana-Champaign: University of Illinois Press, 1984.

Parker, Robert Dale, ed. *Changing Is Not Vanishing: A Collection of American Indian Poetry to 1930*. Philadelphia: University of Pennsylvania Press, 2011.

Peplow, Edward H. *History of Arizona*. New York: Lewis Historical Publishing, 1958.

Prucha, Francis Paul. *American Indian Treaties: The History of a Political Anomaly*. Berkeley: University of California Press, 1997.

Prucha, Francis Paul. *American Indian Policy in Crisis: Christian Reformers and the Indian, 1865–1900*. Norman: University of Oklahoma Press, 2014.

Red Corn, Charles H. *A Pipe for February: A Novel*. Norman: University of Oklahoma Press, 2002.

Russell, Frank. *The Pima Indians*. Re-edition, ed. Bernard L. Fontana. Tucson: University of Arizona Press, 1975.

Shaw, Anna Moore. *A Pima Past*. Tucson: University of Arizona Press, 1974.

Sheridan, Thomas E. *Arizona: A History*. Tucson: University of Arizona Press, 2012.

Speroff, Leon. *Carlos Montezuma, M.D.: A Yavapai American Hero: The Life and Times of an American Indian, 1866–1923*. Portland, Ore.: Arnica Publishing, 2003.

Spicer, Edward H. *Cycles of Conquest: The Impact of Spain, Mexico, and the United States on the Indians of the Southwest, 1533–1960*. Tucson: University of Arizona Press, 1962.

Standing Bear, Luther. *My People the Sioux*. Lincoln: University of Nebraska Press, 1975.

Swazey, Arthur et al. *The Interior*. N.p.: Western Presbyterian Publishing Company, 1913.

Thrapp, Dan L. *Al Sieber, Chief of Scouts*. Norman: University of Oklahoma Press, 2012. Kindle.

Thrapp, Dan L. *The Conquest of Apacheria*. Norman: University of Oklahoma Press, 1975.

Vigil, Kiara. *Indigenous Intellectuals: Sovereignty, Citizenship, and the American Imagination, 1880–1930*. New York: Cambridge University Press, 2015.

Warrior, Robert Allen. *Tribal Secrets: Recovering American Indian Intellectual Traditions*. Minneapolis: University of Minnesota Press, 1995.

Waterstrat, Elaine. *Hoomothya's Long Journey, 1865–1897: The True Story of a Yavapai Indian*. Fountain Hills, Ariz.: Mount McDowell Press, 1998.

Webb, George. *A Pima Remembers*. Tucson: University of Arizona Press, 1959.

Williams, John, Mike Harrison, and Sigrid Khera. *Oral History of the Yavapai*. Tucson: University of Arizona Press, 2015.

Wilson, Raymond. *Ohiyesa: Charles Eastman, Santee Sioux*. Urbana-Champaign: University of Illinois Press, 1983.

Wise, Jennings C. *The Red Man in the New World Drama*. Revised and edited with an introduction by Vine Deloria Jr. New York: Macmillan, 1971.

Book Chapters

Khera, Sigrid, and Patricia S. Mariella. "Yavapai." *Handbook of North American Indians*, edited by William C. Sturtevant. Volume 10, *Southwest*, edited by Alfonso Ortiz, 38–54. Washington, D.C.: Smithsonian, 1983.

Stewart, Kenneth M. "Mohave." *Handbook of North American Indians*, edited by William C. Sturtevant. Volume 10, *Southwest*, edited by Alfonso Ortiz, 55–70. Washington, D.C.: Smithsonian Institution, 1983.

Vollan, Charles. "Yellowtail, Robert (1887/1889–1988)." In *Great Plains Indians*, edited by David J. Wishart. Lincoln: University of Nebraska Press, 2016.

Articles

No author, "Three Countries to Get Rich In," Adventure. United States: Ridgway, 1921: 187–188.

Around the Campus. *Native American*, January 26, 1917.

"ASU Hosts Panel on Dr Carlos Montezuma's WASSAJA Newsletter." *Yavapai News*, May 2015.

August, Jack L. Jr. "Carl Hayden: Born a Politician." *Journal of Arizona History* 26, no. 2 (Summer 1985): 117–44.

August, Jack L. Jr. "Water, Politics, and the Arizona Dream: Carl Hayden and the Modern Origins of the Central Arizona Project, 1922–1963." *Journal of Arizona History* 40, no. 4 (1999): 391–414.

Brown, John B. *Native American*, June 15, 1915.

Camp Notes. *Native American*, April 1, 1916.

Chamberlain, Sue Abbey. "The Fort McDowell Indian Reservation: Water Rights and Indian Removal, 1910–1930." *Journal of the West* 14, no. 4 (October 1975): 27–34.

Coffeen, William R. "The Effects of the Central Arizona Project on the Fort McDowell Indian Community." *Ethnohistory* 19, no. 4 (Autumn 1972): 345–77.

Crandall, Maurice. "Wassaja Comes Home: A Yavapai Perspective on Carlos Montezuma's Search for Identity." *Journal of Arizona History* 55, no. 1 (Spring 2014): 1–26.

Curtis, Natalie. "The Winning of an Indian Reservation: How Theodore Roosevelt and Frank Mead Restored the Mohave-Apaches to Their Own." *Outlook*, June 25, 1919.

DeJong, David H. "An Equal Chance? The Pima Indians and the 1916 Florence-Casa Grande Irrigation Project." *Journal of Arizona History* 45, no. 1 (Spring 2004): 63–102.

DeJong, David H. "Forced to Abandon Their Farms: Water Deprivation and Starvation Among the Gila River Pima, 1892–1904." *American Indian Culture and Research Journal* 28, no. 3 (2004): 29–56.

DeJong, David H. "'Good Samaritans of the Desert': The Pima-Maricopa Villages as Described in California Emigrant Journals, 1846–1852." *Journal of the Southwest* 47, no. 3 (Autmun 2005): 457–96.

DeJong, David H. "'Left High and Dry': Federal Land Policies and Pima Agriculture, 1860–1910." *American Indian Culture and Research Journal* 33, no. 1 (2009): 23–45.

E. L. B. "Things Past." Review of *A Pima Remembers* by George Webb. *New York Times*, October 11, 1959.

"Gem Valley of Them All." *Arizona Republican*, August 10, 1913.

Hospital Notes. *Native American*, November 25, 1916.

"Hurley v. Abbott." *Arizona Republican*, March 2, 1910.

"Indian Boosting Southern Project." *Bisbee Daily Review*, January 16, 1919. https://az memory.azlibrary.gov/digital/collection/sn84024827/id/52013/.

"Indians Hold Reservation of M'Dowell." *Arizona Republican*, August 24, 1912.

Laird, W. David. Review of *A Pima Past* by Anna Moore Shaw. *Arizona and the West* 17, no. 2 (Summer 1975): 178–79.

Martínez, David. "Carlos Montezuma's Fight Against 'Bureauism': An Unexpected Pima Hero." *Studies in American Indian Literatures* 25, no. 2 (Summer 2013): 311–30.

Martínez, David. "Living Large During the Jazz Age: 'Big Chief' Russell Moore, Pima Memories, and the Changing Roles of American Indians in the 20th Century." *Journal of Arizona History* 55, no. 2 (Summer 2014): 127–44.

Montezuma, Carlos. "Light on the Indian Situation." *Quarterly Journal of the Society of American Indians* 1, no. 1 (April 15, 1913): 50–55.

"Changes in Indian Service Employees for the Months of Nov., Dec., 1910," *Native American*, March 25, 1911.

Native American, June 29, 1912.

Native American, April 29, 1916.

Newmark, Julianne. "A Prescription for Freedom: Carlos Montezuma, *Wassaja*, and the Society of American Indians." *American Indian Quarterly* 37, no. 3 (Summer 2013): 139–58.

Peplow, Edward H. Jr. "Seeds of Wounded Knee? Carlos Montezuma Collection, a Timely Acquisition, Boosts Stature of ASU's Hayden Library." *Arizona Statesman* 33, no. 12 (March 1974): 1, 3. Box 13, Folder 2, Montezuma Collection, ASU Library.

"Samuel Adams, 68, Attorney, Is Dead; Chicagoan First Assistant Secretary of the Interior in Taft Administration." *New York Times*, May 21, 1935.

Sands, Kay M. Review of *A Pima Past* by Anna Moore Shaw. *Studies in American Indian Literatures* 5, no. 1 (Winter 1981): 3–5.

Sheridan, Thomas E. "The Other Arizona." *Journal of the Southwest* 36, no. 3 (Autumn 1994): 255–86.

Solomon, Glenn. "Fort McDowell Indians Face Loss of Land." *Wassaja: "Let My People Know"* 1, no. 4 (1973): 1–10.

Southworth, C. H. "A Pima Calendar Stick." *Arizona Historical Review* 4 (1931–1932): 44–51.

Stanciu, Cristina. "'Americanism for Indians': Carlos Montezuma's 'Immigrant Problem,' *Wassaja*, and the Limits of Native Activism." *Studies in American Indian Literatures* 33, nos. 1–2 (Spring–Summer 2021): 126–58.

Trennert, Robert A. "John H. Stout and the Grant Peace Policy Among the Pimas." *Journal of the Southwest* 28, no. 1 (Spring 1986): 45–68.

Zuck, Rochelle Raineri. "'Yours in the Cause': Readers, Correspondents, and the Editorial Politics of Carlos Montezuma's *Wassaja*." *American Periodicals* 22, no. 1 (2012): 72–93.

Government Documents

Citizenship Act, 66 PL 75; 41 Stat. 350, Chap. 95; 66 Enacted HR 5007 (November 6, 1919).

An Act Granting Citizenship to Certain Indians, 66 HR 5007 (1919).

An Act Relating to Rights of Way Through Certain Parks, Reservations, and Other Public Lands, 31 Stat. 790 (1901).

An Act to Amend Section Six of an Act Approved February Eighth, Eighteen Hundred and Eighty-seven, Entitled "An Act to Provide for the Allotment of Lands in Severalty to Indians on the Various Reservations, and to Extend the Protection of the Laws of the United States and the Territories over the Indians, and for Other Purposes," PL 59–149; 34 Stat. 182 (1906).

An Act to Provide for the Allotment of Lands in Severalty to Indians on the Various Reservations, and to Extend the Protection of the Laws of the United States and the Territories over the Indians, and for Other Purposes, 24 Stat. 388 (1887).

Bureau of Indian Affairs. Annual Report of the Commissioner of Indian Affairs, 1913. U.S. Government Printing Office, 1913.

Bureau of Indian Affairs. Annual Report of the Commissioner of Indian Affairs, 1915. U.S. Government Printing Office, 1915.

Bureau of Indian Affairs. Annual Report of the Commissioner of Indian Affairs, 1916. U.S. Government Printing Office, 1916.

Bureau of Indian Affairs. Annual Report of the Commissioner of Indian Affairs, 1920. U.S. Government Printing Office, 1920.

Cherokee Nation v. Georgia. 30 U.S. 1 (1831).

"Colorado River Basin Project." *Congressional Record*, 90th Cong., 2nd Sess., May 16, 1968, 13566–89.

Commissioner of Education. *Annual Reports of the Department of the Interior for the Fiscal Year Ended June 30, 1897: Report of the Commissioner of Education.* Vol. 2, containing parts 2 and 3. Washington, D.C.: Government Printing Office, 1898.

Committee on Indian Affairs. House. *Indians of the United States: Hearings Before the Committee on Indian Affairs, House of Representatives, Sixty-sixth Congress, First Session, on the Condition of Various Tribes of Indians. Act of June 30, 1919.* U.S. Government Printing Office, 1920.

Committee on Indian Affairs. House. *Indians of the U.S.* Vol. 1: *Hearings*, 66th Cong., 1st Sess. (1919).

Committee on Indian Affairs. House. *Indians of the U.S.* Vol 3: *Investigation of the Field Service*, 66th Cong., 2nd Sess. (1920).

Committee on Indian Affairs. House. Memorial and Papers from the Mohave-Apache Indians of McDowell Reservation, Arizona, in Relation to Their Removal from McDowell Reservation to the Salt River Reservation, Arizona. 62nd Cong., 1st Sess. (1911).

Committee on Indian Affairs. House. *Survey of Conditions of the Indians in the United States: Hearings Before a Subcommittee of the Committee on Indian Affairs.* U.S. Government Printing Office, 1929.

Committee on Indian Affairs. Senate. Diversion Dam on the Gila River at a Site Above Florence, Ariz.: Hearing Before the Committee on Indian Affairs, United States Senate, 64th Cong. 2nd Sess. (1917).

Committee on Indian Affairs. Senate. *Survey of Conditions of the Indians in the United States.* Part 10, *Flathead Reservation, Mont.* U.S. Government Printing Office, 1930.

Committee on Interior and Insular Affairs. Senate. *Indian Water Rights of the Five Central Tribes of Arizona: Hearings Before the Committee on Interior and Insular Affairs, United States Senate, Ninety-fourth Congress, First Session . . . October 23 and 24, 1975.* U.S. Government Printing Office, 1976.

Hurley v. Abbott, Arizona Territorial Court, Cause No. 4564 (March 1, 1910).

Leases of Unallotted Mineral Lands Withdrawn from Entry Under Mining Laws, 25 U.S.C. §309.

Lobb v. Avenente. Superior Court of Arizona (1916).

Moore/Swick Partnership. "Hayden Butte Preserve: Management Plan," prepared for the City of Tempe, Ariz., Field Services Division, Public Works Department, May 2017.

Office of Indian Affairs. Annual Report of the Commissioner of Indian Affairs, for the Year 1888. Washington, DC: GPO, [1888].

Oil Lands in Osage Reservation: Hearings on S. Com. Res. 4 (1916).

Reclamation Service. Annual Report of the Reclamation Service. U.S. Government Printing Office, 1911.

Reclamation Service. Ninth Annual Report of the Reclamation Service, 1909–1910. House Committee on Irrigation and Arid Lands, 61st Cong., 3rd Sess. (1910).

Roosevelt, Theodore. "Arizona Territory: Withdrawal of Abandoned Camp McDowell Lands for Mohave-Apache Indians." Unnumbered Executive Order, September 15, 1903.

Salt River Pima-Maricopa Indian Community Water Rights Settlement Agreement (February 12, 1988). Pub. L. 100–512, Oct. 20, 1988, 102 Stat. 2549.

Secretary of the Interior. "Appropriation of Support of Indian Schools, Etc, Fiscal Year 1916." House Committee on Indian Affairs, 64th Cong., 2nd Sess. (1916).

Secretary of the Interior. "Expenditures for Indian School Buildings, 1911." Committee on Expenditures in the Interior Department. House. 6324 H.R. Doc. 196 (1911).

Select Committee on Indian Affairs. To Provide for Allotment of Lands of Crow Indians in Montana. 66th Cong., 1st Sess. (1919).

Smithsonian Institution. *Annual Report of the Board of Regents of the Smithsonian Institution 1920*. U.S. Government Printing Office, 1922.

Treaty of Fort Laramie with the Crow. 15 Stat. 649 (1868).

Theses and Dissertations

Alflen, Louise. "Yavapai Indians Circle Their Wagons: Indians to Arizona: 'It's a Good Day to Declare War.'" MA thesis, Arizona State University, 2011.

Solomon, Glenn. "The Odyssey of Carlos Montezuma." MA thesis, University of Oklahoma, 1973.

Other (Including Online Archives in Addition to Those Listed Above)

Arizona Board of Regents. "Memorial in Re-Investigation of Pima Indians, Arizona." Native American Water Rights. http://water.library.arizona.edu/body.1_div.36.html.

Arizona Department of Transportation. "Arizona Transportation History." December 2011. http://www.ansac.az.gov/UserFiles/PDF/02032016/C040-Engelman BergerCities%20Supplement/Arizona%20Transportation%20History%20Final %20Report%20660%20December%202011%20(00650539xB0704).PDF.

Arizona Department of Transportation. "Good Roads Everywhere: A History of Road Building in Arizona." March 2004. https://azdot.gov/sites/default/files/2019/07 /cultural_good_roads_everywhere.pdf.

Arizona Memory Project. Bisbee Daily Review, 1919-01-16. https://azmemory.azlibrary .gov/digital/collection/sn84024827/id/52013/.

Arizona Memory Project. "Oral History with Manuel Ruiz, January 14, 2011." Capturing Arizona's Stories. https://azmemory.azlibrary.gov/digital/collection/asa capture/id/244/.

Arizona State Parks. "Period History." Fort Verde State Historic Park. https://azstate parks.com/fort-verde/about-the-fort/period-history.

Arizona State University. Labriola National American Indian Data Center. ASU Library. https://lib.asu.edu/labriola.

Biographical Directory of the United States Congress. "Hayden, Carl Trumbull (1877–1972)." https://bioguide.congress.gov/search/bio/H000385.

Butler, Carolina Castillo. Oral History of the Yavapai. https://www.oralhistoryofthe yavapai.com/.

Carlisle Indian School Digital Resource Center. "Grace Thumbo Student Information Card." http://carlisleindian.dickinson.edu/student_files/grace-thumbo-student -information-card.

Carlisle Indian School Digital Resource Center. "Juan Ruiz Student Information Card." http://carlisleindian.dickinson.edu/student_files/juan-ruiz-student-infor mation-card.

Carlisle Indian School Digital Resource Center. "Manuel Ruiz Student Information Card." http://carlisleindian.dickinson.edu/student_files/manuel-ruiz-student -information-card.

Chicago Public Library. "Series 15: R.D. Parker, Civilian, 1896–1901—31 Letters." American Civil War Documents, Manuscripts, Letters and Diaries and Grand Army of the Republic Collections. https://www.chipublib.org/fa-american-civil -war-documents-manuscripts-letters-and-diaries-and-grand-army-of-the-republic -collection/#P1S15.

Cornell Law School. "Consideration." Legal Information Institute. https://www.law .cornell.edu/wex/consideration.

Cornerstone Environmental. "History of Horseshoe Ranch." https://www.cornerstone -environmental.com/publications/item/a-brief-history-of-horseshoe-ranch.

Fort McDowell Yavapai Nation. https://www.fmyn.org/.

Library of Congress. "'The N*gger' in the Woodpile." Prints and Photographs Online Catalog. https://www.loc.gov/pictures/item/2003674571/.

Library of Congress. "Salt River Project." American Folklife Center. http://memory .loc.gov/diglib/legacies/loc.afc.afc-legacies.200002705/.

Lindauer, Owen. "Archaeology of the Phoenix Indian School." *Archaeology*, March 27, 1998. https://archive.archaeology.org/online/features/phoenix/.

MapQuest. "Rio Verde, AZ." https://www.mapquest.com/us/arizona/business-rio -verde/rio-verde-az-282031090

Masonic Lodge of Education. "AF and AM vs F and AM States." https://www.masonic -lodge-of-education.com/af-and-am-vs-f-and-am-states.html.

Meyers, Donald W. "It Happened Here: Native American Advocate, Actor Nipo Strongheart Born in White Swan." *Yakima Herald-Republic*, February 25, 2019.

https://www.yakimaherald.com/news/local/it-happened-here-native-american
-advocate-actor-nipo-strongheart-born-in-white-swan/article_4658b610-37c3
-11e9-b585-db75711b7292.html.

National Governors Association. "Gov. George Wylie Hunt." https://www.nga.org
/governor/george-wylie-hunt/.

Office of the Historian, United States Department of State. "U.S. Entry into World
War I, 1917." Milestones in the History of US Foreign Relations. https://history
.state.gov/milestones/1914-1920/wwi.

Ohio State University. "SAI Centennial Symposium Archive." American Indian Studies. https://americanindianstudies.osu.edu/symposium.

Smithsonian Institution. "Revised Yavapai Vocabularies." Smithsonian Online Vir-
tual Archives. https://sova.si.edu/record/NAA.MS2249BC?s=0&n=10&t=C&q
=Yavapai&i=0.

SRP. "A History of Canals in Arizona." https://www.srpnet.com/water/canals/history
.aspx.

SRP. "Timeline." A History of Service. https://www.srpnet.com/about/history/time
line.aspx.

Tatro, M. Kaye. "Curtis Act (1898)." *The Encyclopedia of Oklahoma History and Culture*. Oklahoma Historical Society. https://www.okhistory.org/publications/enc
/entry.php?entry=CU006.

UChicago Medicine. "2008 DeLee Humanitarian Award Goes to Leon Speroff, MD,
of Oregon Health Sciences University." February 22, 2008. https://www.uchicago
medicine.org/forefront/news/2008-delee-humanitarian-award-goes-to-leon
-speroff-md-of-oregon-health-sciences-university.

U.S. Department of the Interior. "Past Secretaries." Who We Are. https://www.doi
.gov/whoweare/past-secretaries#fisher.

US Inflation Calculator. https://www.usinflationcalculator.com/.

Woolley, John, and Gerhard Peters. The American Presidency Project. https://www
.presidency.ucsb.edu.

Yale Law School. "President Woodrow Wilson's Fourteen Points." Avalon Project,
Lillian Goldman Law Library. https://avalon.law.yale.edu/20th_century/wilson
14.asp.

Index

Note: Figures are indicated by page numbers in *italics*.

About the Author

David Martínez (Akimel O'odham/Hia Ced O'odham/Mexican) is professor of American Indian studies at Arizona State University. He is also the author of *Life of the Indigenous Mind: Vine Deloria Jr. and the Birth of the Red Power Movement*. Enrolled in the Gila River Indian Community, he is currently writing *Elder Brother's Forgotten People: How the Hia Ced O'odham Survived an Epidemic to Claim a Place in Arizona's Transborder History*.